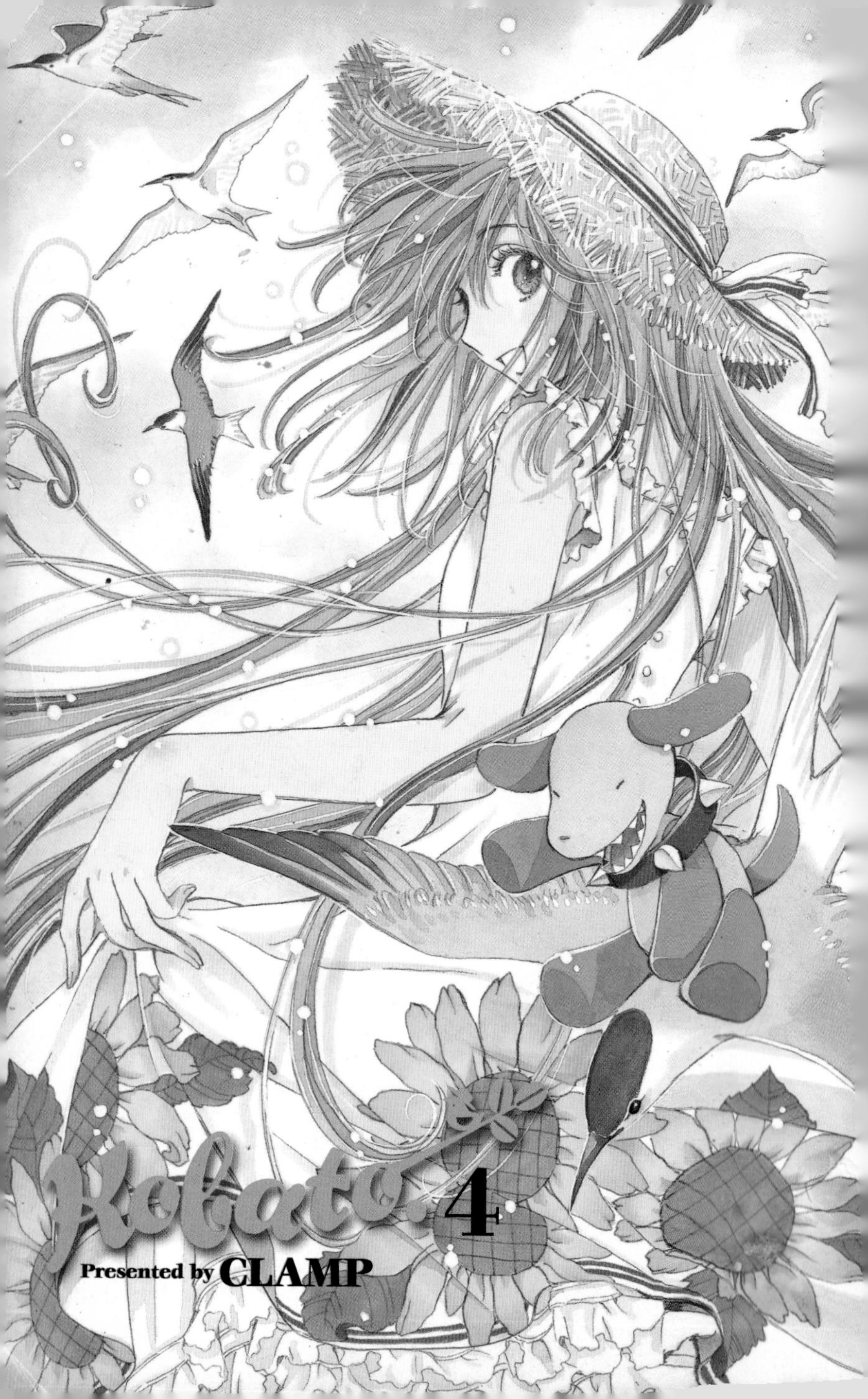
Kobato. 4
Presented by CLAMP

KOBATO.

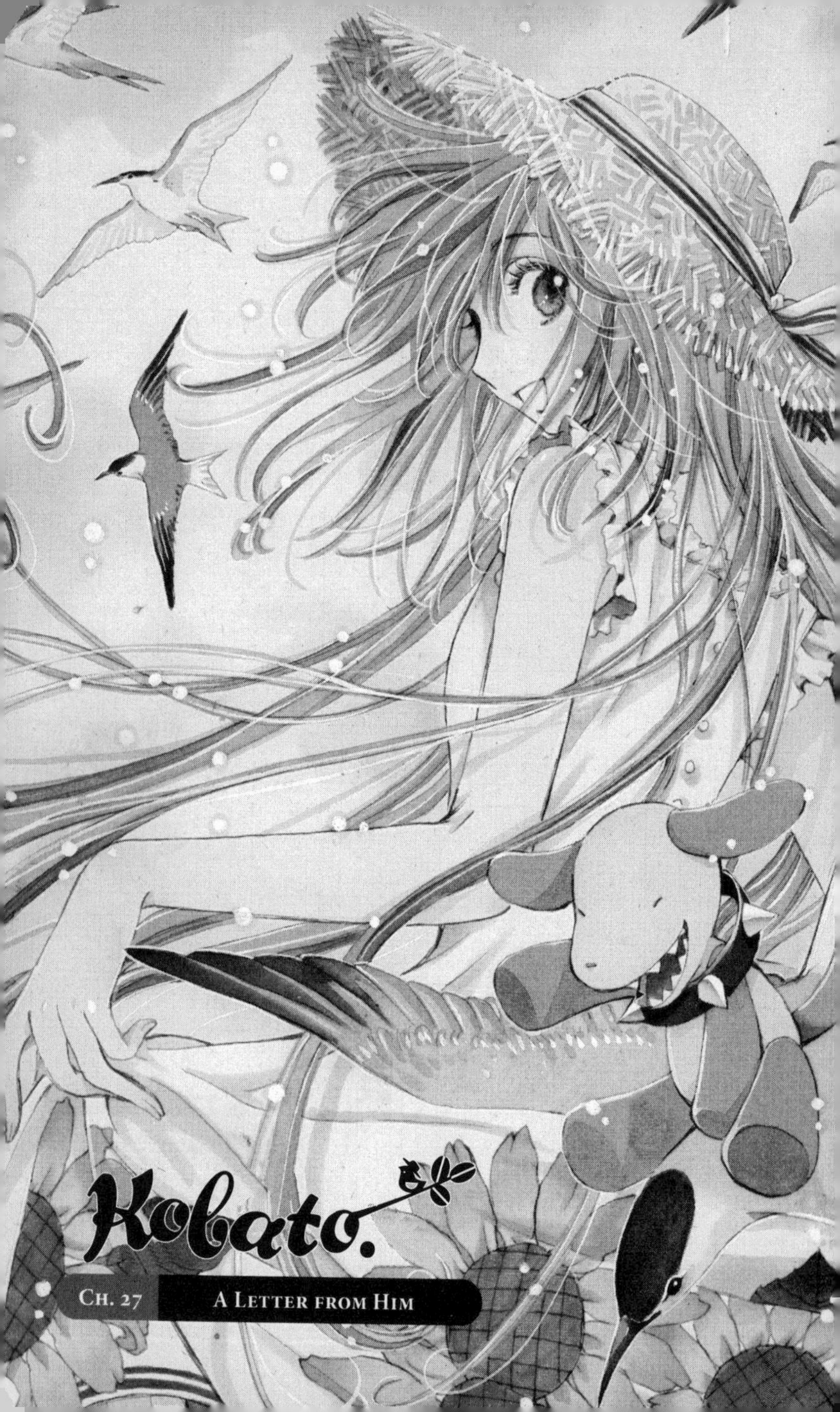
Kobato.
Ch. 27
A Letter from Him

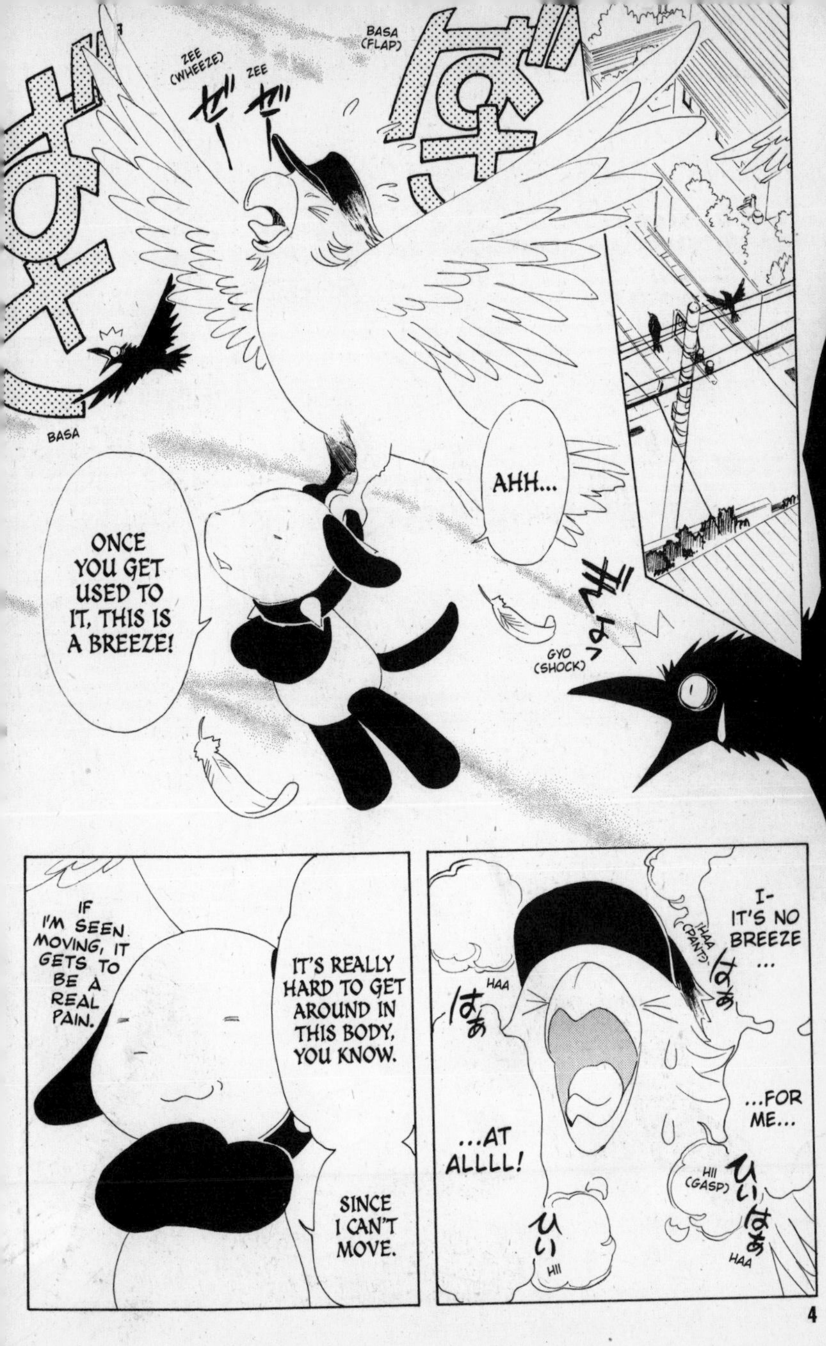
BASA (FLAP)
ZEE (WHEEZE)
ZEE
AHH...
GYO (SHOCK)
ONCE YOU GET USED TO IT, THIS IS A BREEZE!
BASA
I- IT'S NO BREEZE ...
HAA (PANT)
HAA
...FOR ME...
...AT ALLLL!
HII (GASP)
HAA
HII
IT'S REALLY HARD TO GET AROUND IN THIS BODY, YOU KNOW.
IF I'M SEEN MOVING, IT GETS TO BE A REAL PAIN.
SINCE I CAN'T MOVE.

[redacted]

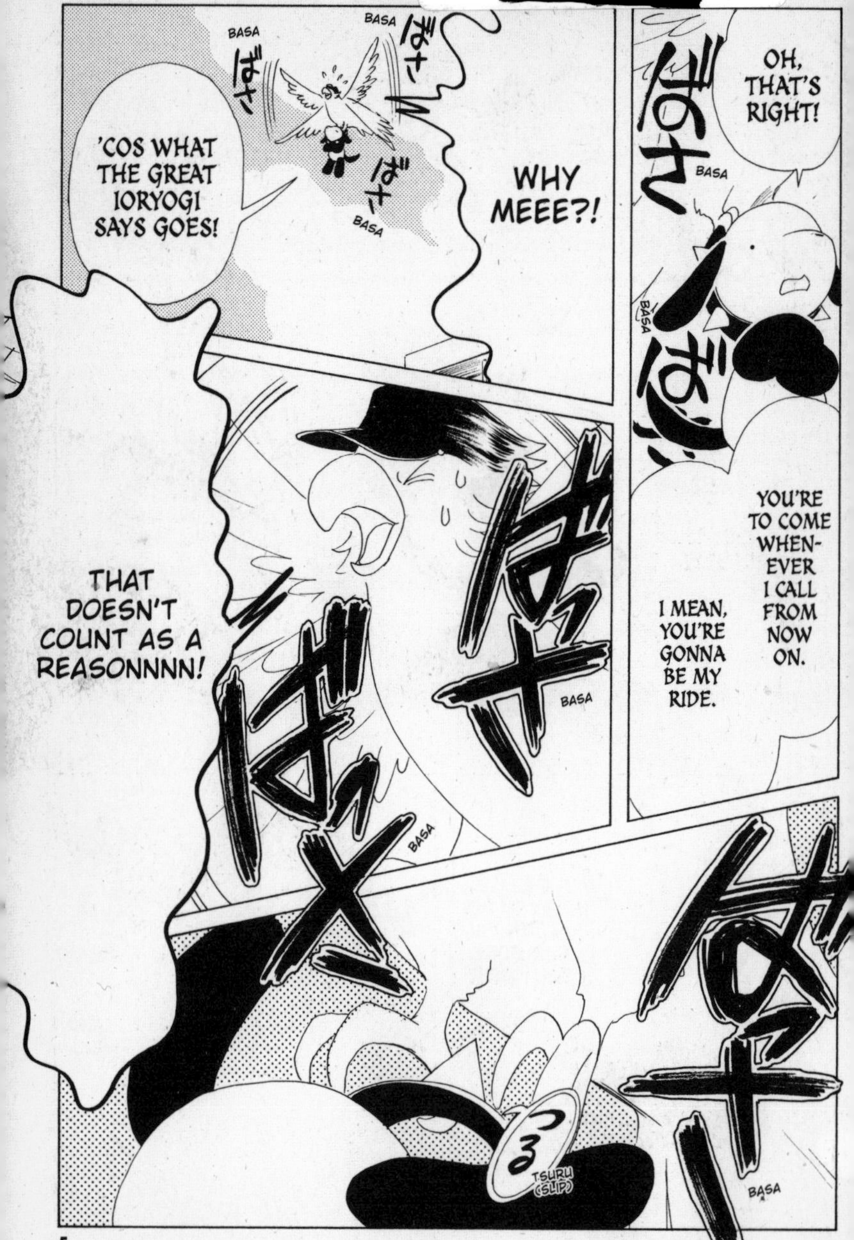

OH, THAT'S RIGHT!
BASA
BASA
YOU'RE TO COME WHEN-EVER I CALL FROM NOW ON.
I MEAN, YOU'RE GONNA BE MY RIDE.
WHY MEEE?!
BASA
BASA
BASA
'COS WHAT THE GREAT IORYOGI SAYS GOES!
BASA
BASA
THAT DOESN'T COUNT AS A REASONNNN!
BASA
TSURU (SLIP)

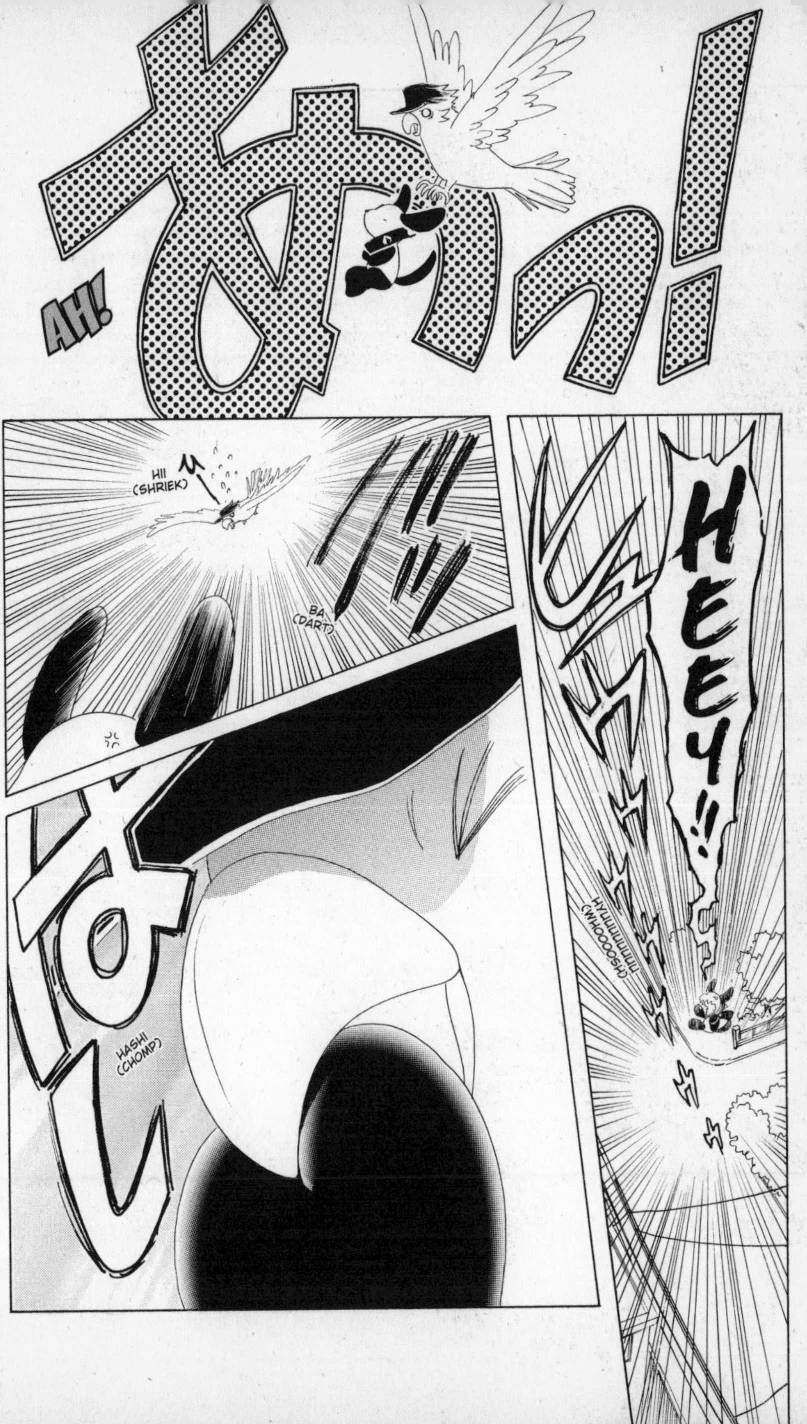
AH!
HEEY!!
HYUUUUUUN
(WHOOOOSH)
HII
(SHRIEK)
BA
(DART)
HASHI
(CHOMP)

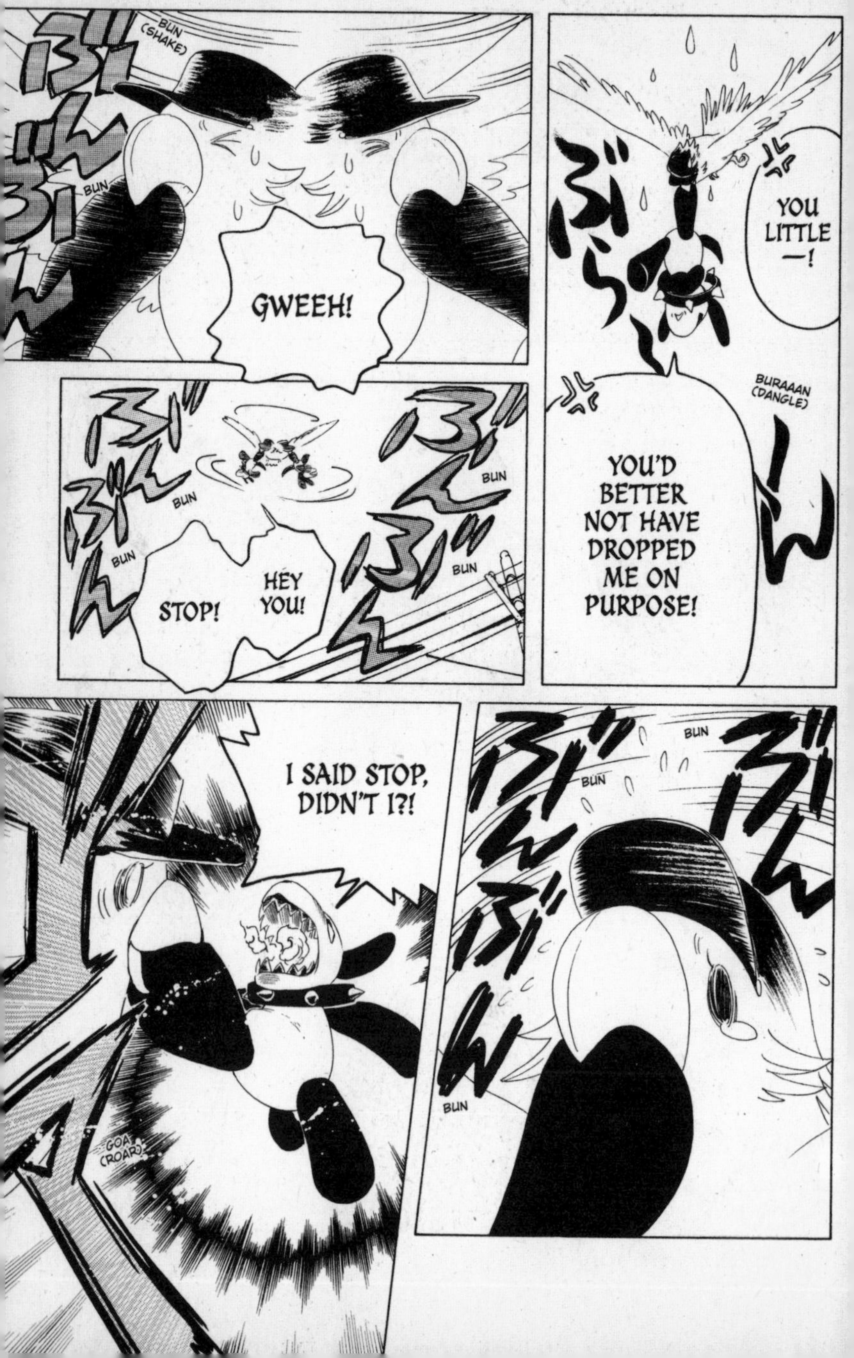
YOU LITTLE—!
BURAAAN (DANGLE)
YOU'D BETTER NOT HAVE DROPPED ME ON PURPOSE!
BUN (SHAKE)
BUN
GWEEH!
BUN
BUN
HEY YOU!
STOP!
BUN
BUN
BUN
BUN
BUN
I SAID STOP, DIDN'T I?!
GOA (ROAR)

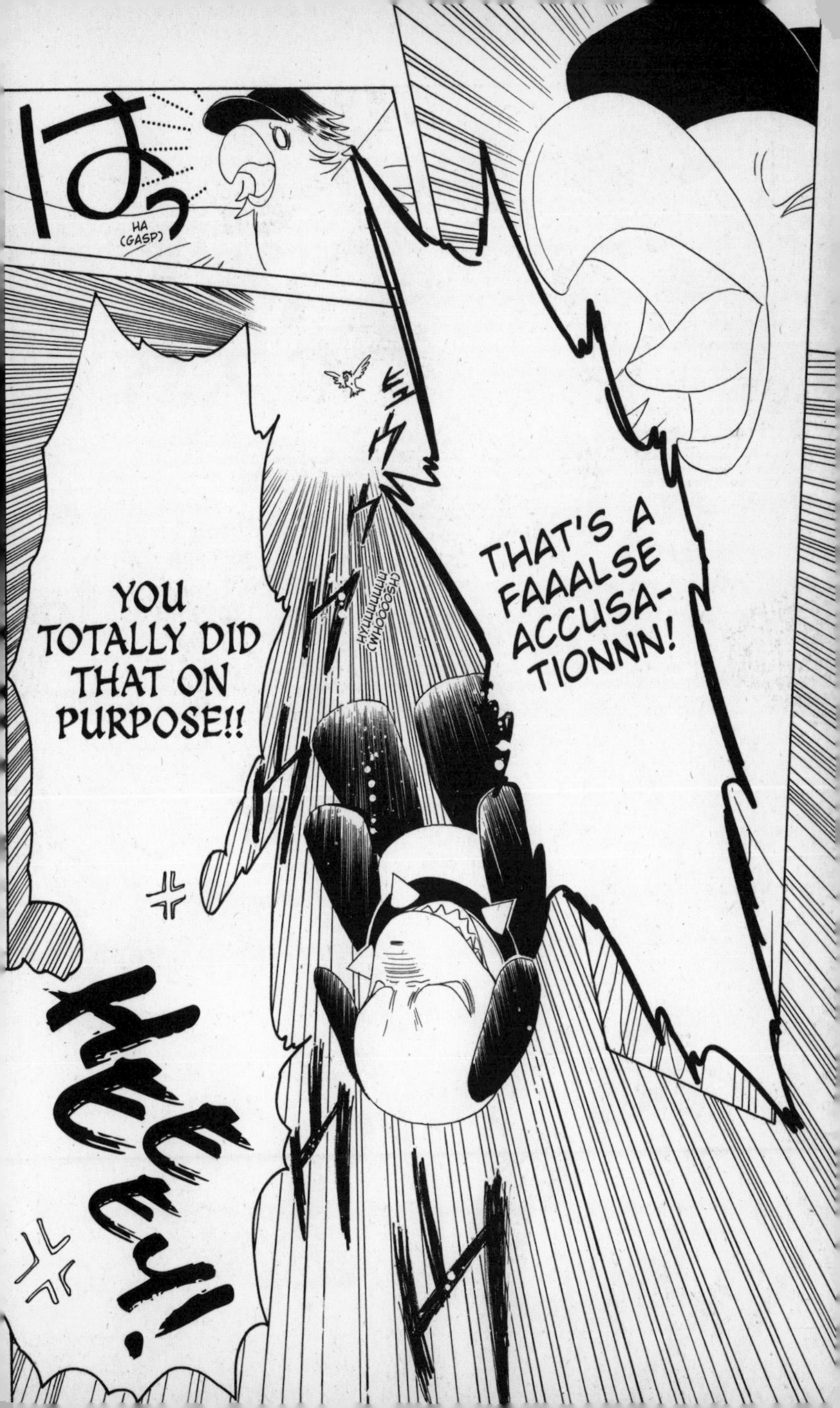
はっ
HA (GASP)
THAT'S A FAAALSE ACCUSATIONNN!
HYUUUUUUU (WHOOOOSH)
YOU TOTALLY DID THAT ON PURPOSE!!
HEEEY!

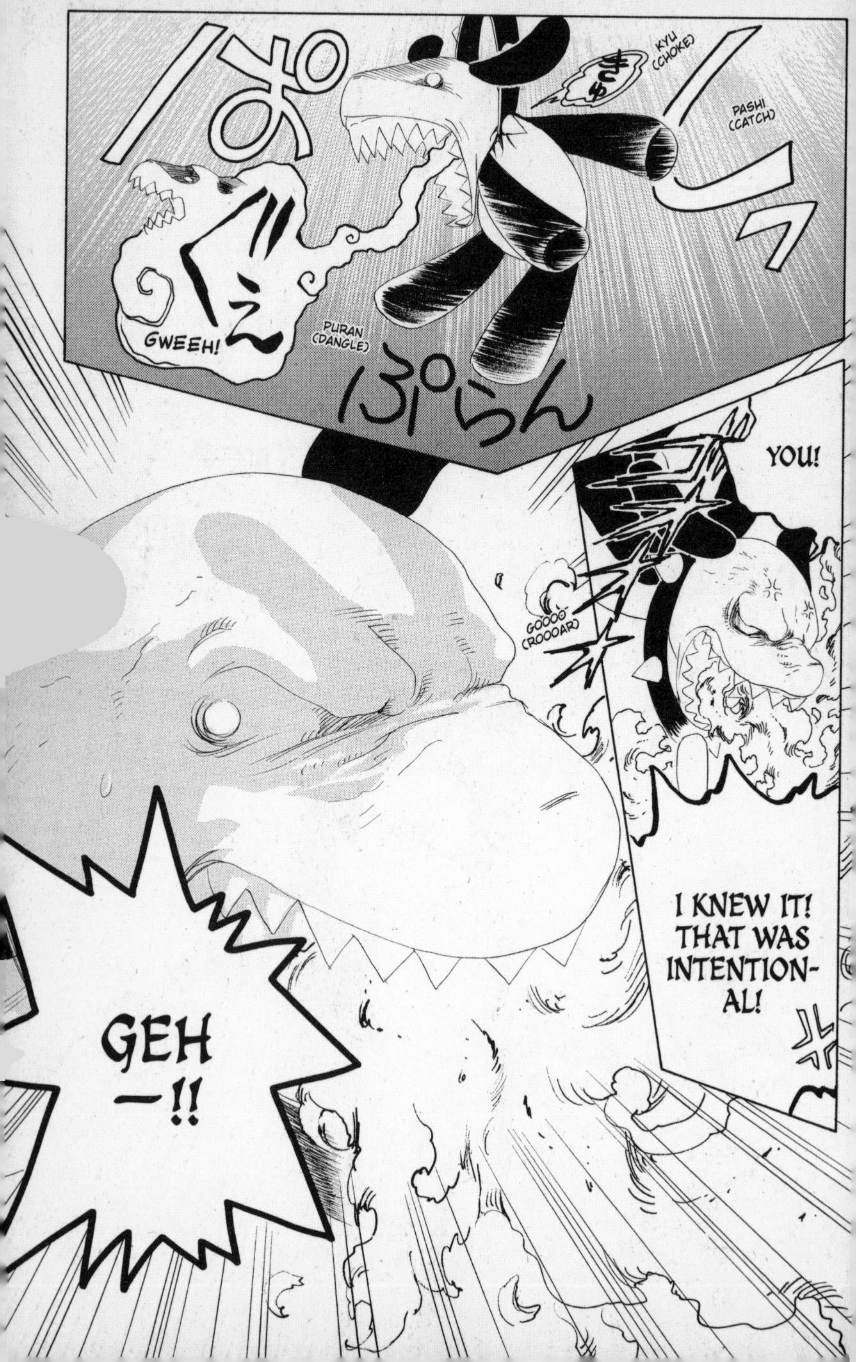

KYU (CHOKE)
PASHI (CATCH)
GWEEH!
PURAN (DANGLE)
YOU!
GOOOO (ROOOAR)
I KNEW IT! THAT WAS INTENTION-AL!
GEH —!!

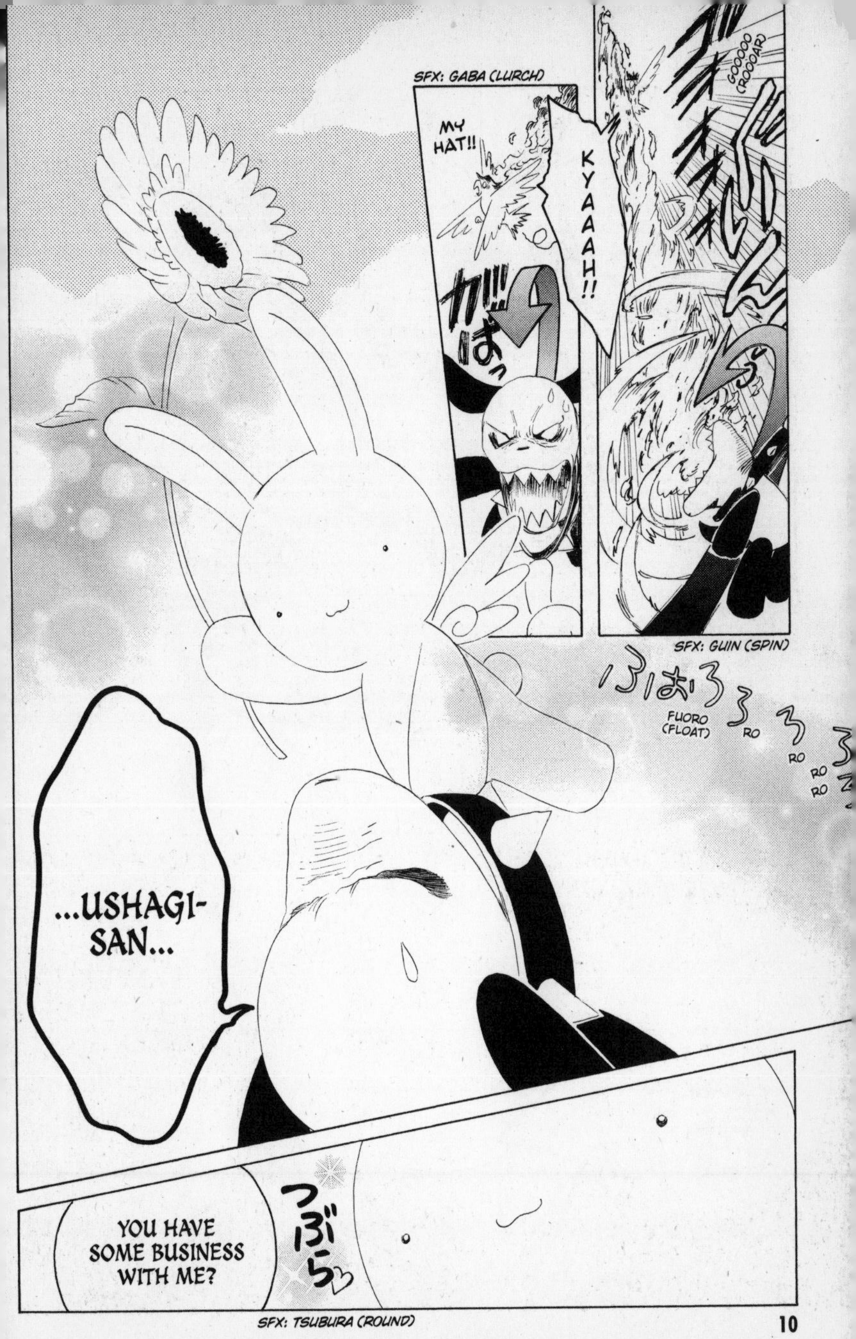
GOOOOO (ROOOAR)
SFX: GUIN (SPIN)
MY HAT!!
KYAAAH!!
SFX: GABA (LURCH)
FUORO (FLOAT) RO RO RO RO
...USHAGI-SAN...
YOU HAVE SOME BUSINESS WITH ME?
SFX: TSUBURA (ROUND)

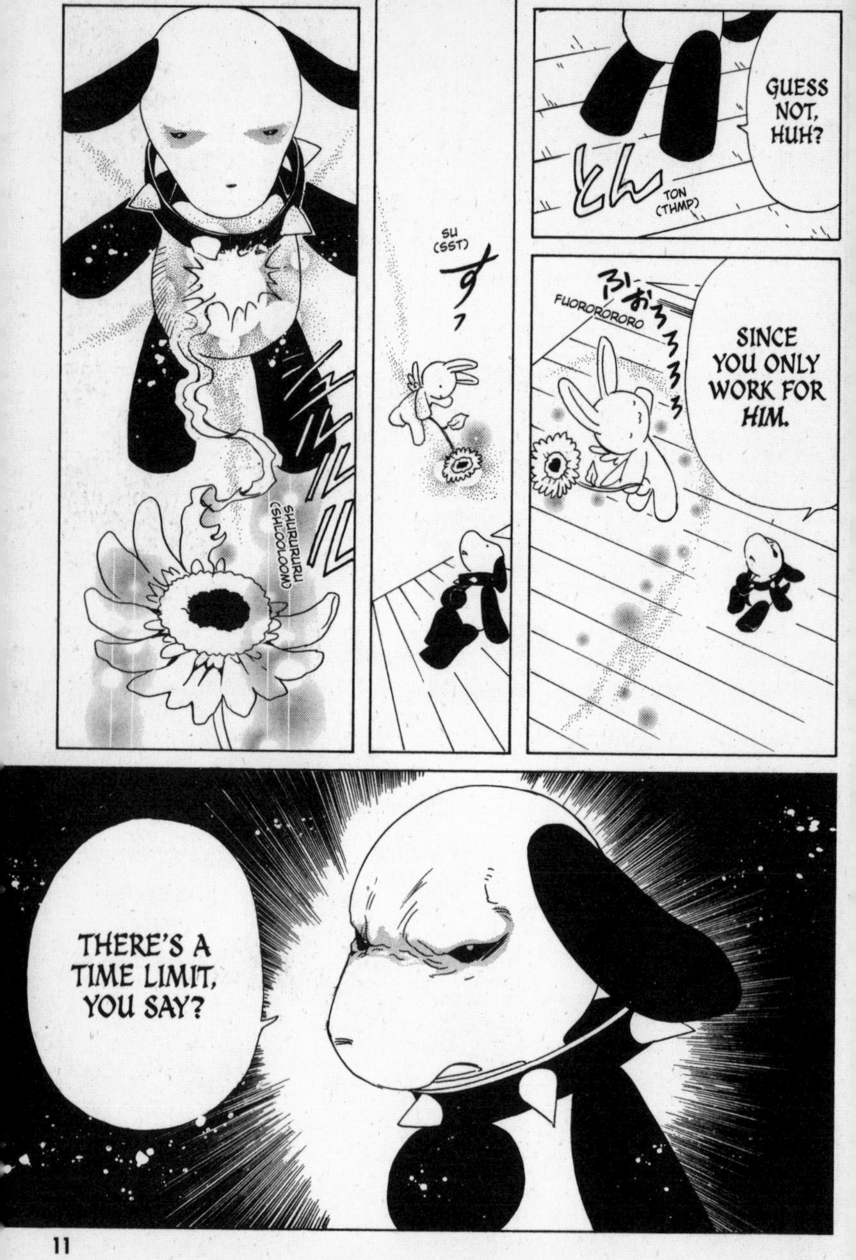
GUESS NOT, HUH?
とん
TON (THMP)
FUORORORORO
SINCE YOU ONLY WORK FOR *HIM.*
SU (SST)
SHURURURU (SHULOOLOOM)
THERE'S A TIME LIMIT, YOU SAY?

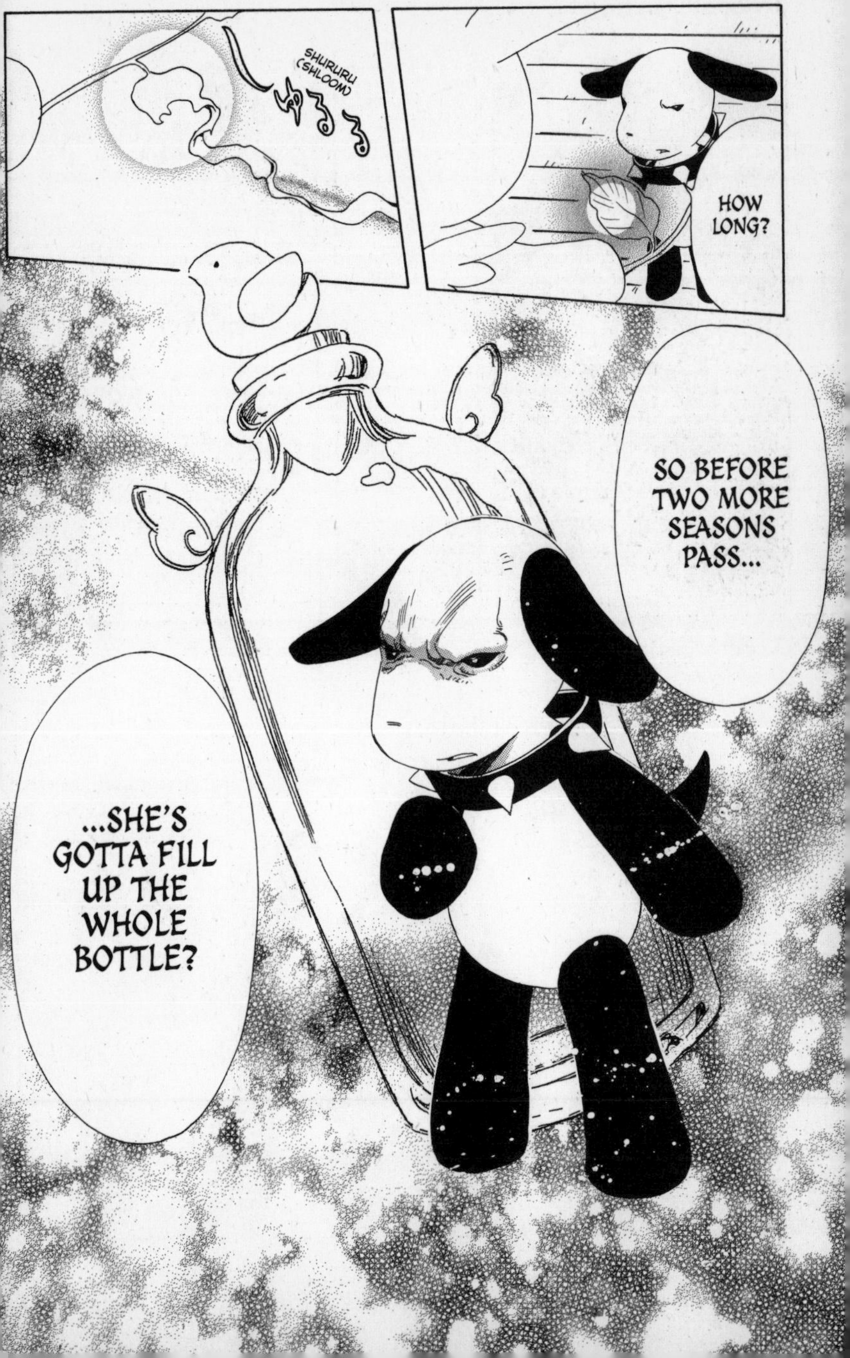
HOW LONG?
SHURURU (SHLOOM)
SO BEFORE TWO MORE SEASONS PASS...
...SHE'S GOTTA FILL UP THE WHOLE BOTTLE?

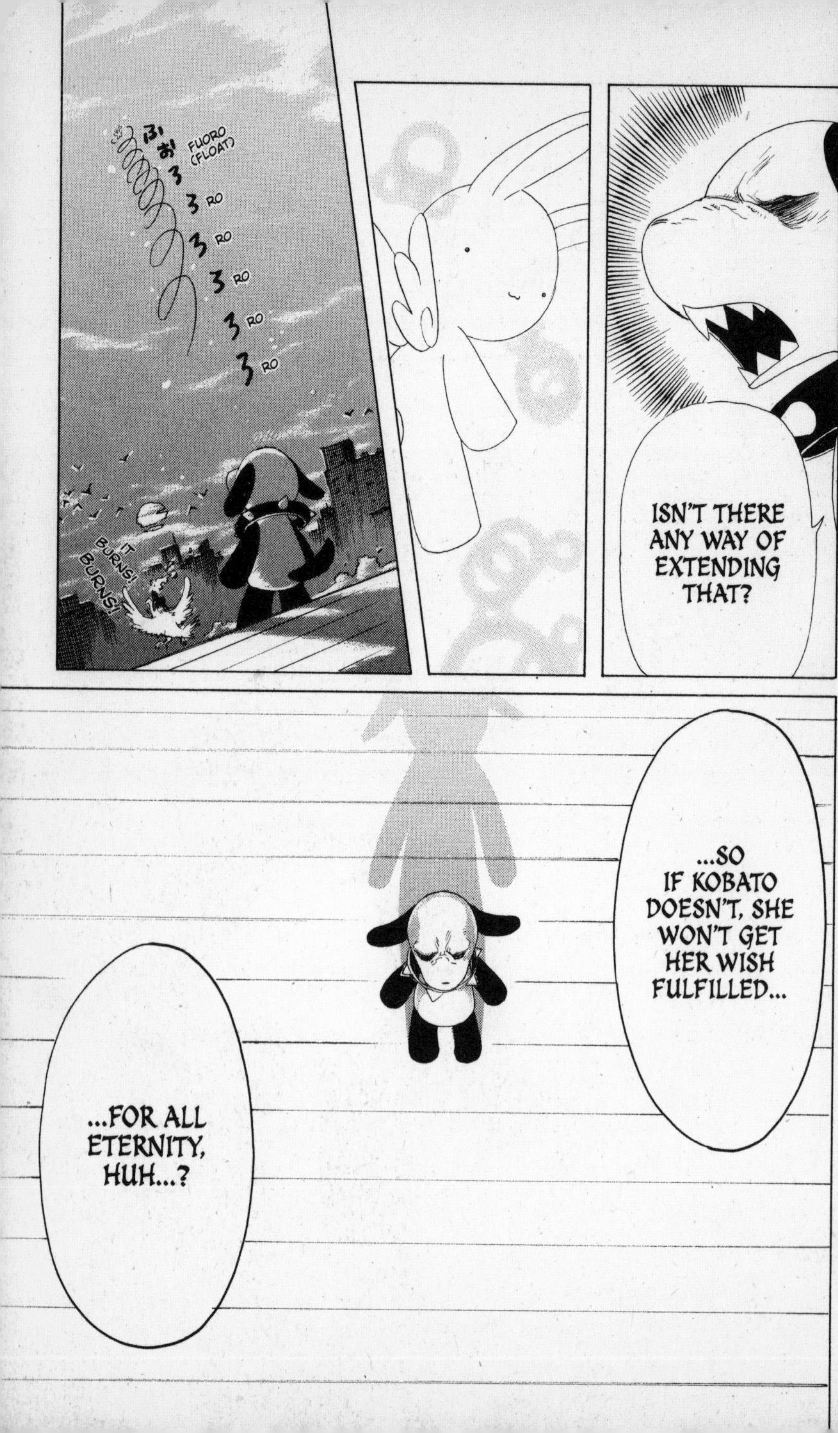
ISN'T THERE ANY WAY OF EXTENDING THAT?
ふお
FUORO (FLOAT)
ろ RO
ろ RO
ろ RO
ろ RO
ろ RO
IT BURNS! BURNS!
...SO IF KOBATO DOESN'T, SHE WON'T GET HER WISH FULFILLED...
...FOR ALL ETERNITY, HUH...?

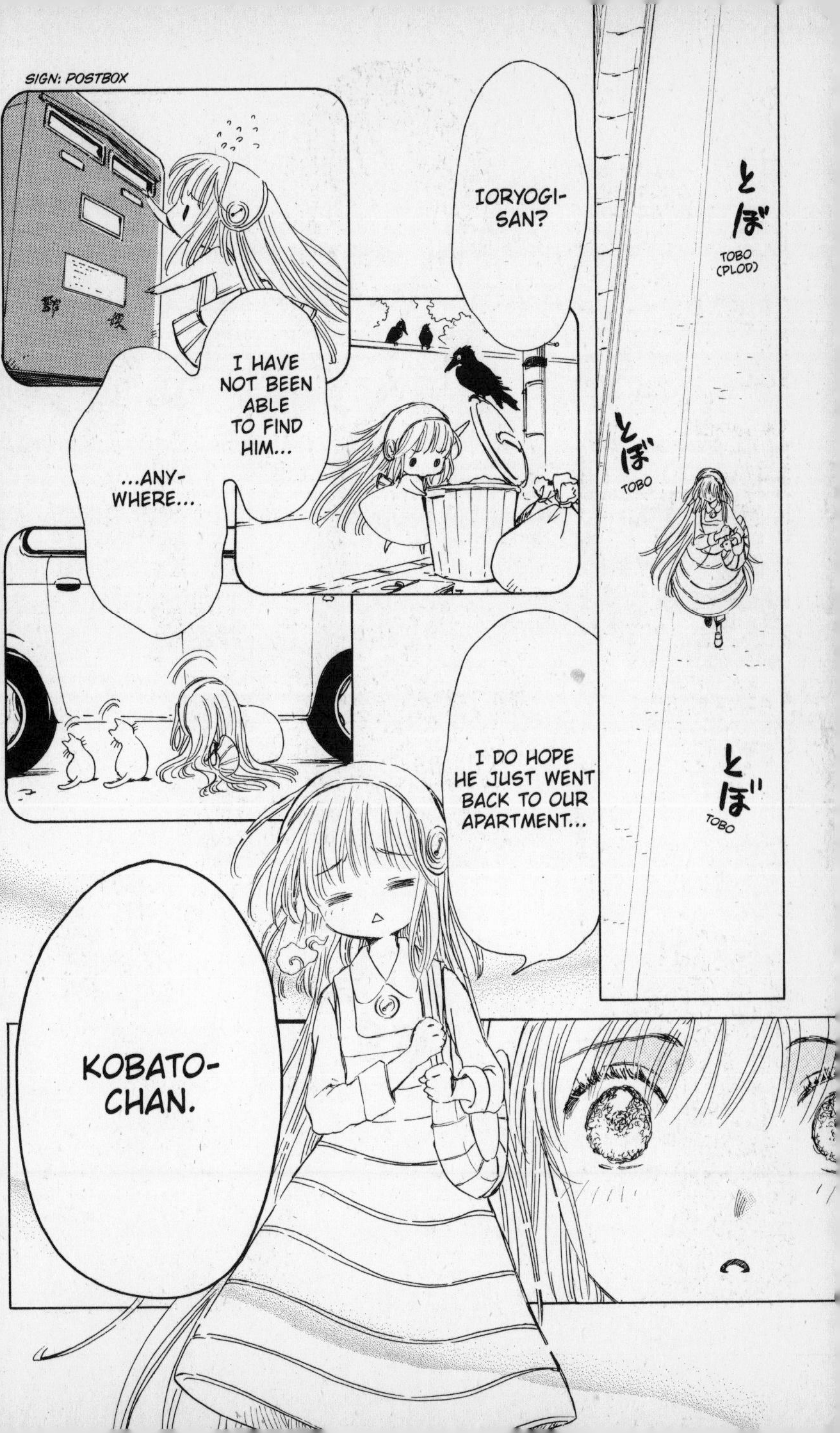

とぼ
TOBO (PLOD)
とぼ
TOBO
とぼ
TOBO
SIGN: POSTBOX
郵便
IORYOGI-SAN?
I HAVE NOT BEEN ABLE TO FIND HIM...
...ANY-WHERE...
I DO HOPE HE JUST WENT BACK TO OUR APARTMENT...
KOBATO-CHAN.

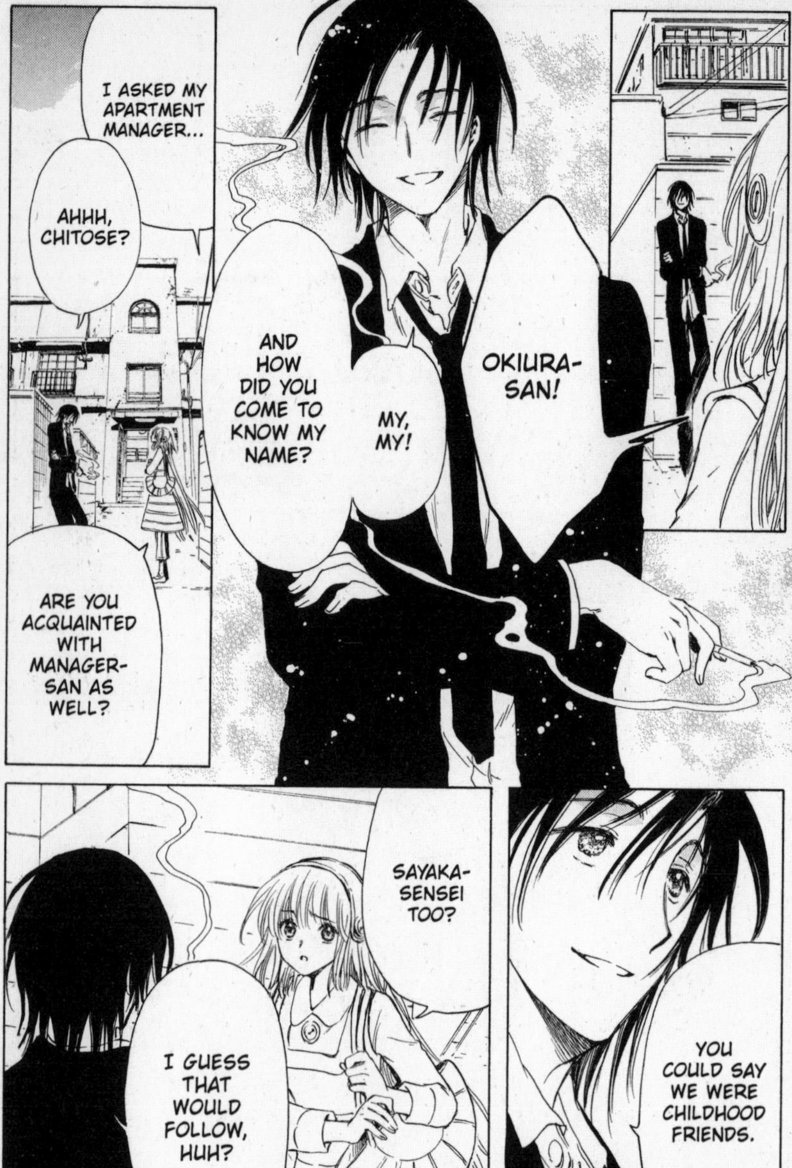
OKIURA-SAN!
MY, MY!
AND HOW DID YOU COME TO KNOW MY NAME?
I ASKED MY APARTMENT MANAGER...
AHHH, CHITOSE?
ARE YOU ACQUAINTED WITH MANAGER-SAN AS WELL?
YOU COULD SAY WE WERE CHILDHOOD FRIENDS.
SAYAKA-SENSEI TOO?
I GUESS THAT WOULD FOLLOW, HUH?

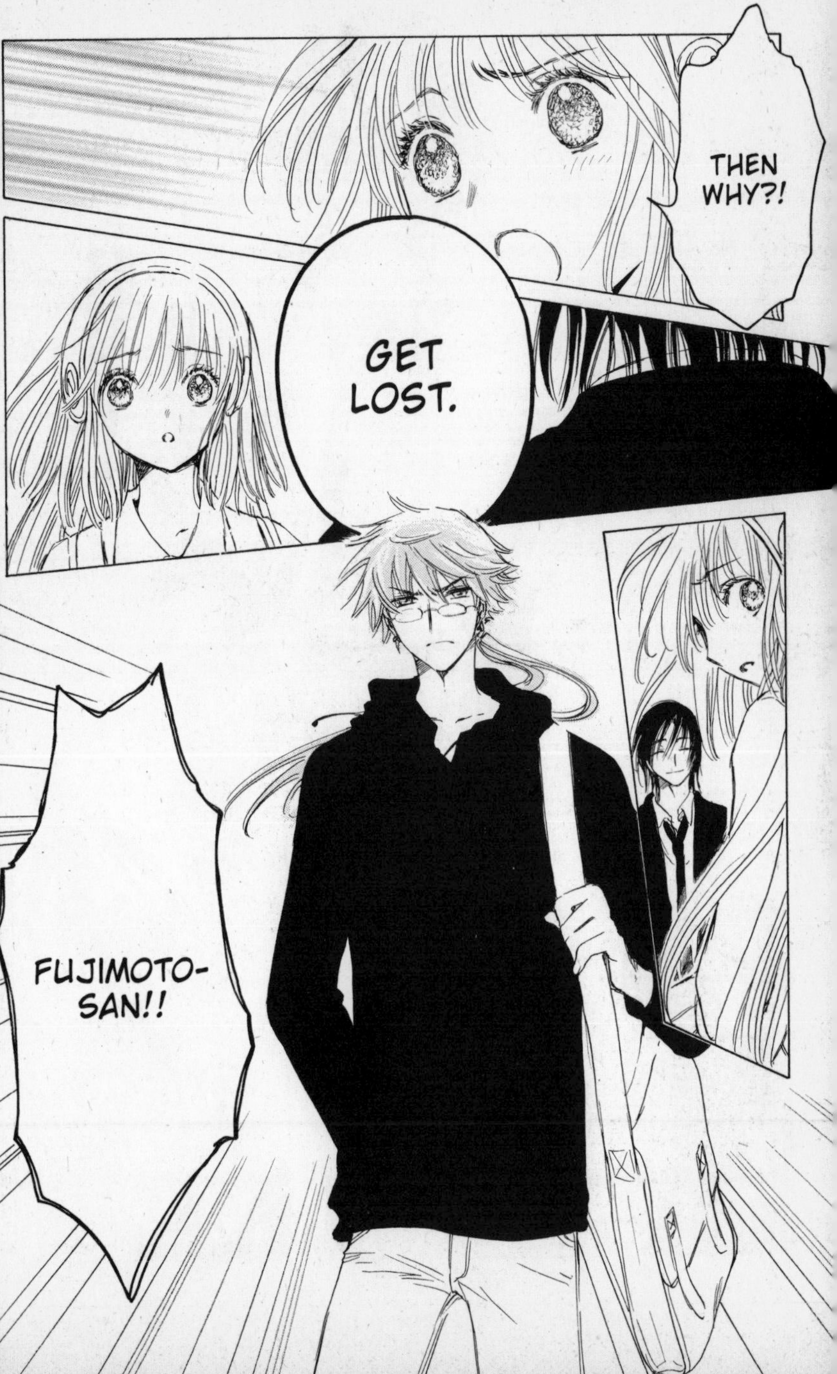
THEN WHY?!
GET LOST.
FUJIMOTO-SAN!!

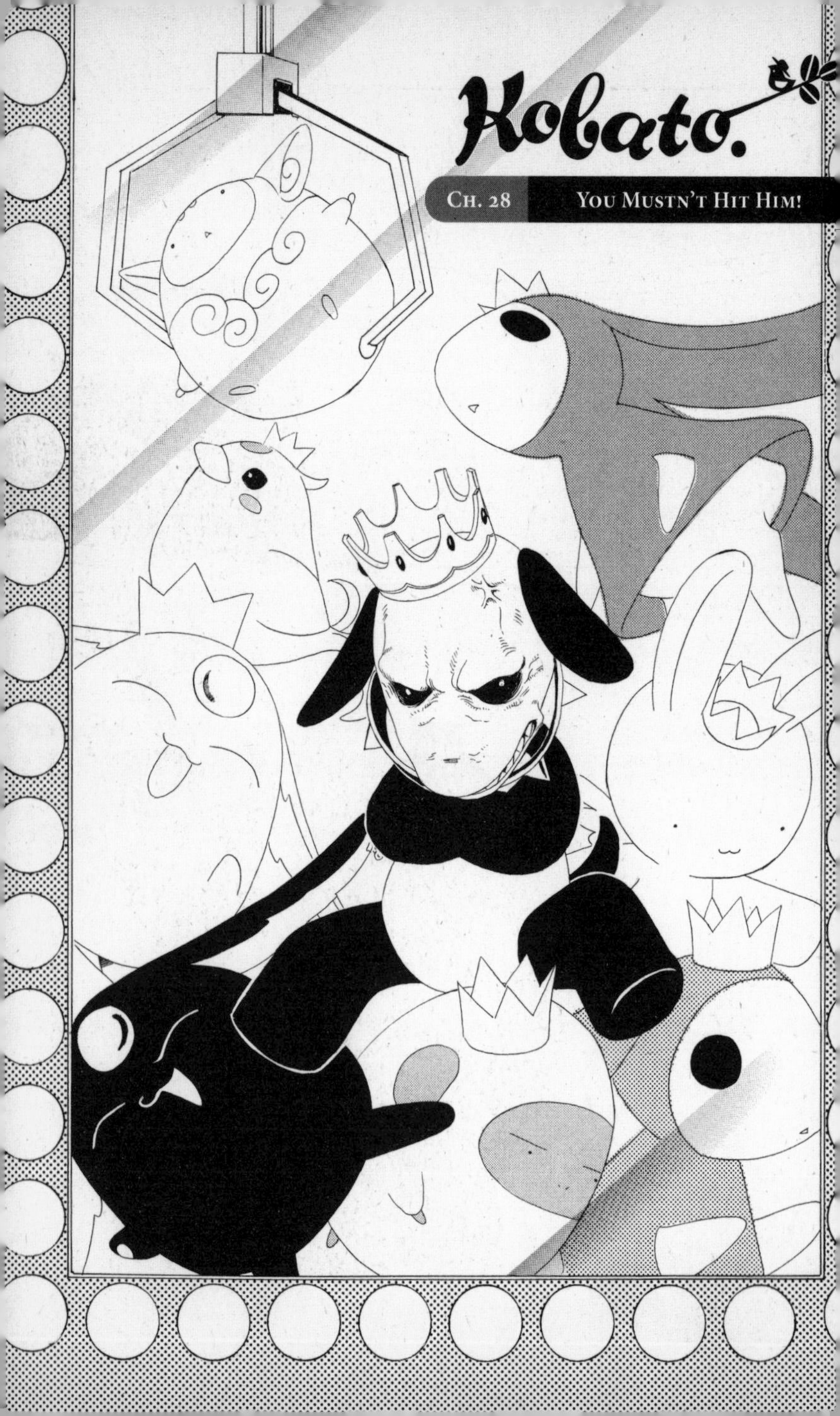

Kobato.

Ch. 28 You Mustn't Hit Him!

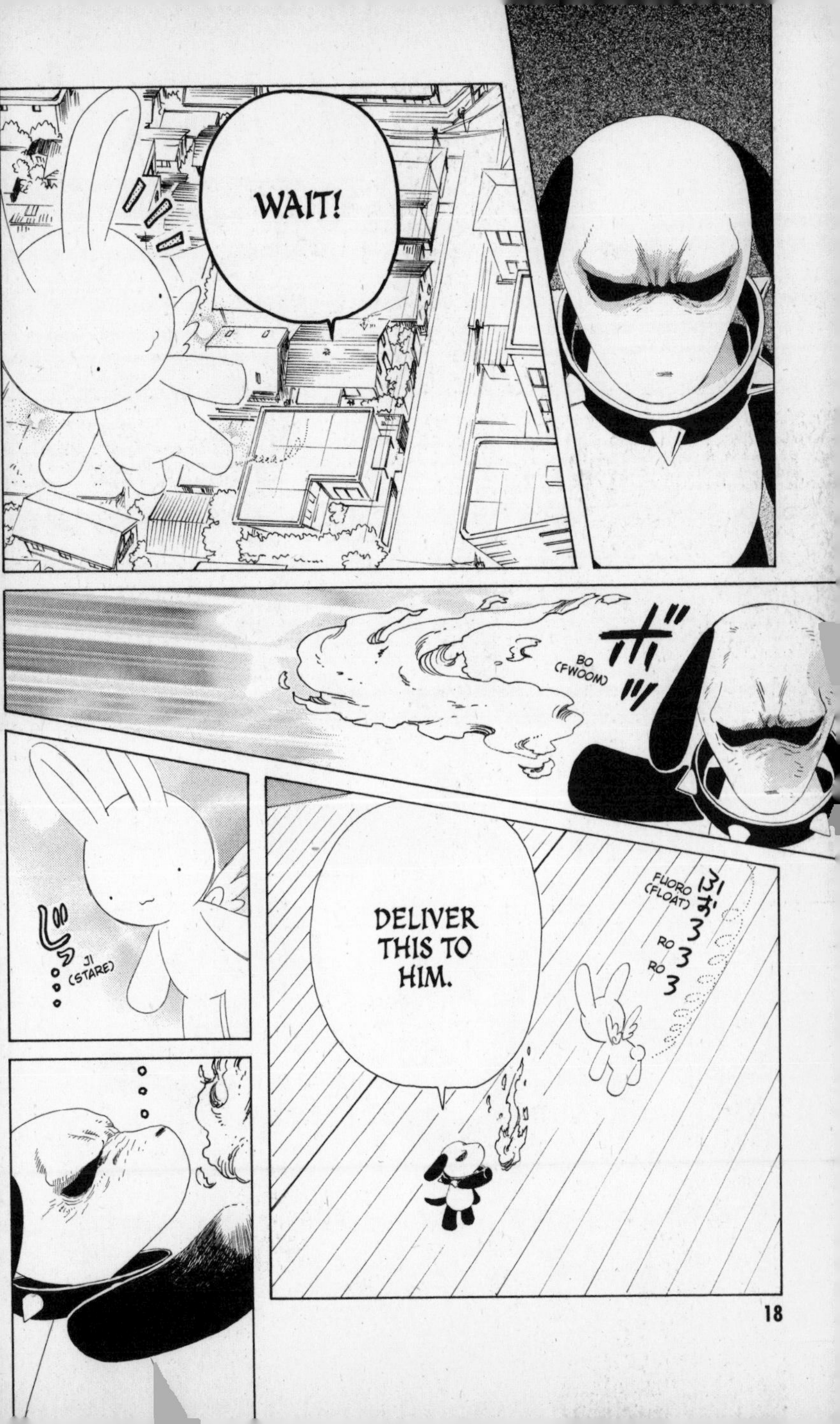
WAIT!
ボッ
BO (FWOOM)
DELIVER THIS TO HIM.
FUORO (FLOAT)
RO
RO
JI (STARE)

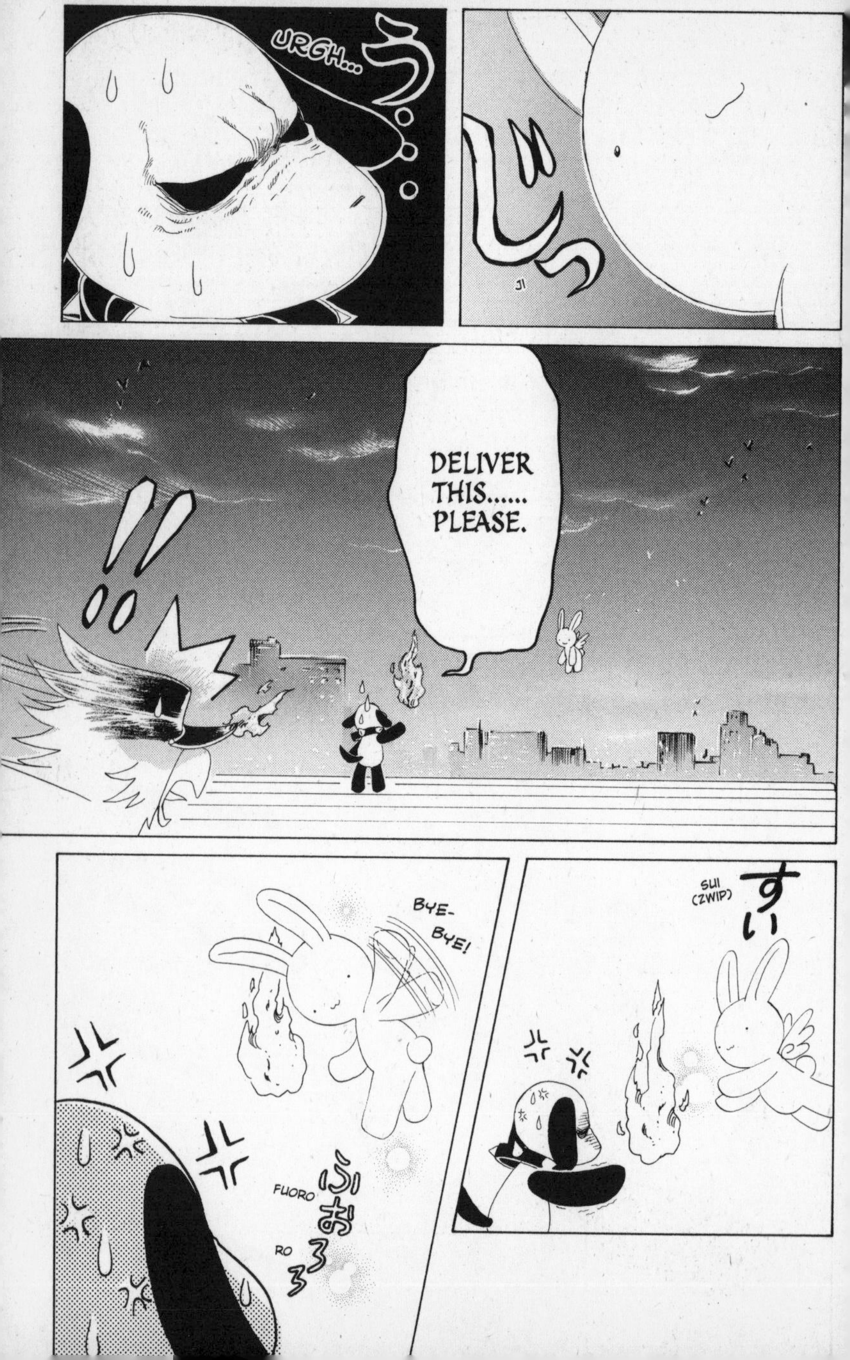
JI
URGH...
DELIVER THIS...... PLEASE.
SUI (ZWIP)
すい
BYE-BYE!
FUORO
RO
ふおろろ

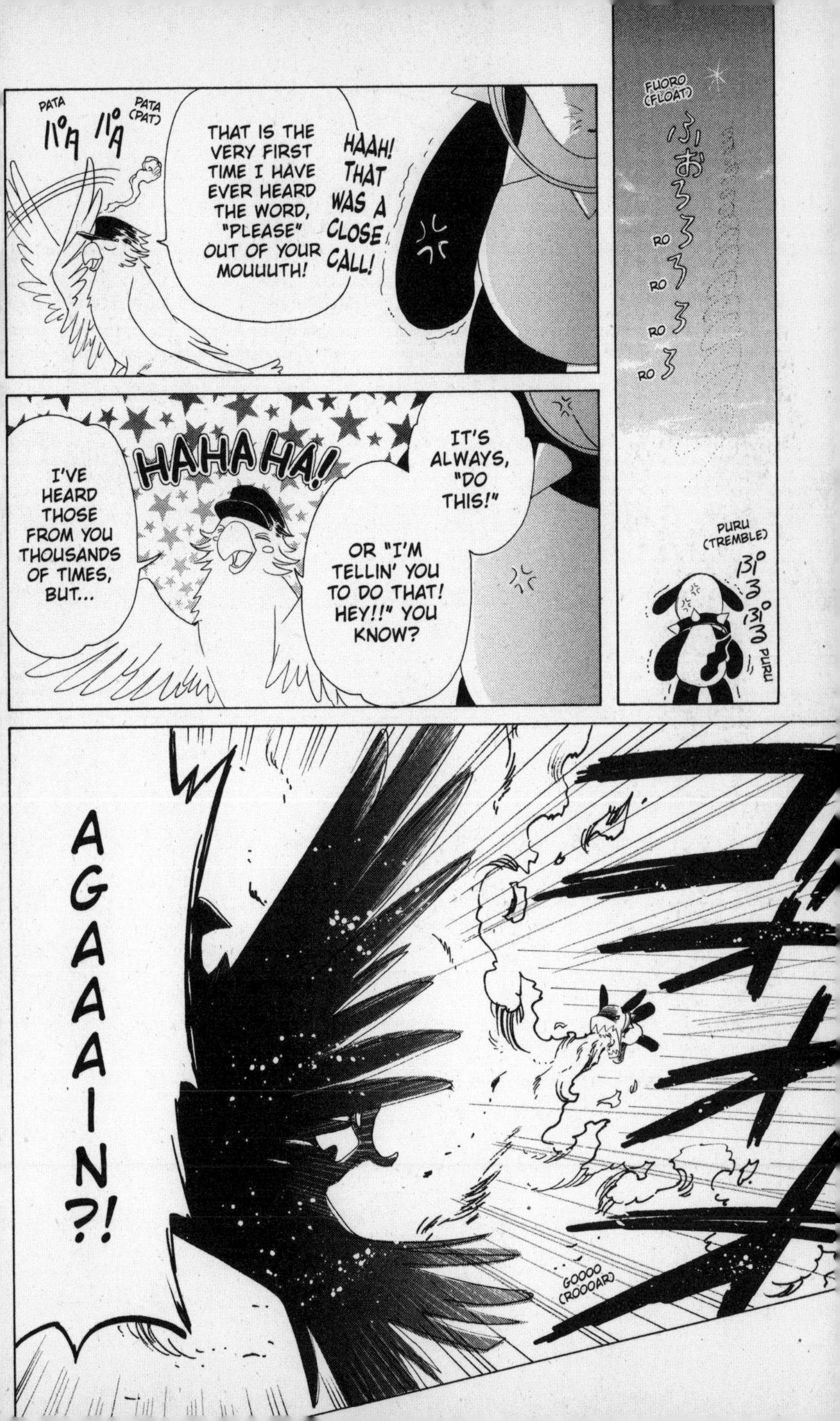
FUORO (FLOAT)
ふおろろろろ
RO
RO
RO
RO
PURU (TREMBLE)
ぷるぷる
PURU
HAAH! THAT WAS A CLOSE CALL!
THAT IS THE VERY FIRST TIME I HAVE EVER HEARD THE WORD, "PLEASE" OUT OF YOUR MOUUUTH!
PATA (PAT)
パタ
PATA
パタ
IT'S ALWAYS, "DO THIS!"
OR "I'M TELLIN' YOU TO DO THAT! HEY!!" YOU KNOW?
HAHAHA!
I'VE HEARD THOSE FROM YOU THOUSANDS OF TIMES, BUT...
GOOOO (ROOOAR)
AGAAAIN?!

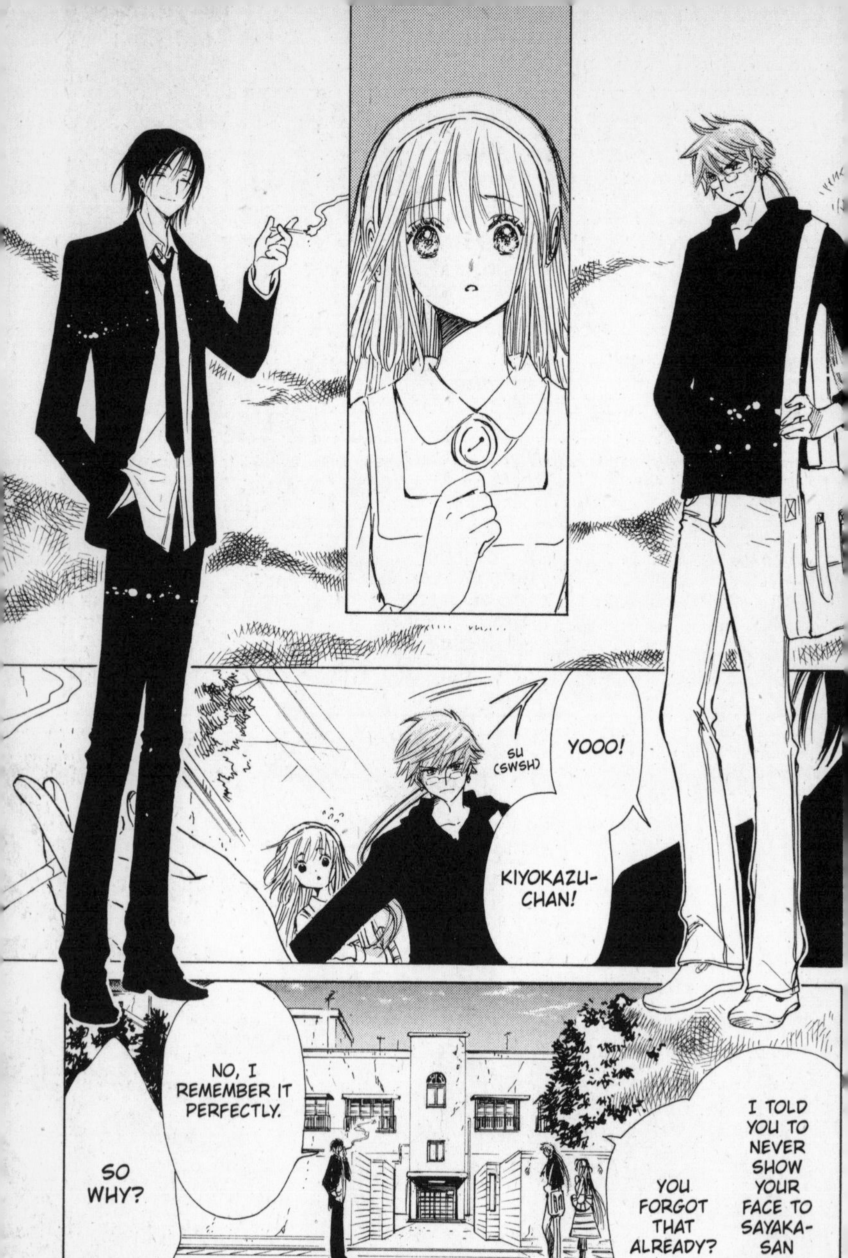
YOOO!
KIYOKAZU-CHAN!
SU (SWSH)
I TOLD YOU TO NEVER SHOW YOUR FACE TO SAYAKA-SAN AGAIN!
YOU FORGOT THAT ALREADY?
NO, I REMEMBER IT PERFECTLY.
SO WHY?

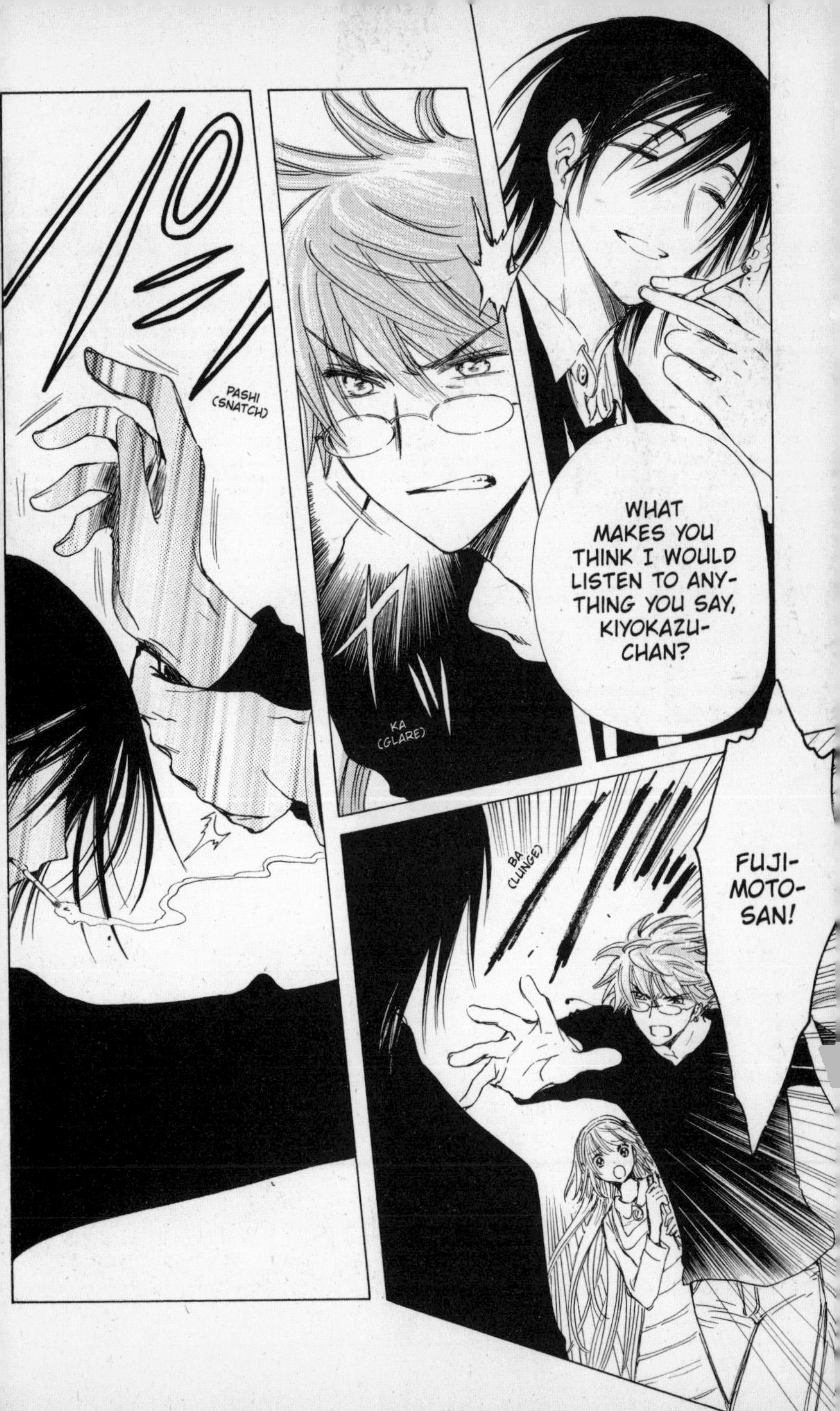
WHAT MAKES YOU THINK I WOULD LISTEN TO ANYTHING YOU SAY, KIYOKAZU-CHAN?
KA (GLARE)
FUJI-MOTO-SAN!
BA (LUNGE)
PASHI (SNATCH)

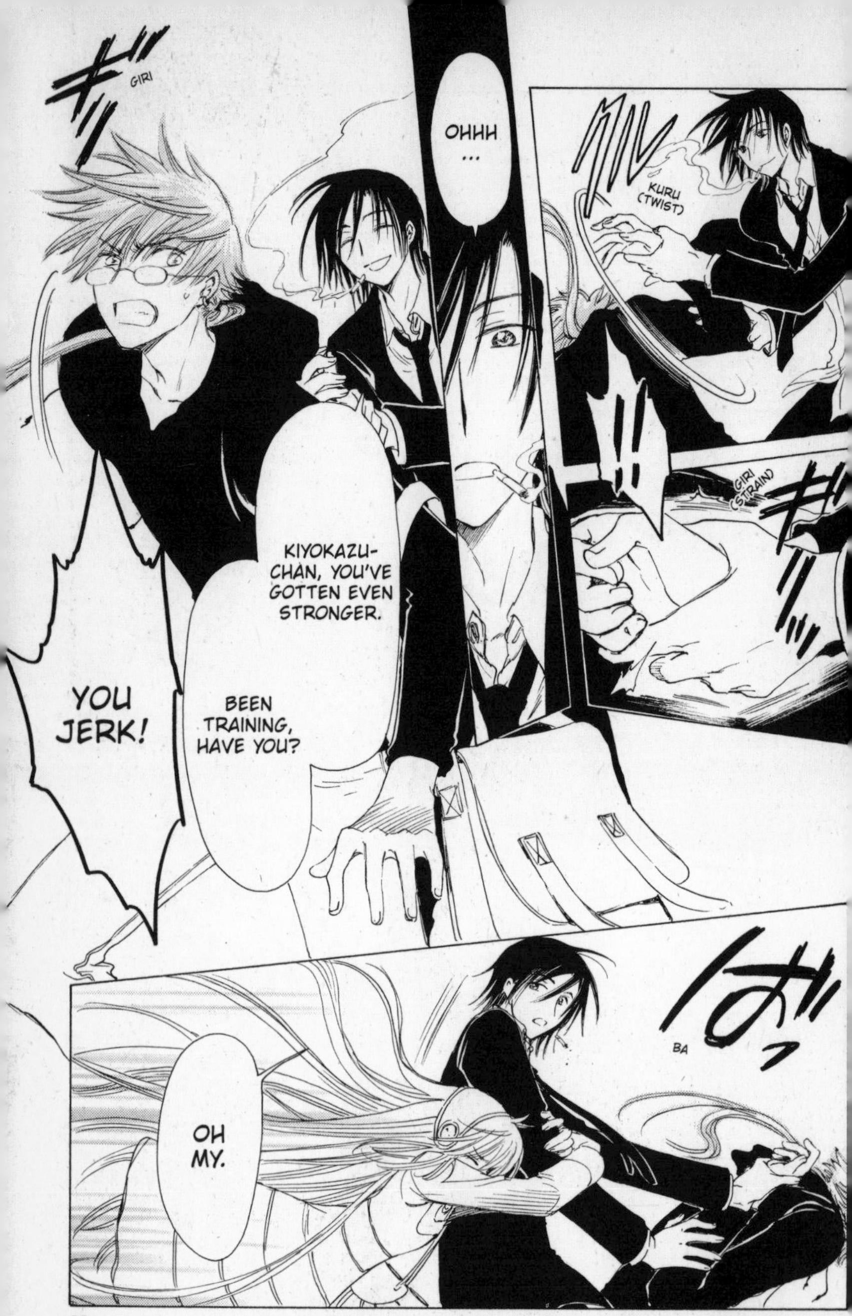
KURU (TWIST)
GIRI (STRAIN)
OHHH ...
GIRI
KIYOKAZU-CHAN, YOU'VE GOTTEN EVEN STRONGER.
BEEN TRAINING, HAVE YOU?
YOU JERK!
BA
OH MY.

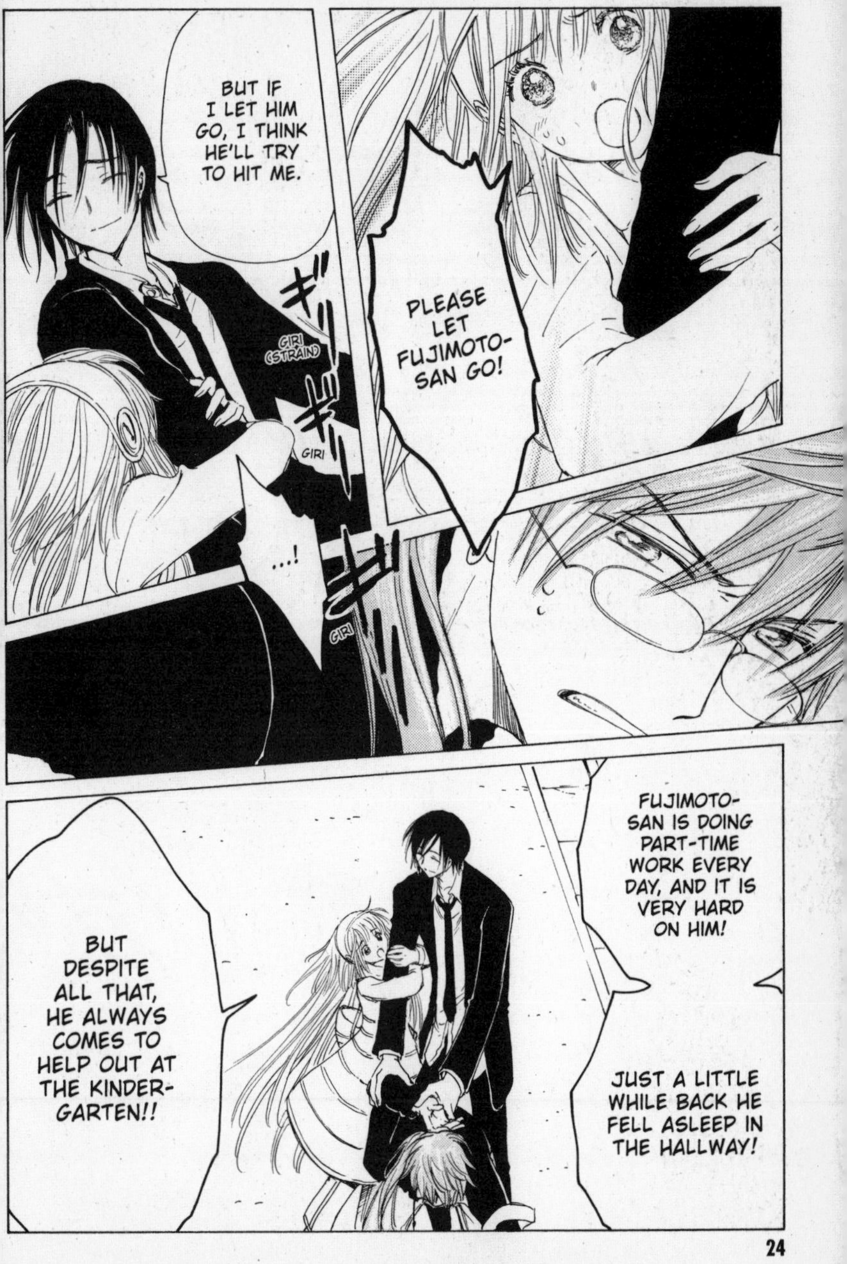
PLEASE LET FUJIMOTO-SAN GO!
BUT IF I LET HIM GO, I THINK HE'LL TRY TO HIT ME.
GIRI (STRAIN)
GIRI
GIRI
...!
FUJIMOTO-SAN IS DOING PART-TIME WORK EVERY DAY, AND IT IS VERY HARD ON HIM!
JUST A LITTLE WHILE BACK HE FELL ASLEEP IN THE HALLWAY!
BUT DESPITE ALL THAT, HE ALWAYS COMES TO HELP OUT AT THE KINDER-GARTEN!!

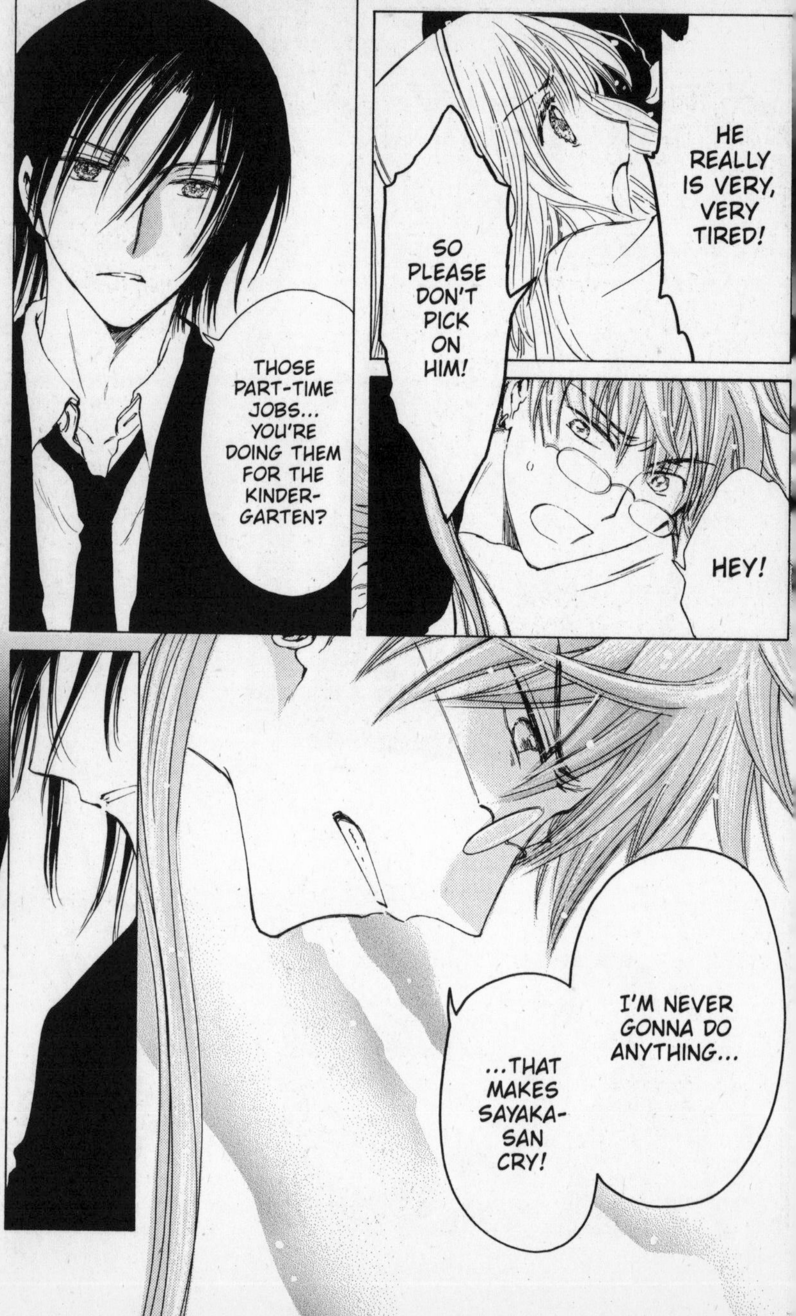
HE REALLY IS VERY, VERY TIRED!
SO PLEASE DON'T PICK ON HIM!
HEY!
THOSE PART-TIME JOBS... YOU'RE DOING THEM FOR THE KINDER-GARTEN?
I'M NEVER GONNA DO ANYTHING...
...THAT MAKES SAYAKA-SAN CRY!

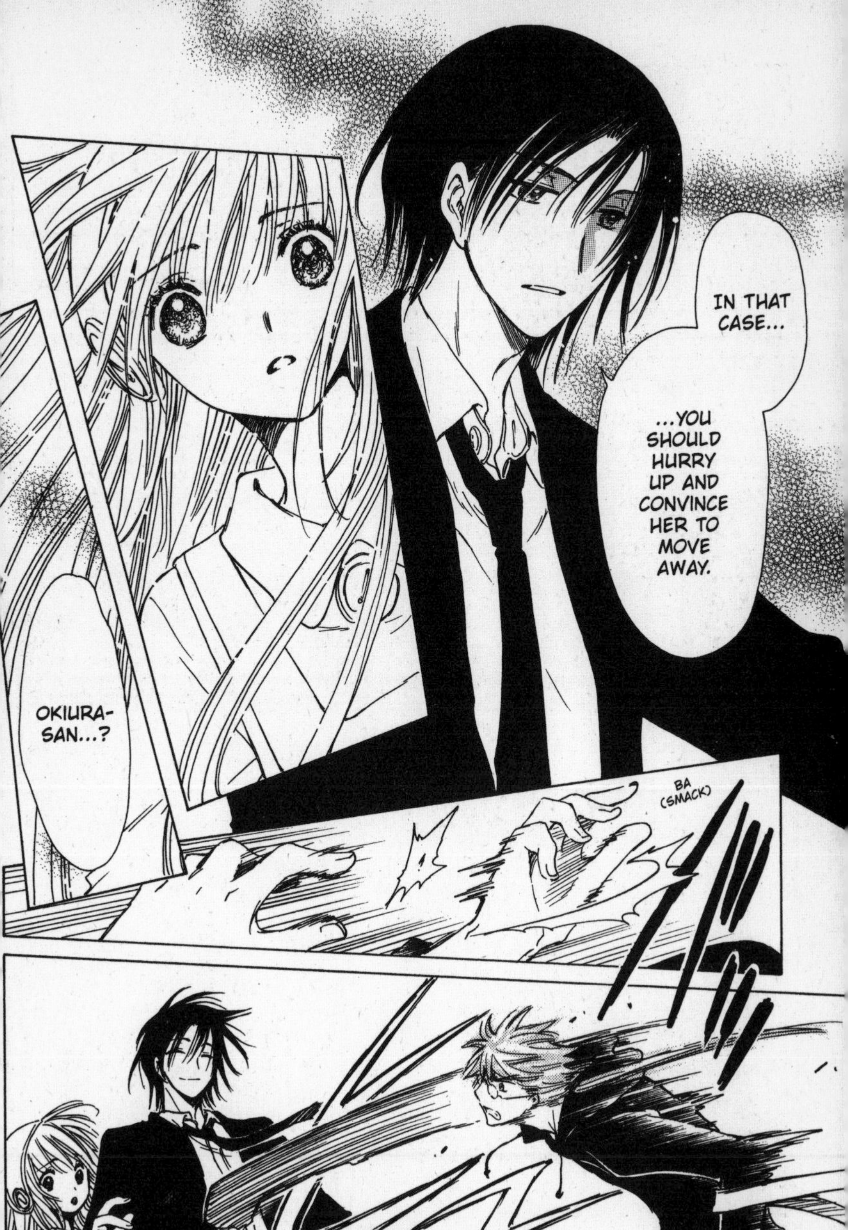
IN THAT CASE...
...YOU SHOULD HURRY UP AND CONVINCE HER TO MOVE AWAY.
OKIURA-SAN...?
BA (SMACK)
HYU (WHOOSH)

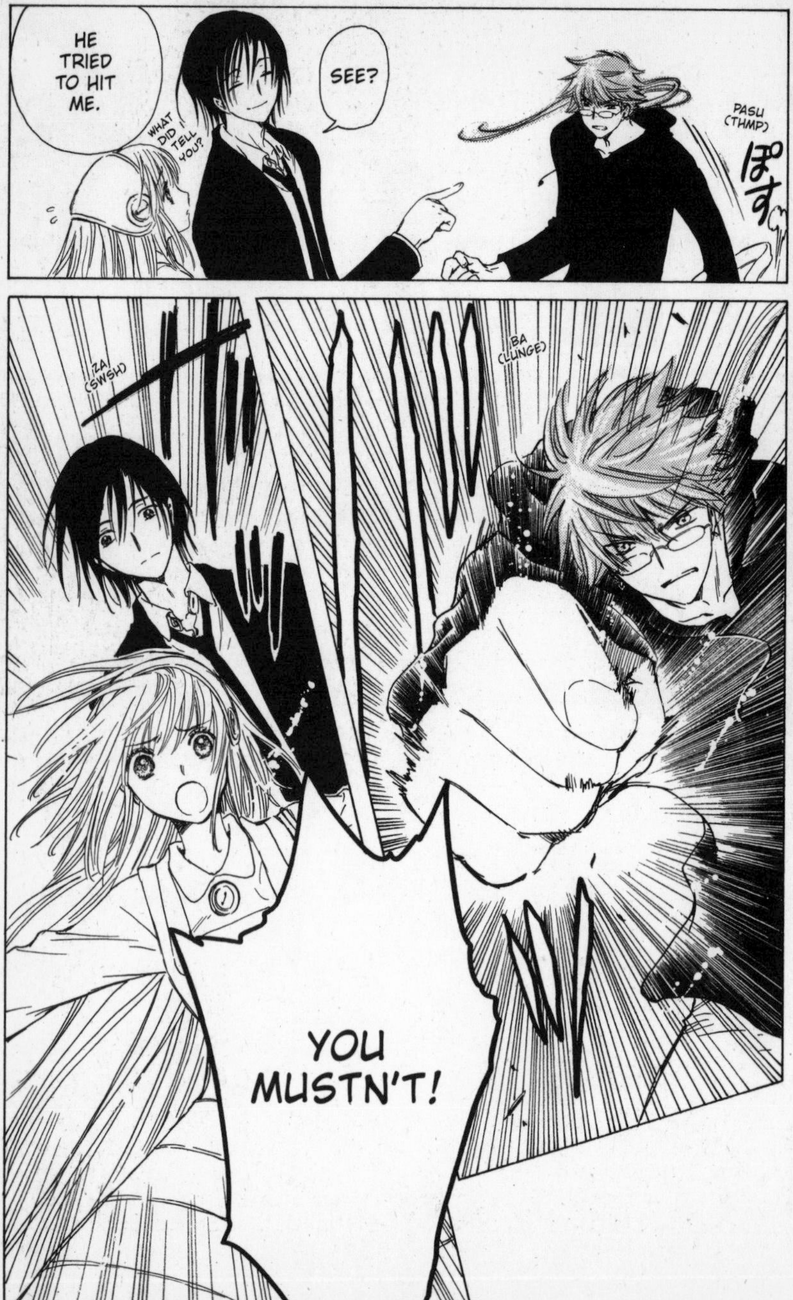

PASU (THMP)
ぽす
SEE?
WHAT DID I TELL YOU?
HE TRIED TO HIT ME.
BA (LUNGE)
ZA (SWSH)
YOU MUSTN'T!

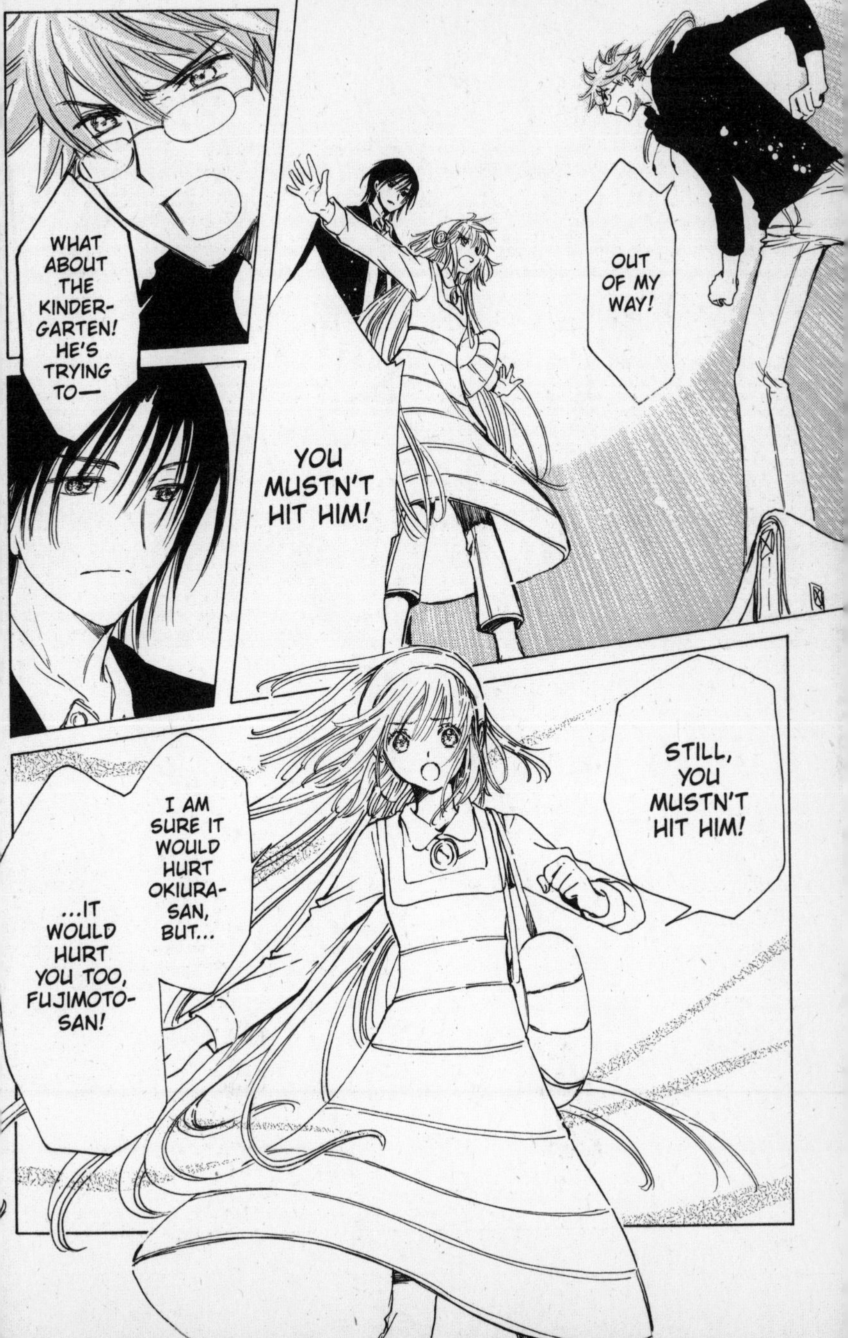
OUT OF MY WAY!
YOU MUSTN'T HIT HIM!
WHAT ABOUT THE KINDERGARTEN! HE'S TRYING TO—
STILL, YOU MUSTN'T HIT HIM!
I AM SURE IT WOULD HURT OKIURA-SAN, BUT...
...IT WOULD HURT YOU TOO, FUJIMOTO-SAN!

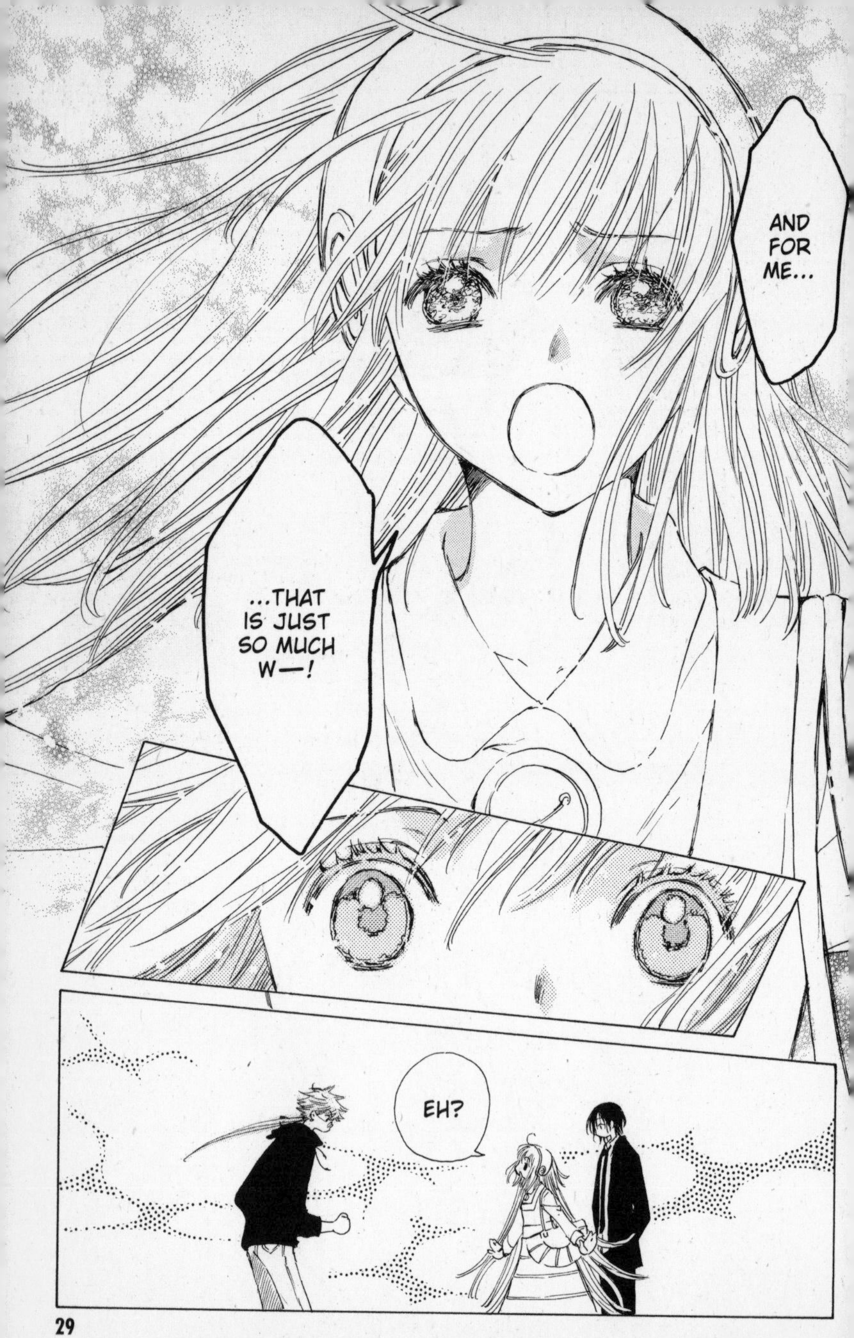
AND FOR ME...
...THAT IS JUST SO MUCH W—!
EH?

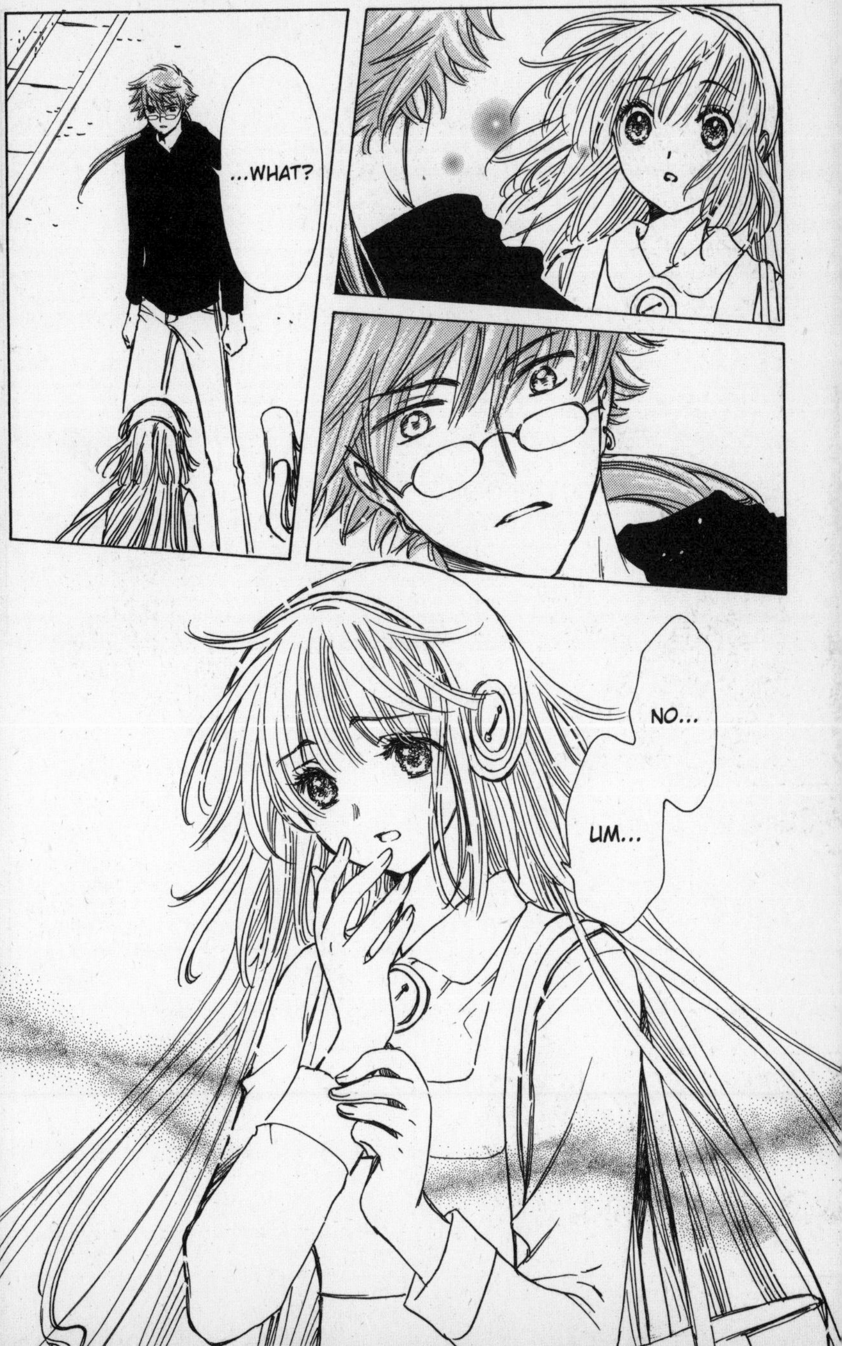
...WHAT?
NO...
UM...

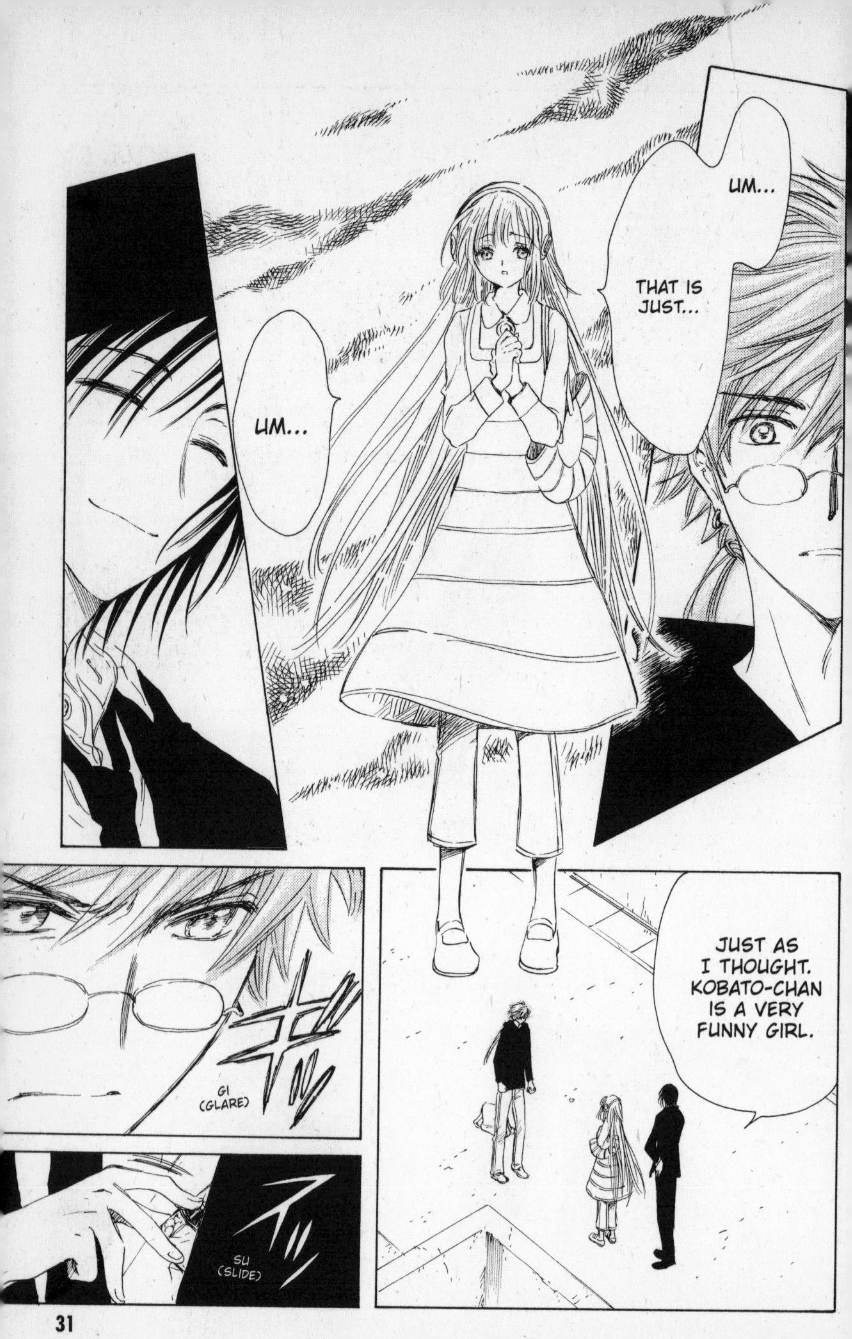
UM...
THAT IS JUST...
UM...
JUST AS I THOUGHT. KOBATO-CHAN IS A VERY FUNNY GIRL.
GI (GLARE)
SU (SLIDE)

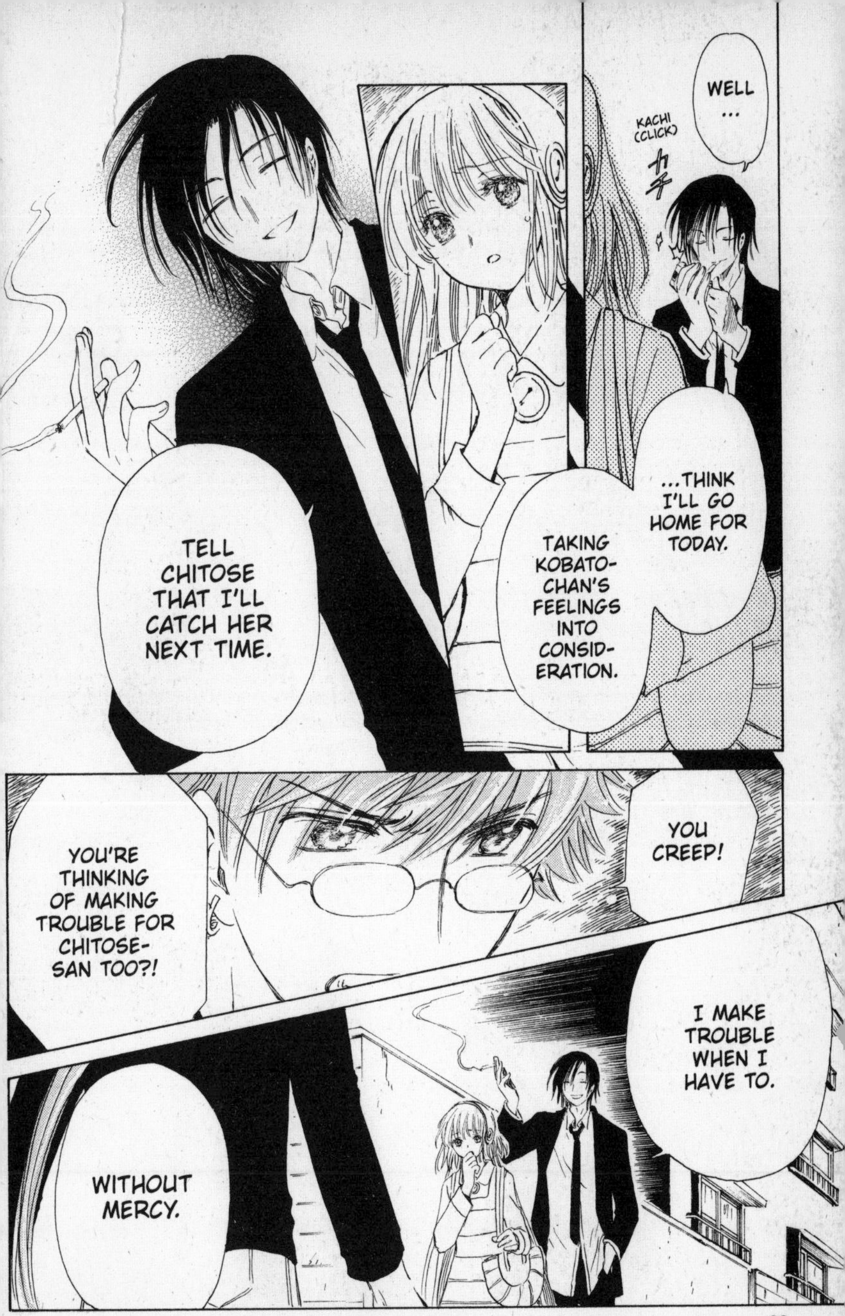
WELL ...
KACHI (CLICK)
カチ
...THINK I'LL GO HOME FOR TODAY.
TAKING KOBATO-CHAN'S FEELINGS INTO CONSID-ERATION.
TELL CHITOSE THAT I'LL CATCH HER NEXT TIME.
YOU CREEP!
YOU'RE THINKING OF MAKING TROUBLE FOR CHITOSE-SAN TOO?!
I MAKE TROUBLE WHEN I HAVE TO.
WITHOUT MERCY.

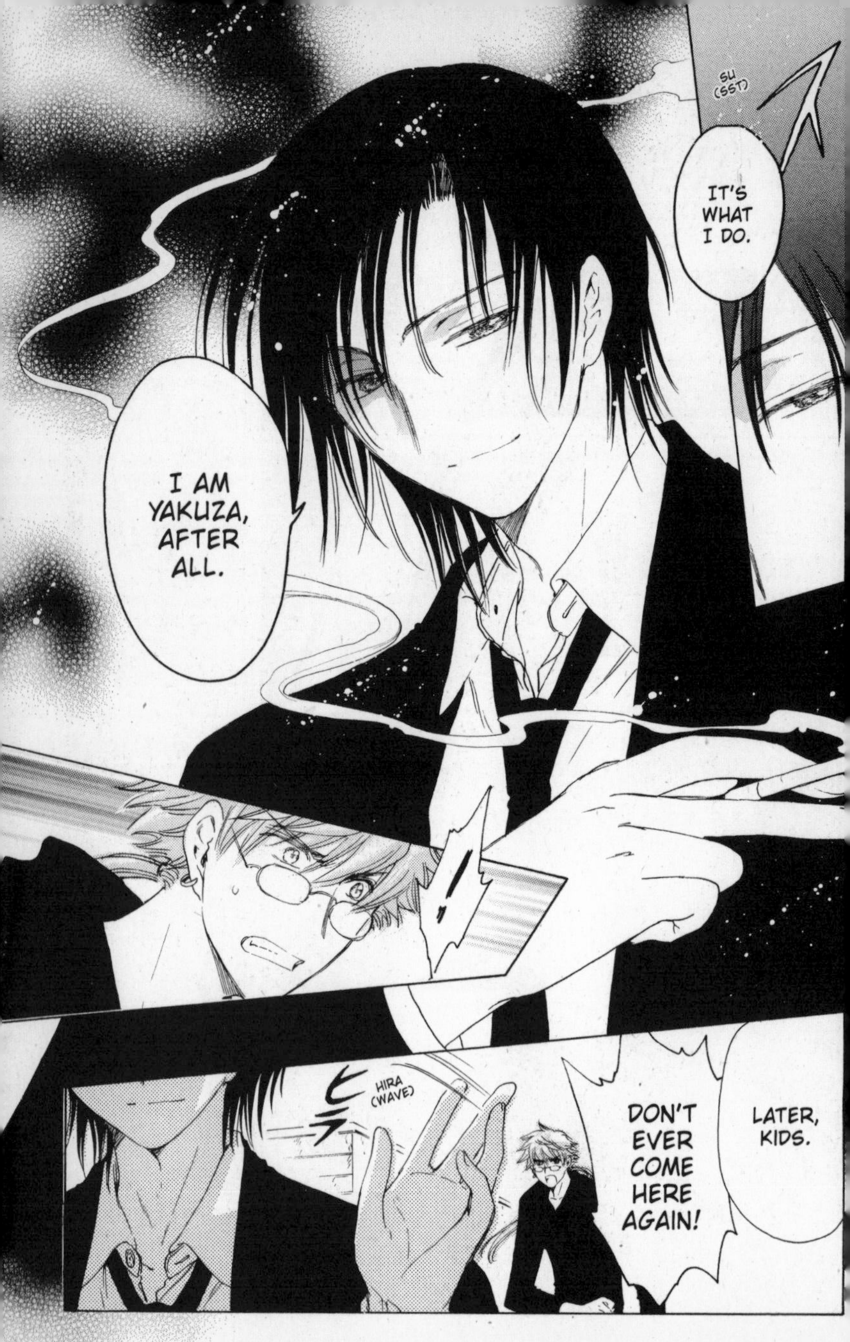
SU (SST)
IT'S WHAT I DO.
I AM YAKUZA, AFTER ALL.
LATER, KIDS.
DON'T EVER COME HERE AGAIN!
HIRA (WAVE)

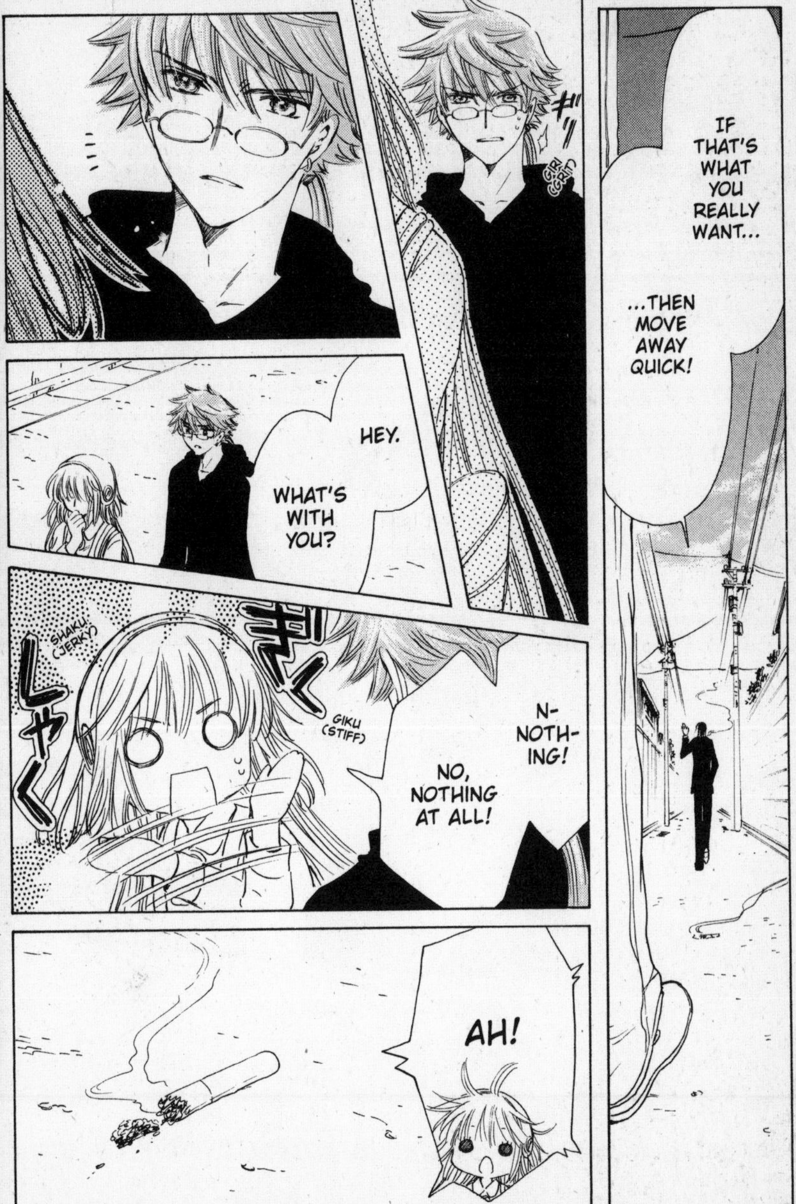
IF THAT'S WHAT YOU REALLY WANT...
...THEN MOVE AWAY QUICK!
GIRI (GRIT)
HEY.
WHAT'S WITH YOU?
GIKU (STIFF)
N-NOTH-ING!
NO, NOTHING AT ALL!
SHAKU (JERKY)
AH!

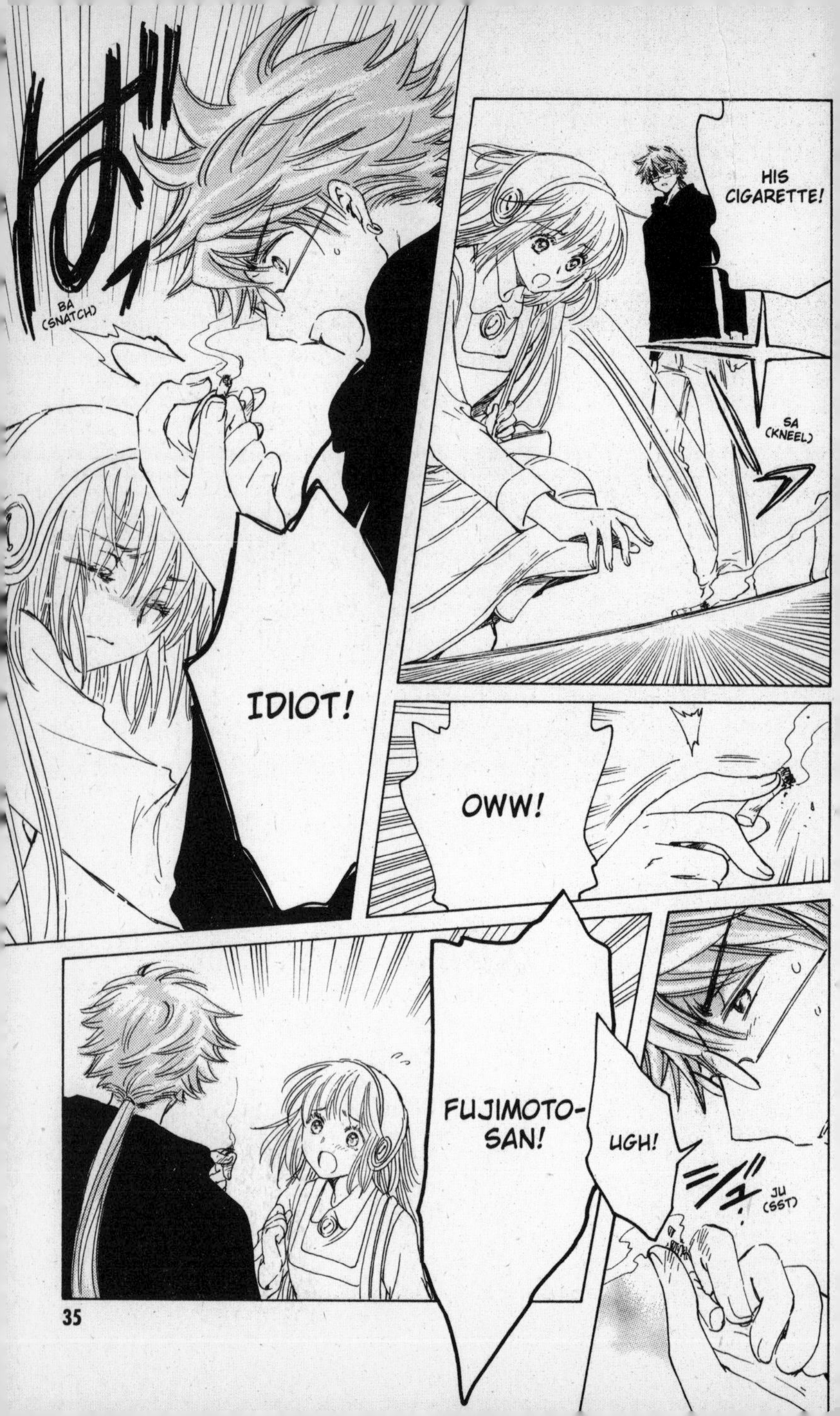
HIS CIGARETTE!
SA (KNEEL)
OWW!
BA (SNATCH)
IDIOT!
UGH!
JU (SST)
FUJIMOTO-SAN!

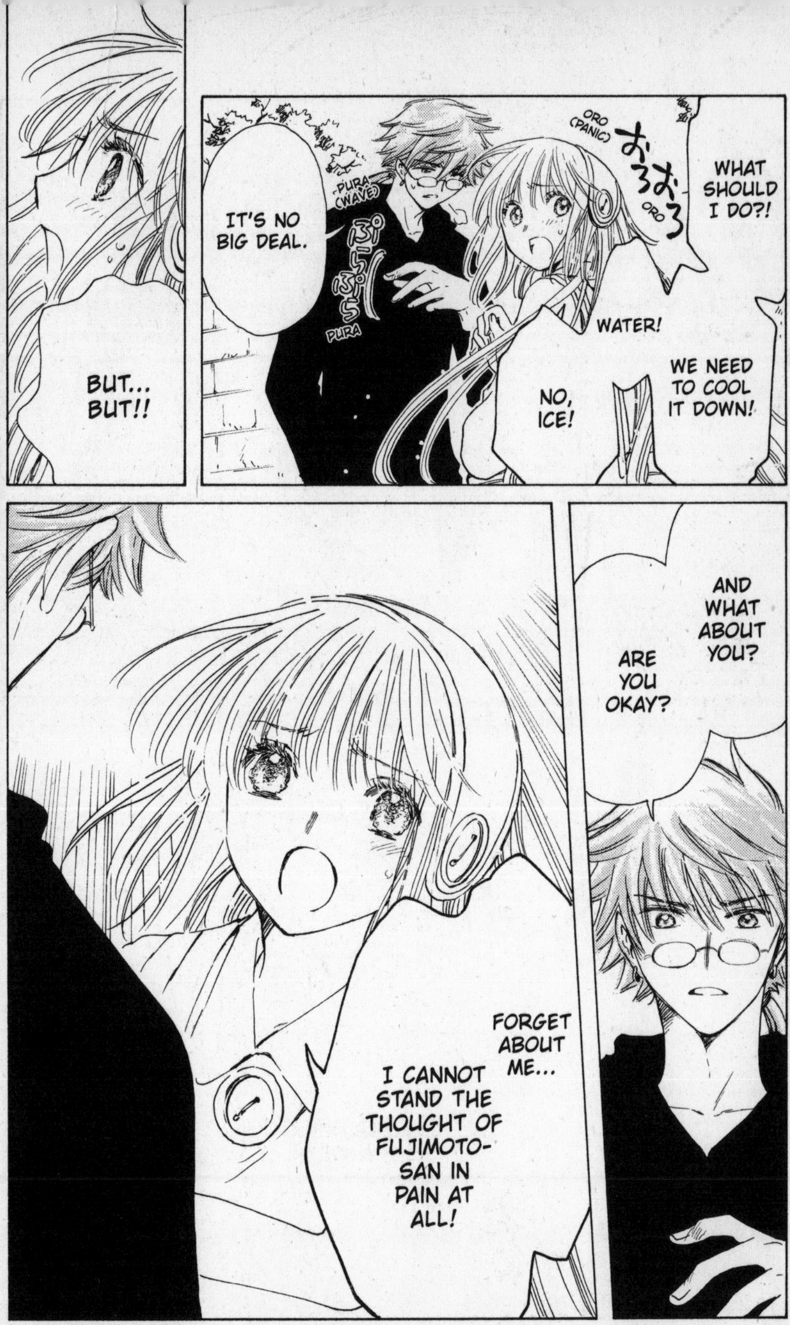
WHAT SHOULD I DO?!
ORO (PANIC) おろおろ ORO
WATER!
WE NEED TO COOL IT DOWN!
NO, ICE!
PURA (WAVE) ぷらぷら PURA
IT'S NO BIG DEAL.
BUT... BUT!!
AND WHAT ABOUT YOU?
ARE YOU OKAY?
FORGET ABOUT ME...
I CANNOT STAND THE THOUGHT OF FUJIMOTO-SAN IN PAIN AT ALL!

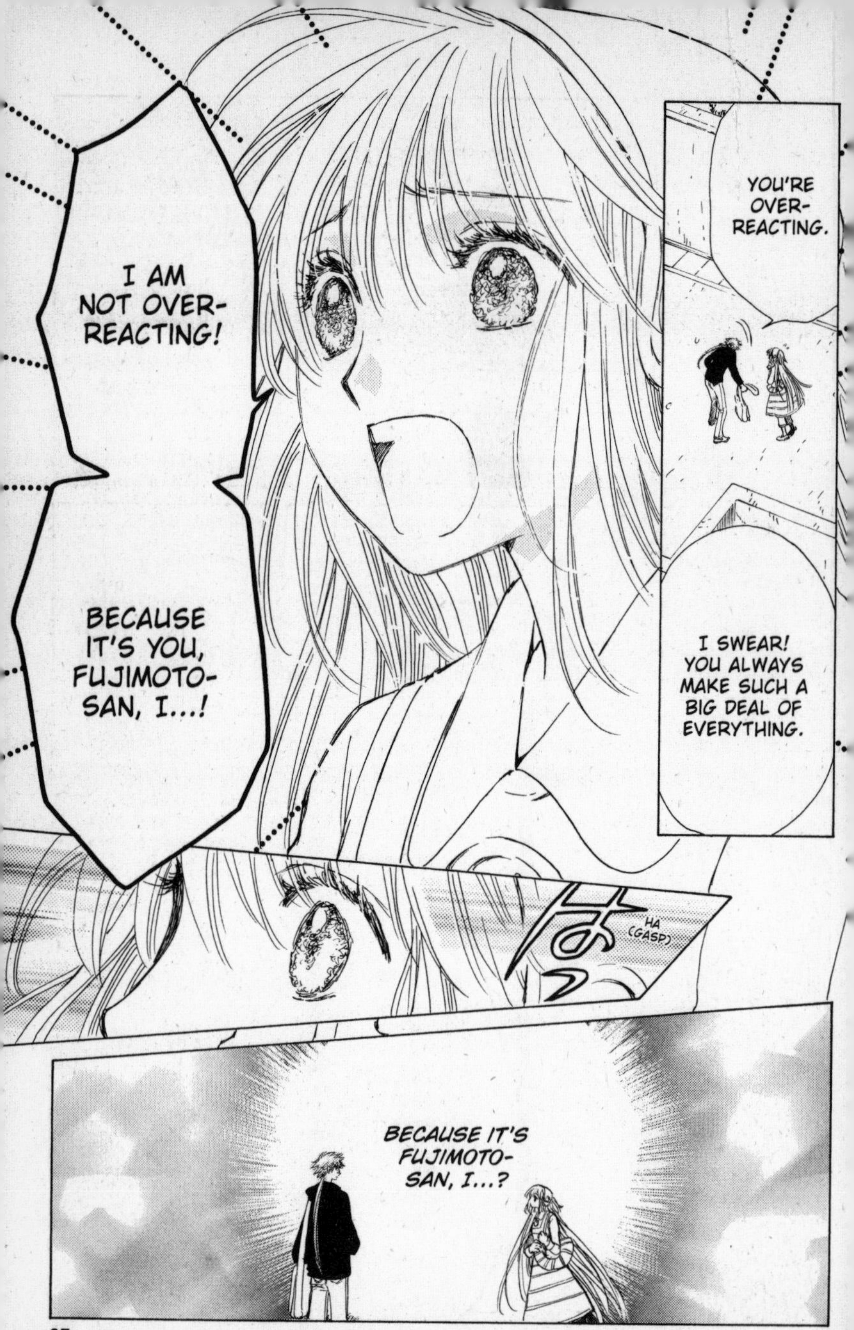
YOU'RE OVER-REACTING.
I SWEAR! YOU ALWAYS MAKE SUCH A BIG DEAL OF EVERYTHING.
I AM NOT OVER-REACTING!
BECAUSE IT'S YOU, FUJIMOTO-SAN, I...!
はっ
HA (GASP)
BECAUSE IT'S FUJIMOTO-SAN, I...?

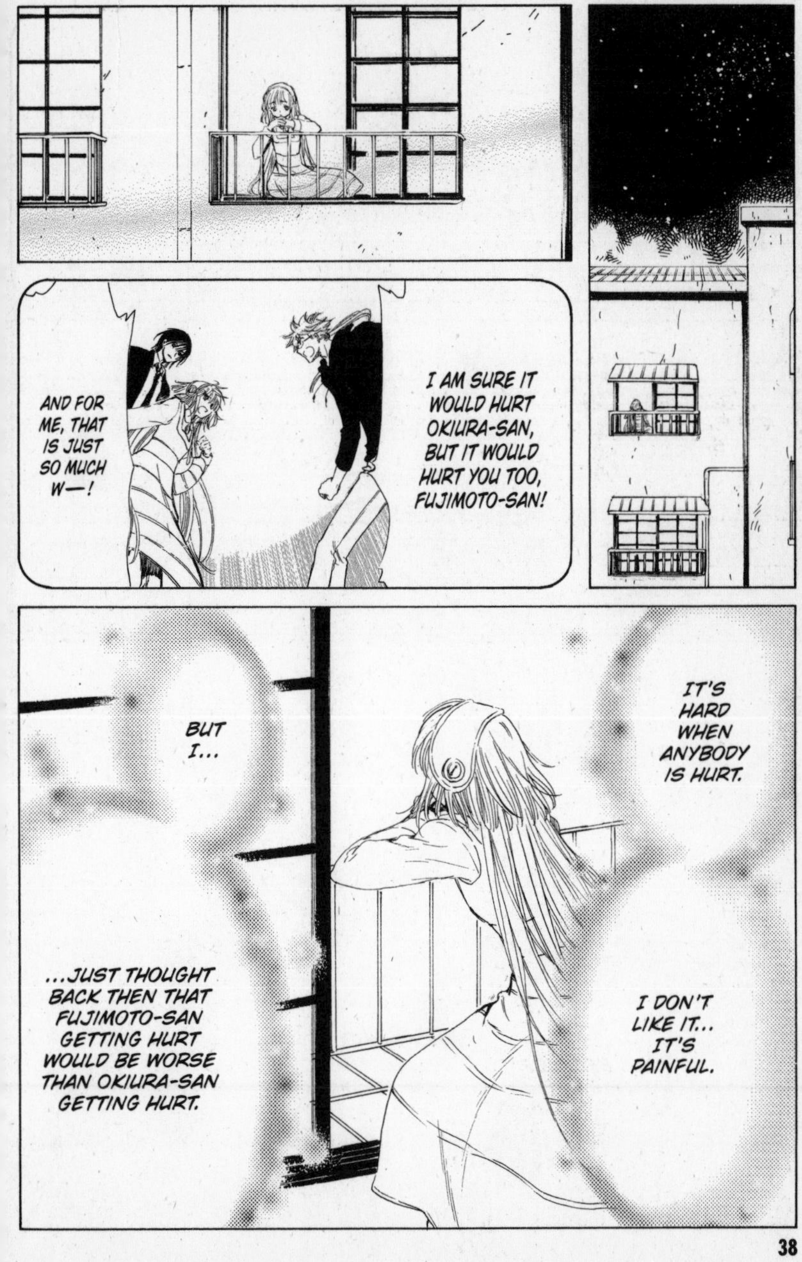
I AM SURE IT WOULD HURT OKIURA-SAN, BUT IT WOULD HURT YOU TOO, FUJIMOTO-SAN!
AND FOR ME, THAT IS JUST SO MUCH W—!
IT'S HARD WHEN ANYBODY IS HURT.
BUT I...
I DON'T LIKE IT... IT'S PAINFUL.
...JUST THOUGHT BACK THEN THAT FUJIMOTO-SAN GETTING HURT WOULD BE WORSE THAN OKIURA-SAN GETTING HURT.

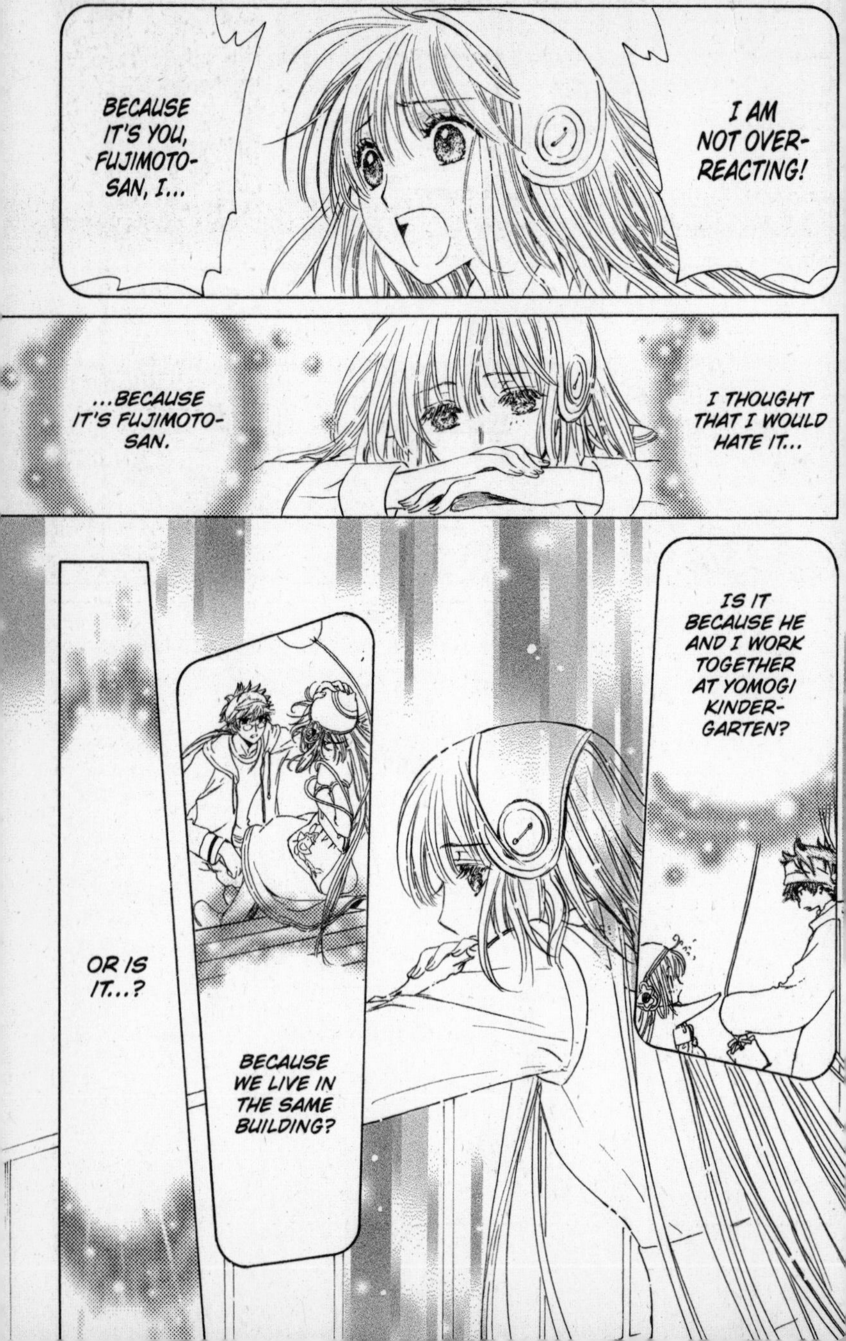
I AM NOT OVER-REACTING!
BECAUSE IT'S YOU, FUJIMOTO-SAN, I...
I THOUGHT THAT I WOULD HATE IT...
...BECAUSE IT'S FUJIMOTO-SAN.
IS IT BECAUSE HE AND I WORK TOGETHER AT YOMOGI KINDER-GARTEN?
OR IS IT...?
BECAUSE WE LIVE IN THE SAME BUILDING?

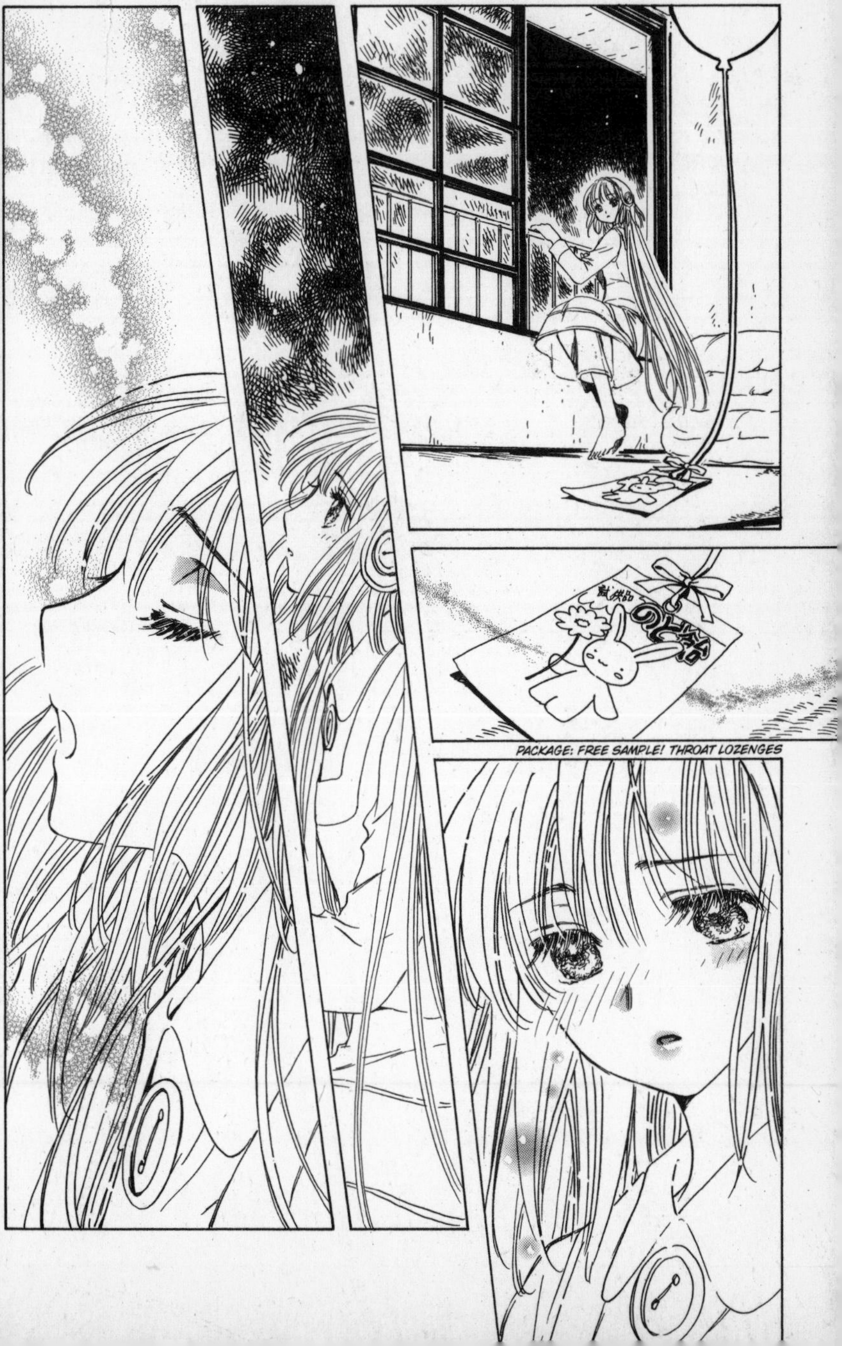
試供品
のど飴
PACKAGE: FREE SAMPLE! THROAT LOZENGES

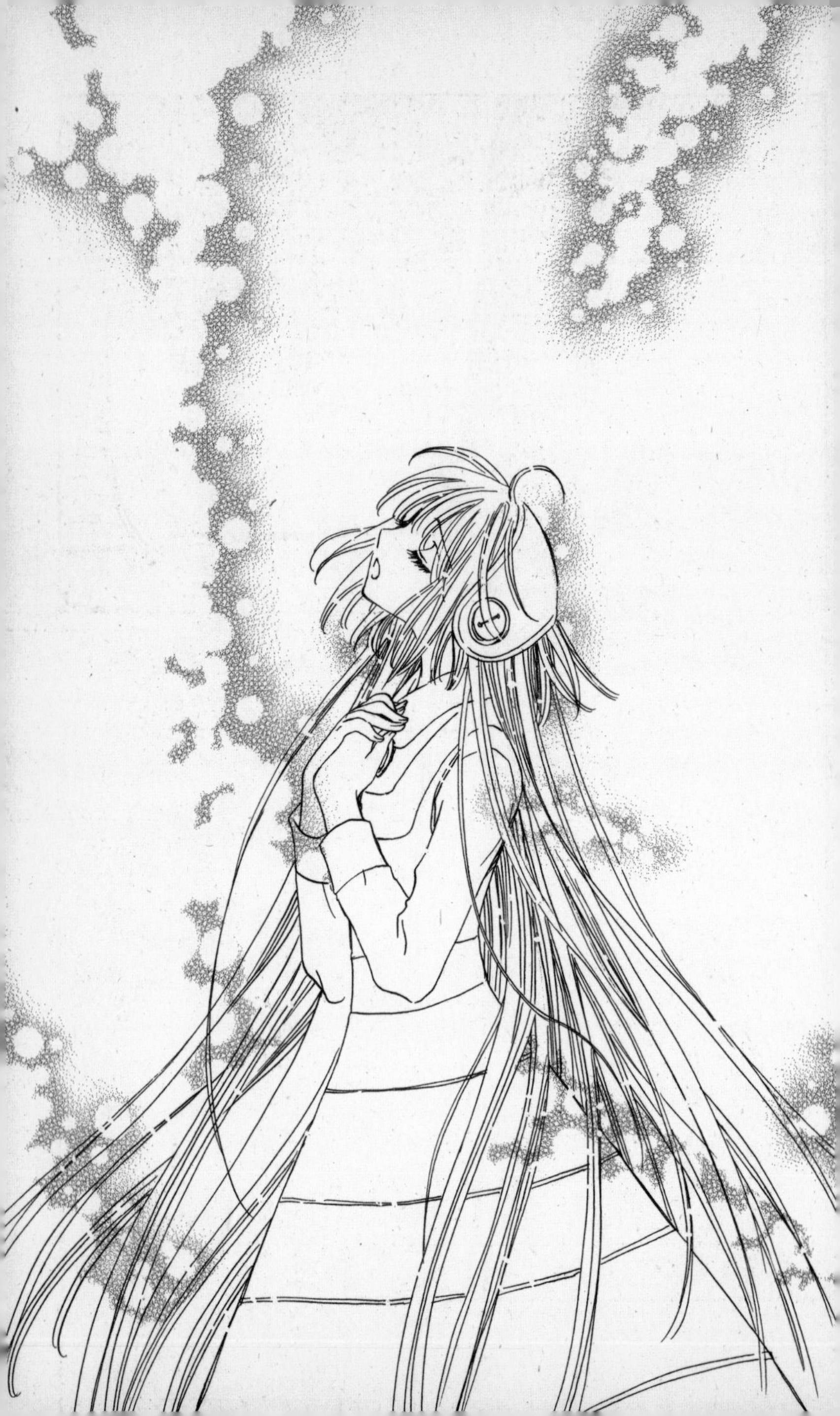

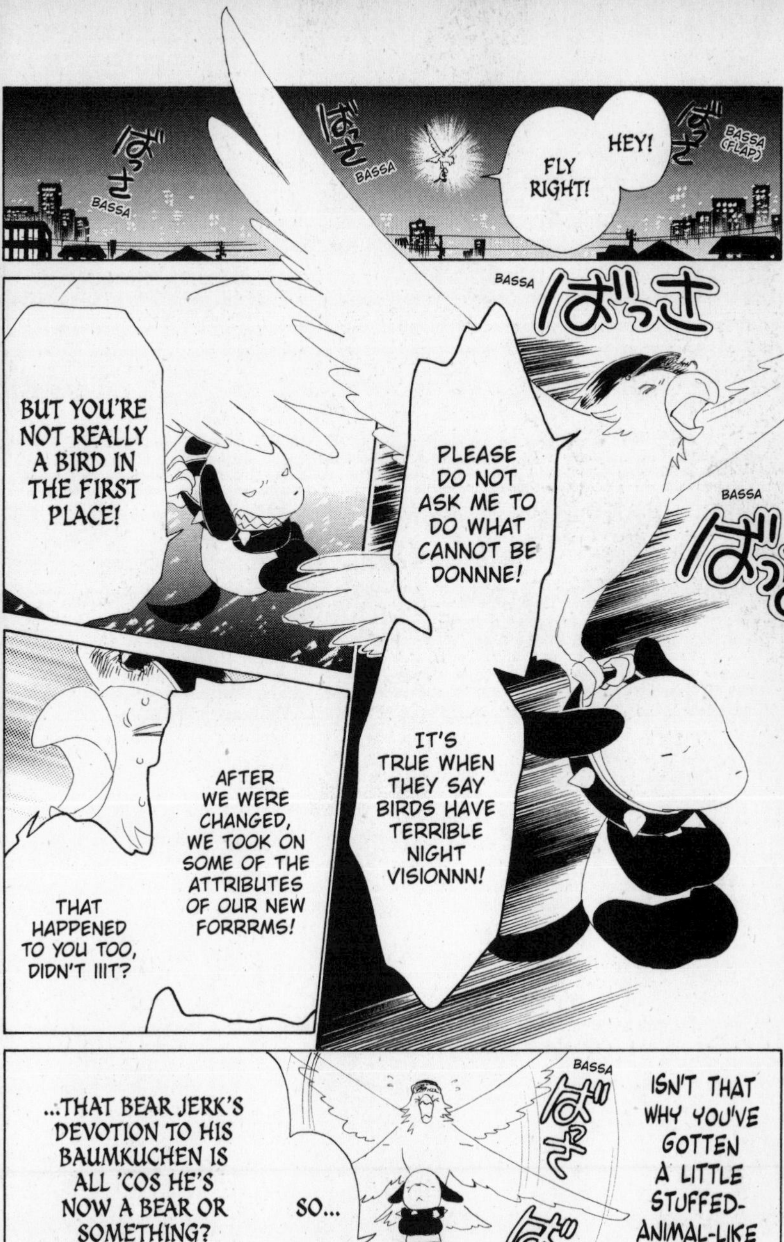
ばさ
BASSA (FLAP)
HEY!
FLY RIGHT!
ばさ
BASSA
ばさ
BASSA
BASSA
ばっさ
PLEASE DO NOT ASK ME TO DO WHAT CANNOT BE DONNNE!
BASSA
ばっさ
IT'S TRUE WHEN THEY SAY BIRDS HAVE TERRIBLE NIGHT VISIONNN!
BUT YOU'RE NOT REALLY A BIRD IN THE FIRST PLACE!
AFTER WE WERE CHANGED, WE TOOK ON SOME OF THE ATTRIBUTES OF OUR NEW FORRRMS!
THAT HAPPENED TO YOU TOO, DIDN'T IIIT?
ISN'T THAT WHY YOU'VE GOTTEN A LITTLE STUFFED-ANIMAL-LIKE YOURSELLLF?
BASSA
ばさ
ばさ
BASSA
SO...
...THAT BEAR JERK'S DEVOTION TO HIS BAUMKUCHEN IS ALL 'COS HE'S NOW A BEAR OR SOMETHING?
THAT'S SOME FAIRY-TALE TRIP! HEY!

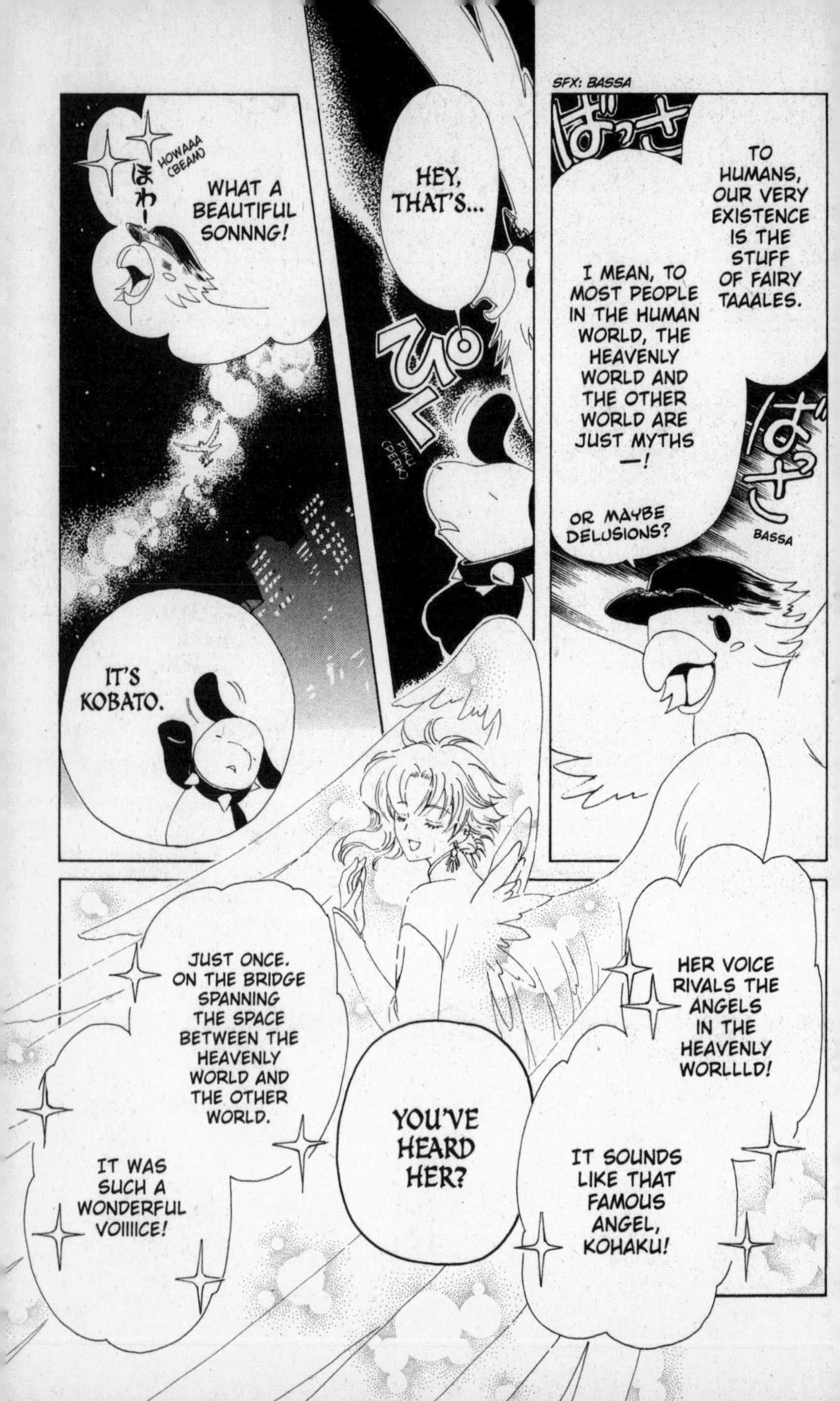
SFX: BASSA
TO HUMANS, OUR VERY EXISTENCE IS THE STUFF OF FAIRY TAAALES.
I MEAN, TO MOST PEOPLE IN THE HUMAN WORLD, THE HEAVENLY WORLD AND THE OTHER WORLD ARE JUST MYTHS—!
OR MAYBE DELUSIONS?
BASSA
HEY, THAT'S...
PIKU (PERK)
HOWAAA (BEAM)
WHAT A BEAUTIFUL SONNNG!
IT'S KOBATO.
HER VOICE RIVALS THE ANGELS IN THE HEAVENLY WORLLLD!
IT SOUNDS LIKE THAT FAMOUS ANGEL, KOHAKU!
YOU'VE HEARD HER?
JUST ONCE. ON THE BRIDGE SPANNING THE SPACE BETWEEN THE HEAVENLY WORLD AND THE OTHER WORLD.
IT WAS SUCH A WONDERFUL VOIIIICE!

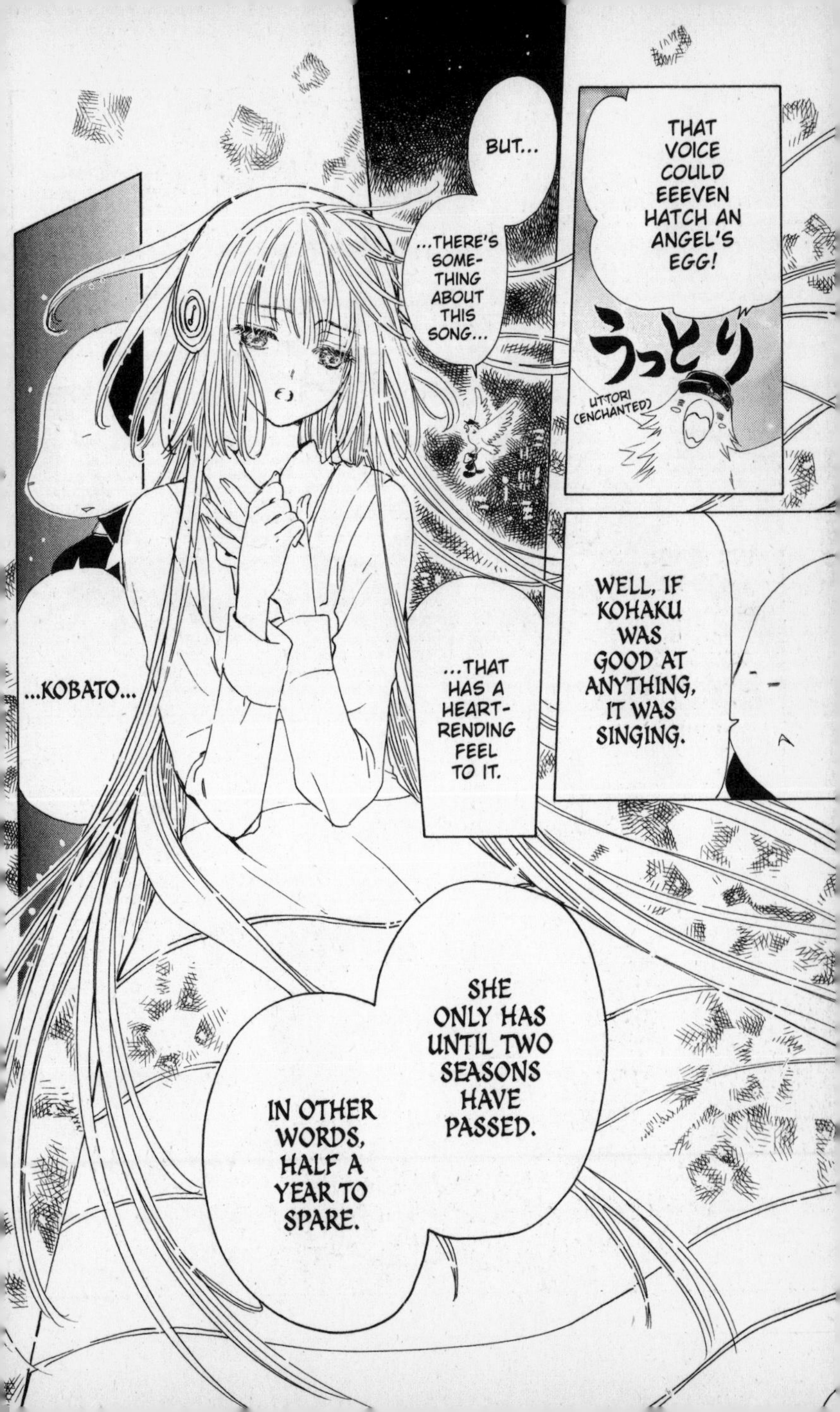
THAT VOICE COULD EEEVEN HATCH AN ANGEL'S EGG!
うっとり
UTTORI (ENCHANTED)
BUT...
...THERE'S SOMETHING ABOUT THIS SONG...
WELL, IF KOHAKU WAS GOOD AT ANYTHING, IT WAS SINGING.
...THAT HAS A HEART-RENDING FEEL TO IT.
...KOBATO...
SHE ONLY HAS UNTIL TWO SEASONS HAVE PASSED.
IN OTHER WORDS, HALF A YEAR TO SPARE.

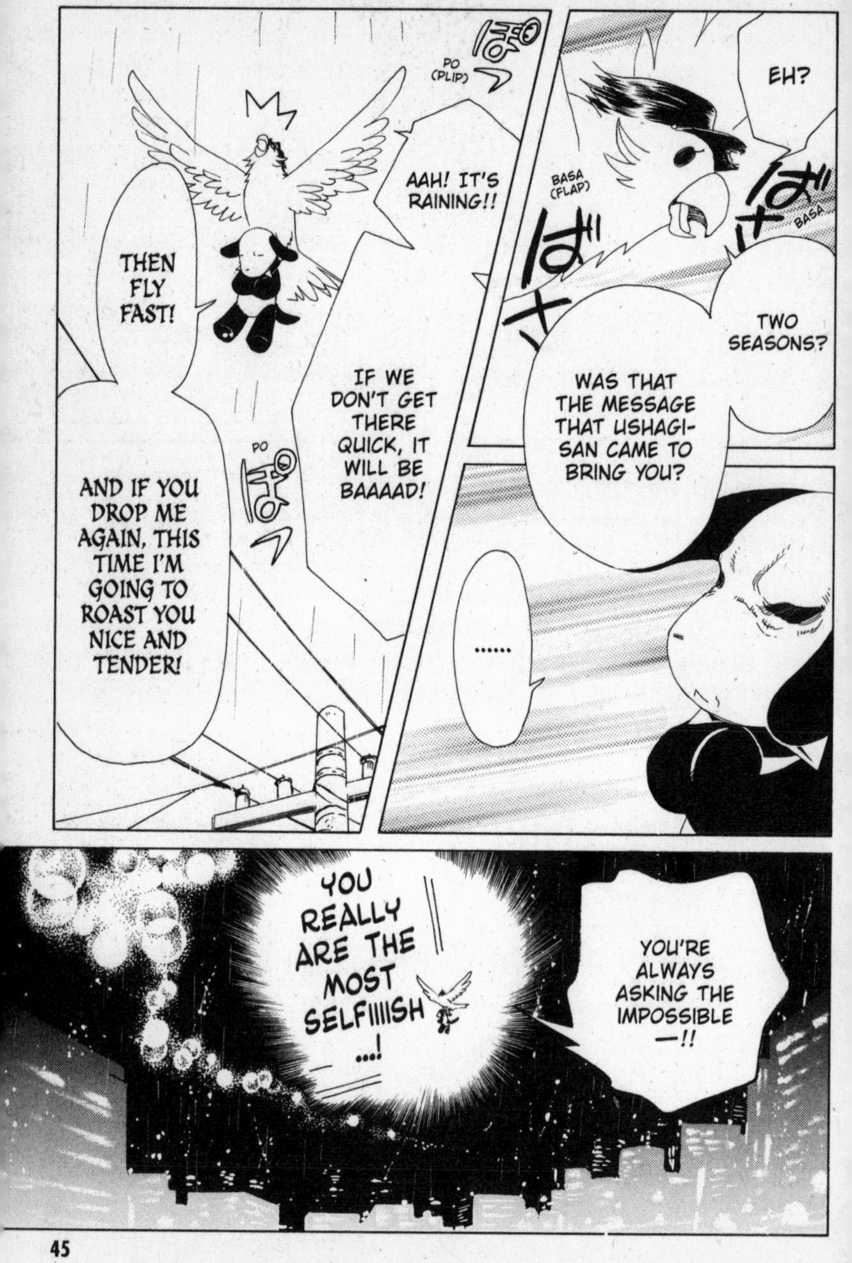
EH?
BASA (FLAP)
BASA
TWO SEASONS?
WAS THAT THE MESSAGE THAT USHAGI-SAN CAME TO BRING YOU?
......
PO (PLIP)
AAH! IT'S RAINING!!
THEN FLY FAST!
IF WE DON'T GET THERE QUICK, IT WILL BE BAAAAD!
PO
AND IF YOU DROP ME AGAIN, THIS TIME I'M GOING TO ROAST YOU NICE AND TENDER!
YOU'RE ALWAYS ASKING THE IMPOSSIBLE—!!
YOU REALLY ARE THE MOST SELFIIIISH ...!

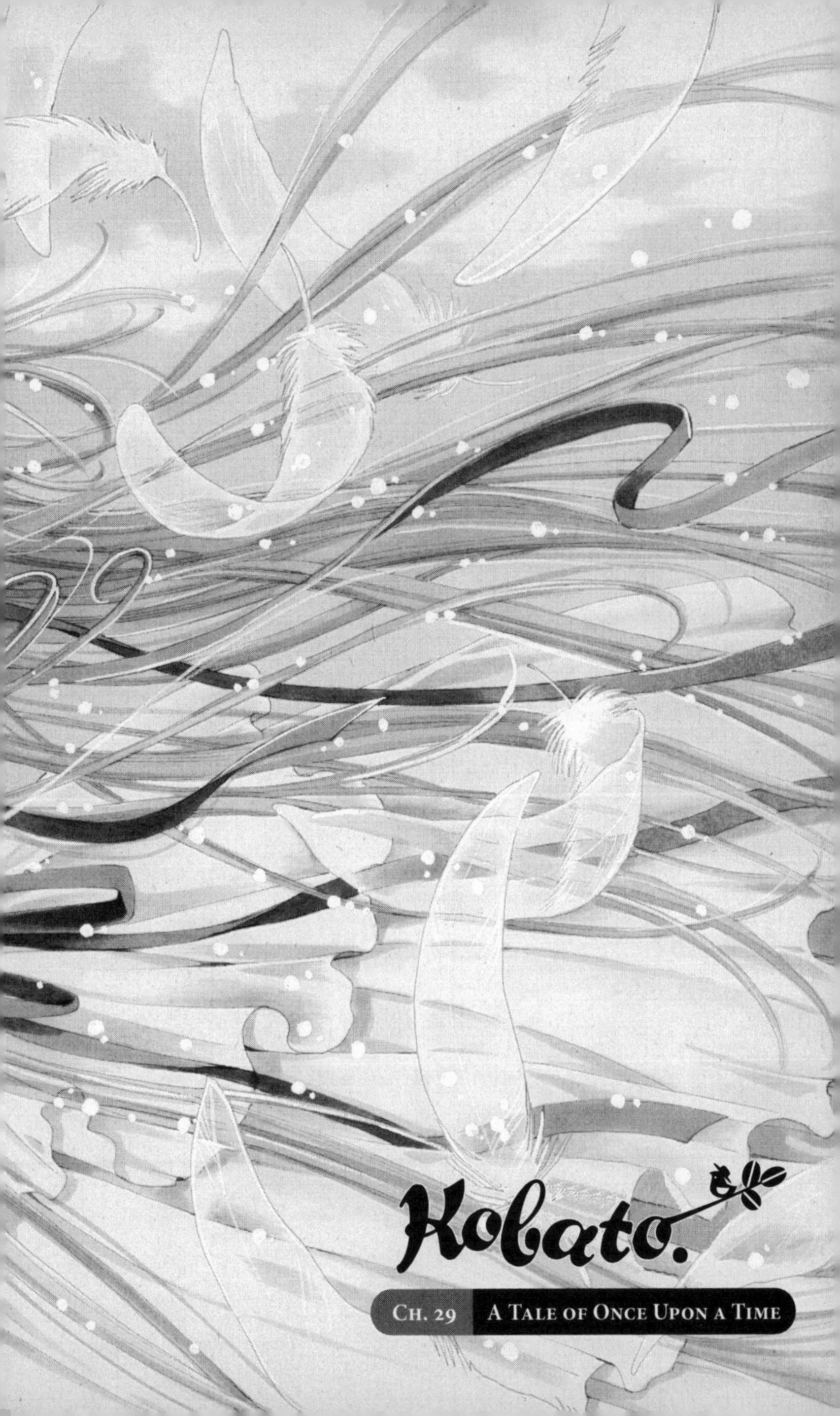
Kobato.
Ch. 29 A Tale of Once Upon a Time

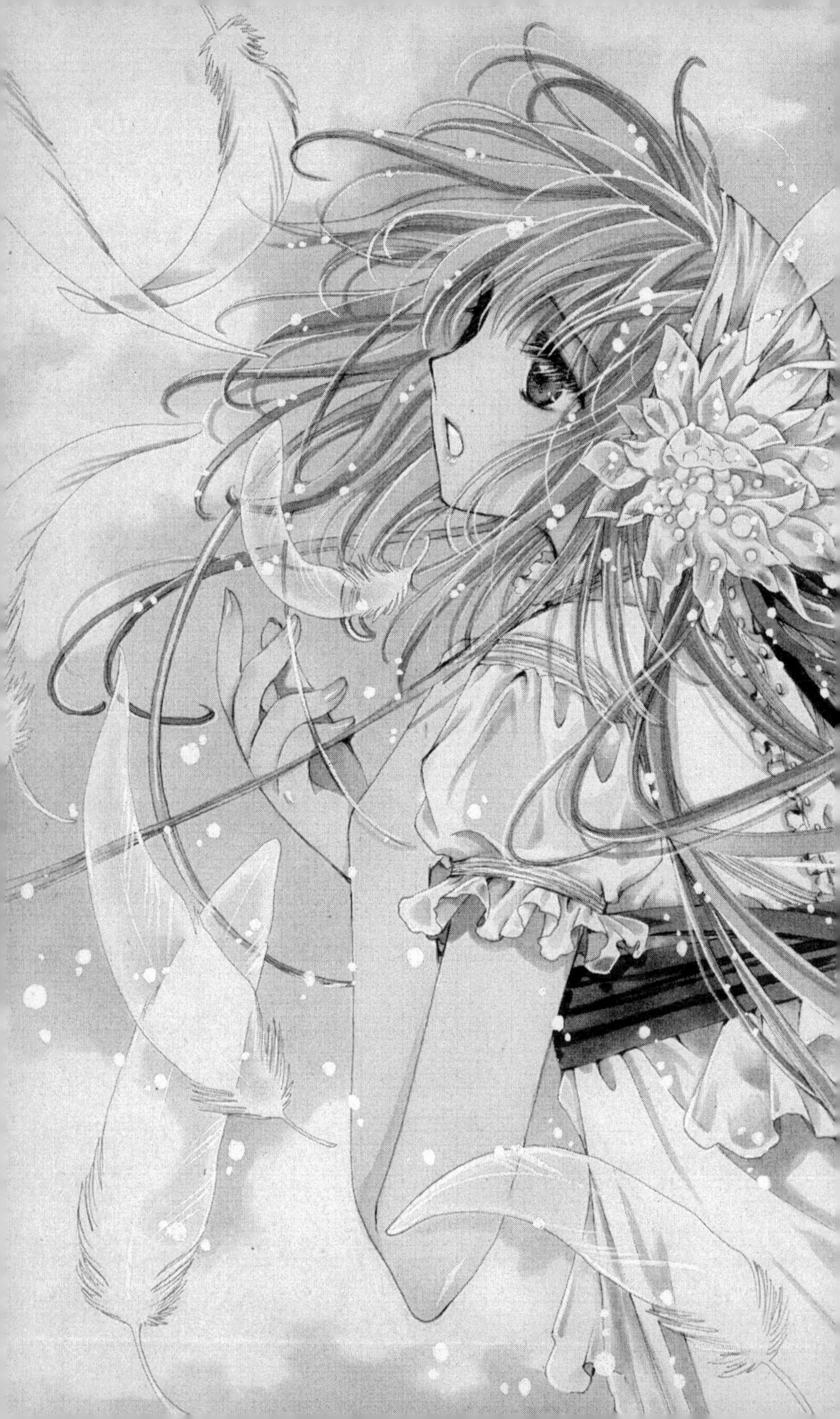

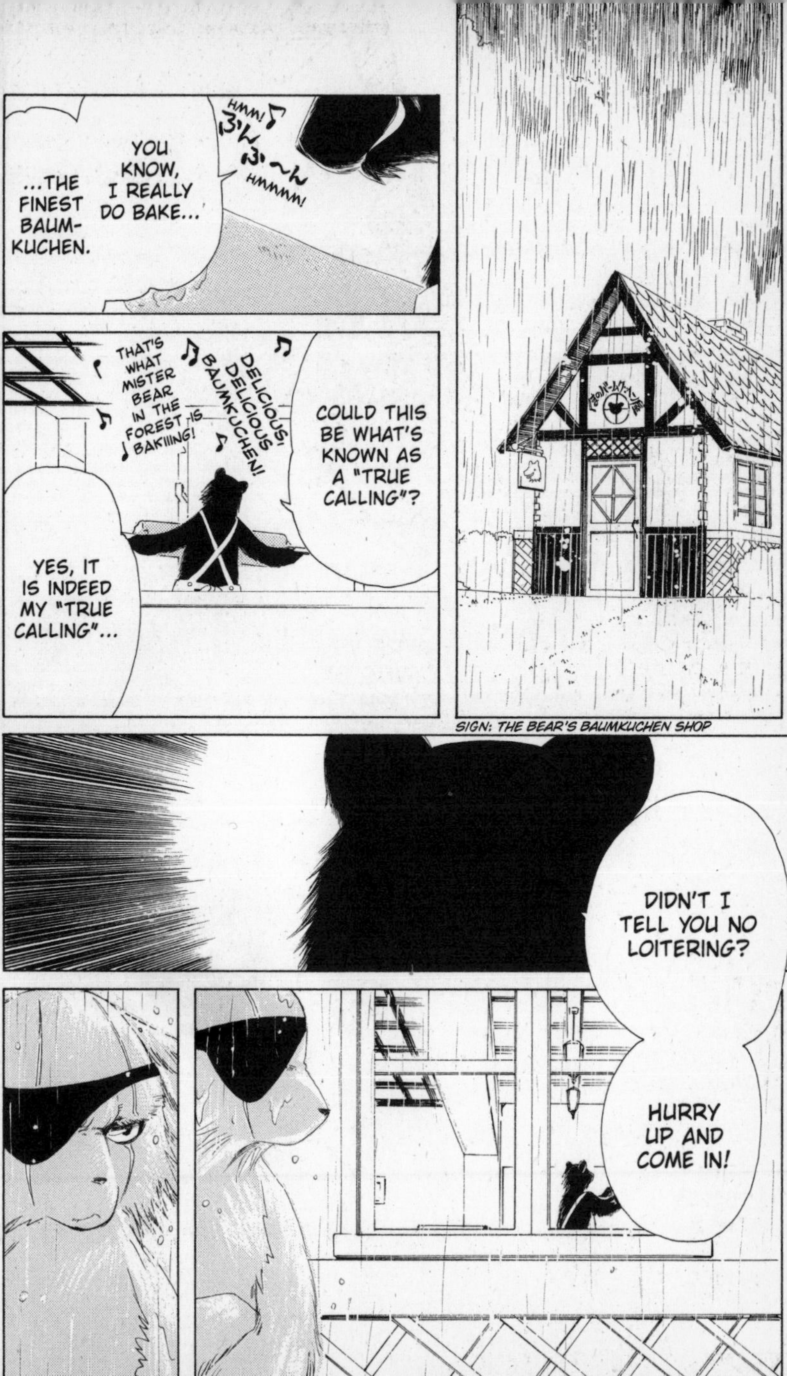
SIGN: THE BEAR'S BAUMKUCHEN SHOP
HMM! ぷんふ〜ん HMMMM!
YOU KNOW, I REALLY DO BAKE...
...THE FINEST BAUMKUCHEN.
COULD THIS BE WHAT'S KNOWN AS A "TRUE CALLING"?
DELICIOUS, DELICIOUS BAUMKUCHEN!
THAT'S WHAT MISTER BEAR IN THE FOREST IS BAKIIING!
YES, IT IS INDEED MY "TRUE CALLING"...
DIDN'T I TELL YOU NO LOITERING?
HURRY UP AND COME IN!

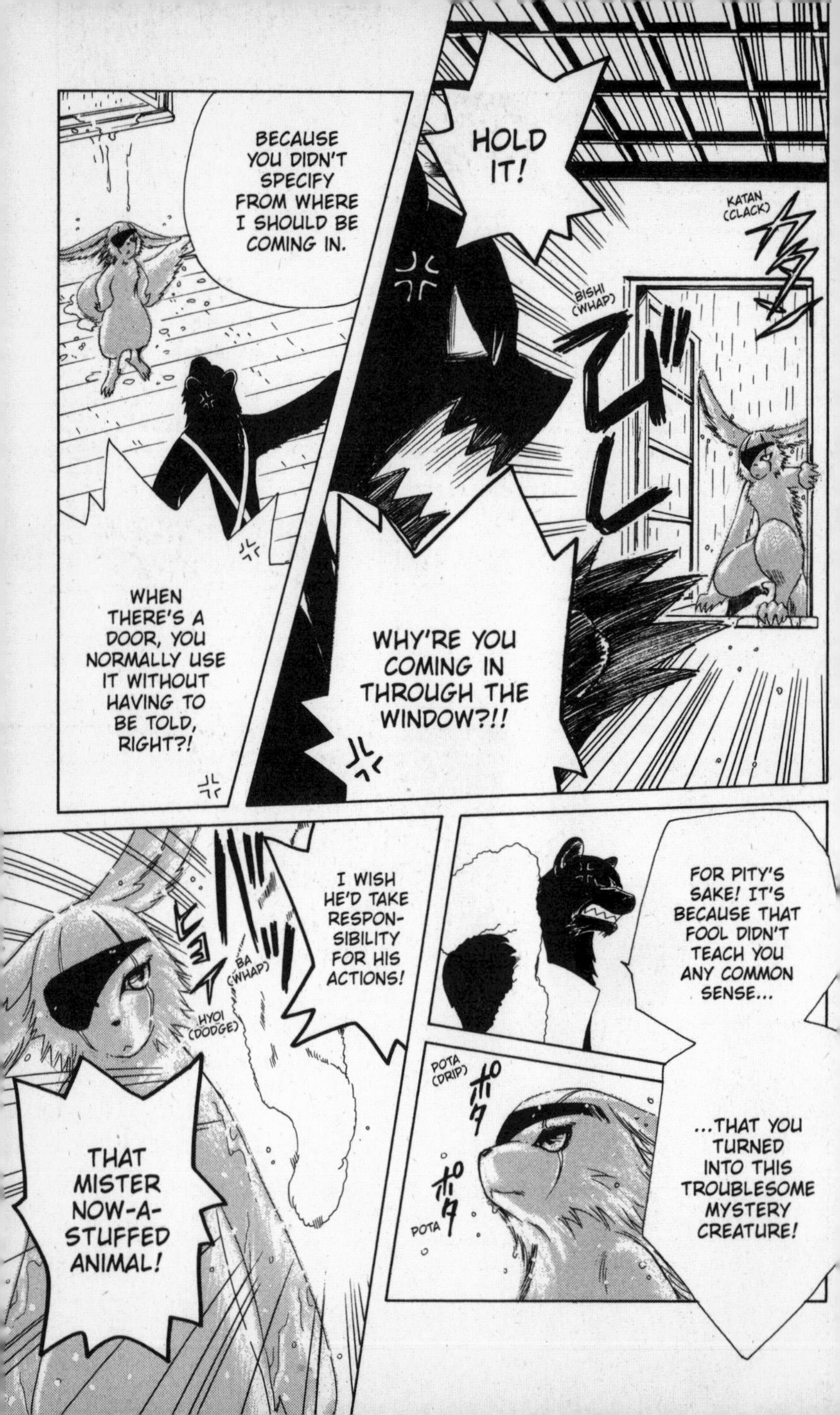

HOLD IT!
KATAN (CLACK)
BISHI (WHAP)
WHY'RE YOU COMING IN THROUGH THE WINDOW?!!
BECAUSE YOU DIDN'T SPECIFY FROM WHERE I SHOULD BE COMING IN.
WHEN THERE'S A DOOR, YOU NORMALLY USE IT WITHOUT HAVING TO BE TOLD, RIGHT?!
FOR PITY'S SAKE! IT'S BECAUSE THAT FOOL DIDN'T TEACH YOU ANY COMMON SENSE...
POTA (DRIP)
POTA
...THAT YOU TURNED INTO THIS TROUBLESOME MYSTERY CREATURE!
I WISH HE'D TAKE RESPON-SIBILITY FOR HIS ACTIONS!
BA (WHAP)
HYOI (DODGE)
THAT MISTER NOW-A-STUFFED ANIMAL!

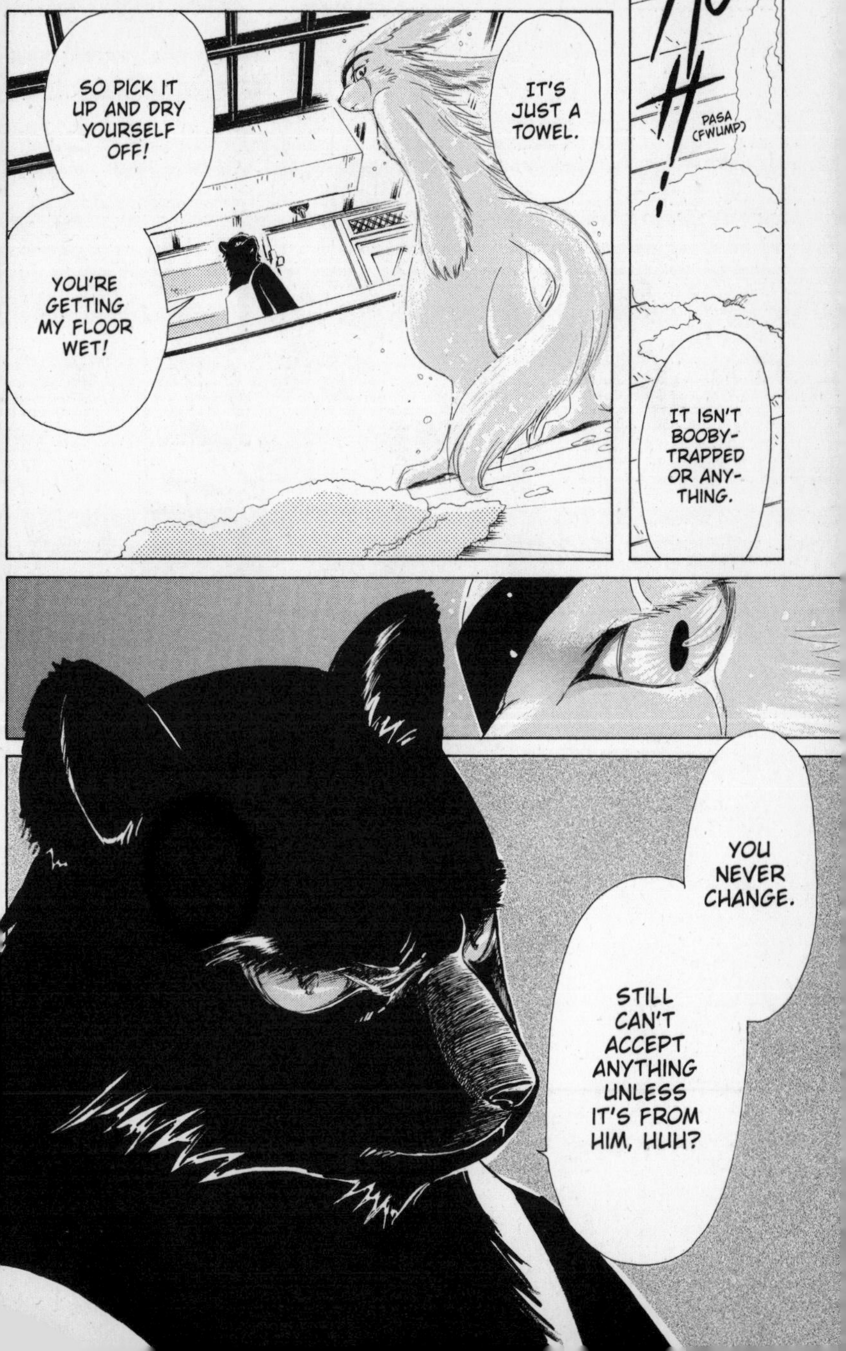
PASA (FWUMP)
IT ISN'T BOOBY-TRAPPED OR ANYTHING.
IT'S JUST A TOWEL.
SO PICK IT UP AND DRY YOURSELF OFF!
YOU'RE GETTING MY FLOOR WET!
YOU NEVER CHANGE.
STILL CAN'T ACCEPT ANYTHING UNLESS IT'S FROM HIM, HUH?

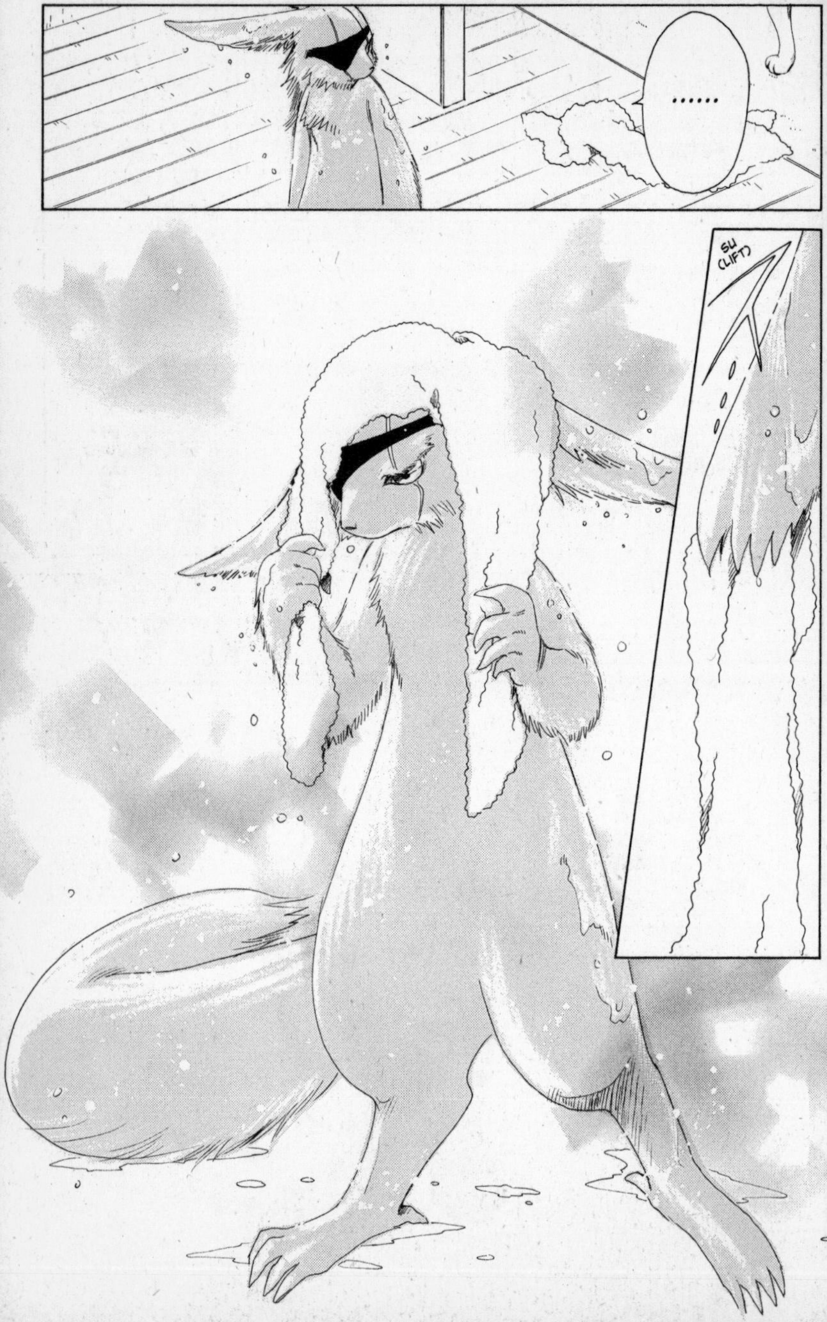
......
SU (LIFT)

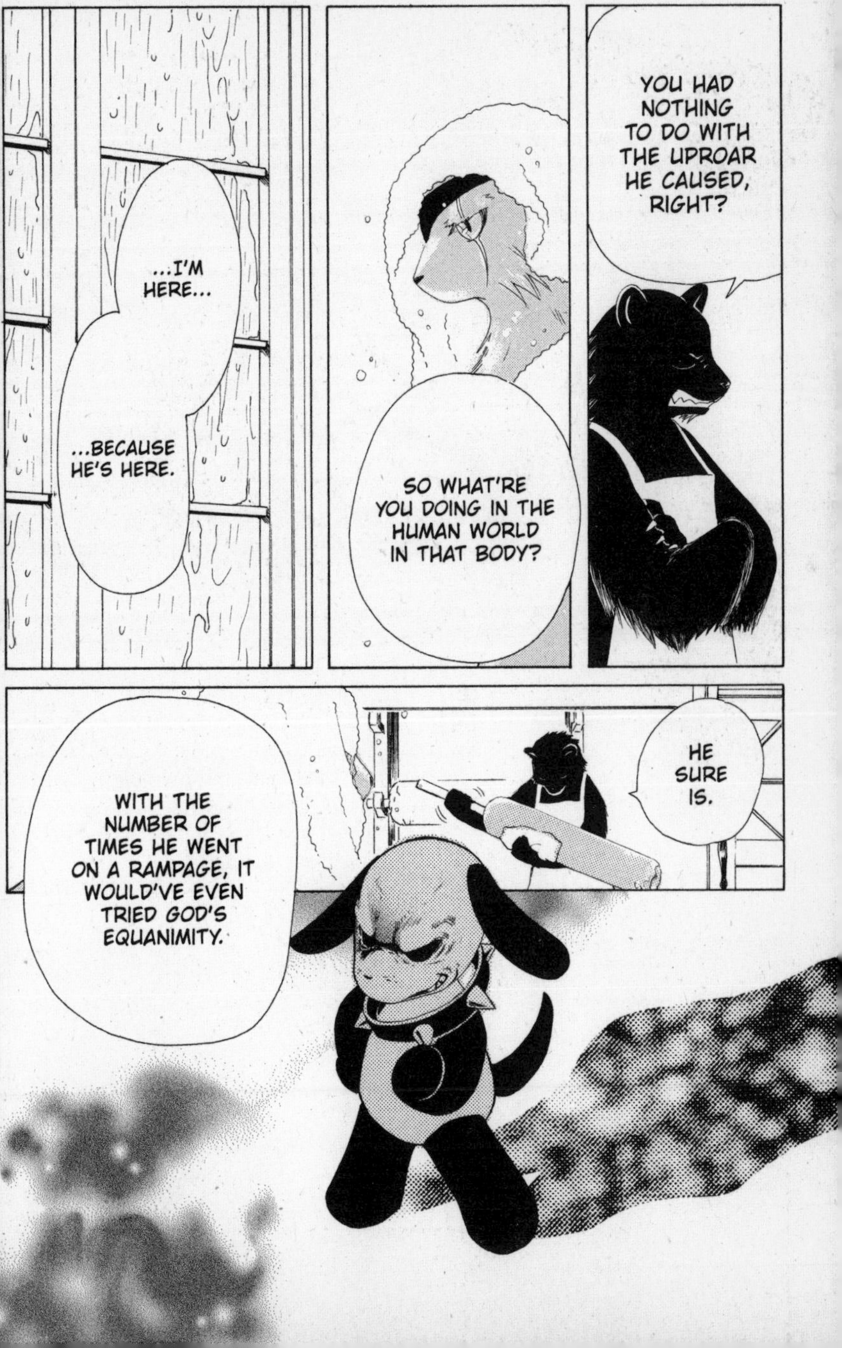
YOU HAD NOTHING TO DO WITH THE UPROAR HE CAUSED, RIGHT?
SO WHAT'RE YOU DOING IN THE HUMAN WORLD IN THAT BODY?
...I'M HERE...
...BECAUSE HE'S HERE.
HE SURE IS.
WITH THE NUMBER OF TIMES HE WENT ON A RAMPAGE, IT WOULD'VE EVEN TRIED GOD'S EQUANIMITY.

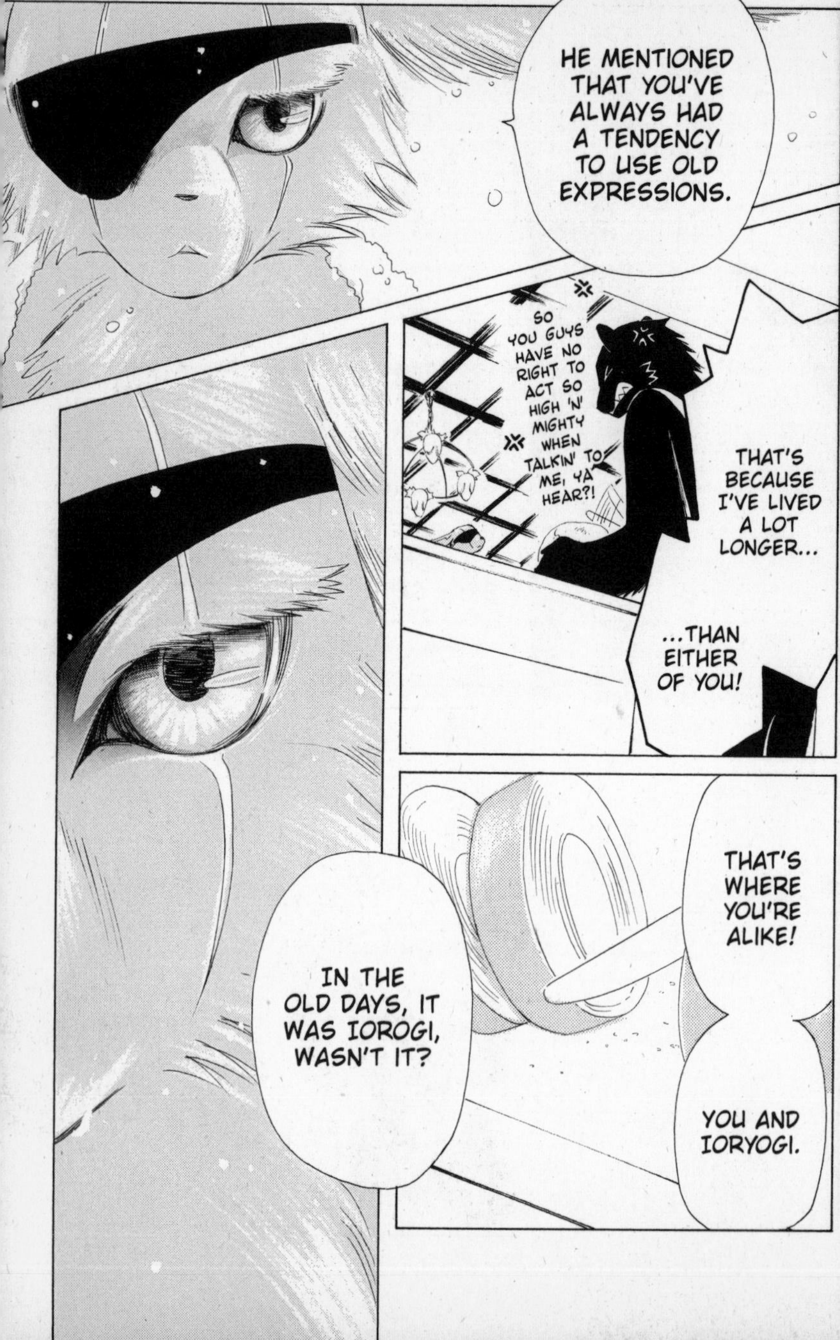
HE MENTIONED THAT YOU'VE ALWAYS HAD A TENDENCY TO USE OLD EXPRESSIONS.
THAT'S BECAUSE I'VE LIVED A LOT LONGER...
...THAN EITHER OF YOU!
SO YOU GUYS HAVE NO RIGHT TO ACT SO HIGH 'N' MIGHTY WHEN TALKIN' TO ME, YA HEAR?!
THAT'S WHERE YOU'RE ALIKE!
YOU AND IORYOGI.
IN THE OLD DAYS, IT WAS IOROGI, WASN'T IT?

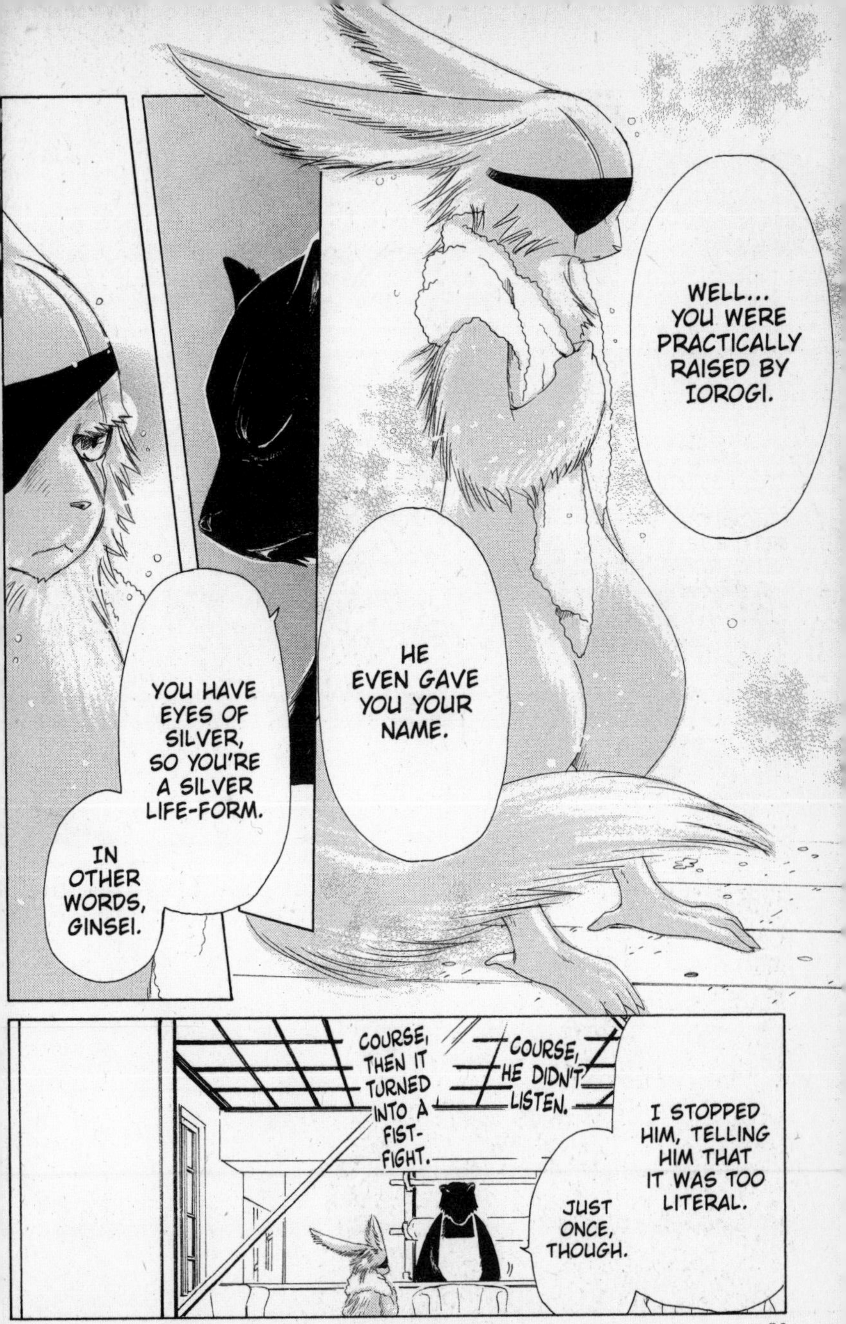
WELL... YOU WERE PRACTICALLY RAISED BY IOROGI.
HE EVEN GAVE YOU YOUR NAME.
YOU HAVE EYES OF SILVER, SO YOU'RE A SILVER LIFE-FORM.
IN OTHER WORDS, GINSEI.
I STOPPED HIM, TELLING HIM THAT IT WAS TOO LITERAL.
JUST ONCE, THOUGH.
COURSE, HE DIDN'T LISTEN.
COURSE, THEN IT TURNED INTO A FIST-FIGHT.

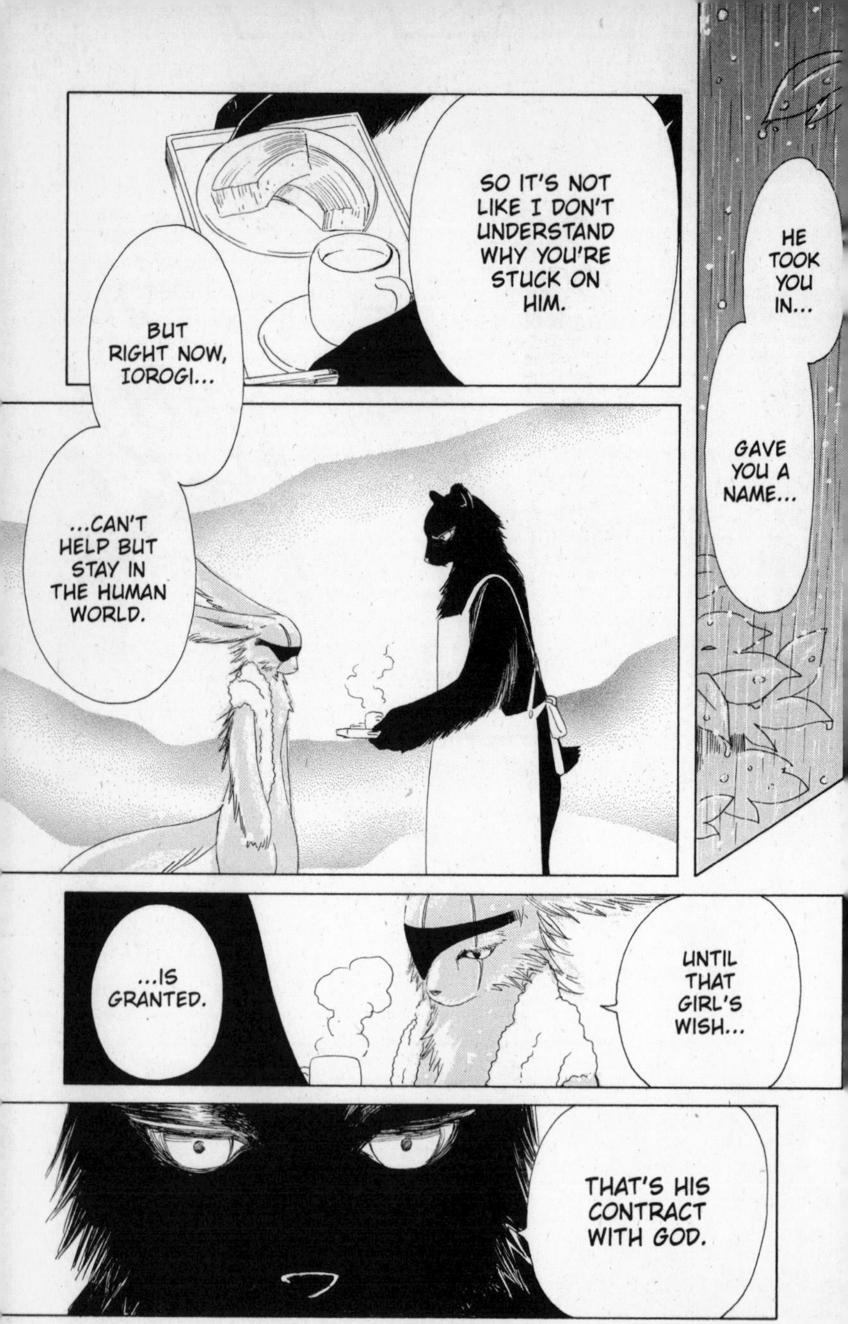
HE TOOK YOU IN...
GAVE YOU A NAME...
SO IT'S NOT LIKE I DON'T UNDERSTAND WHY YOU'RE STUCK ON HIM.
BUT RIGHT NOW, IOROGI...
...CAN'T HELP BUT STAY IN THE HUMAN WORLD.
UNTIL THAT GIRL'S WISH...
...IS GRANTED.
THAT'S HIS CONTRACT WITH GOD.

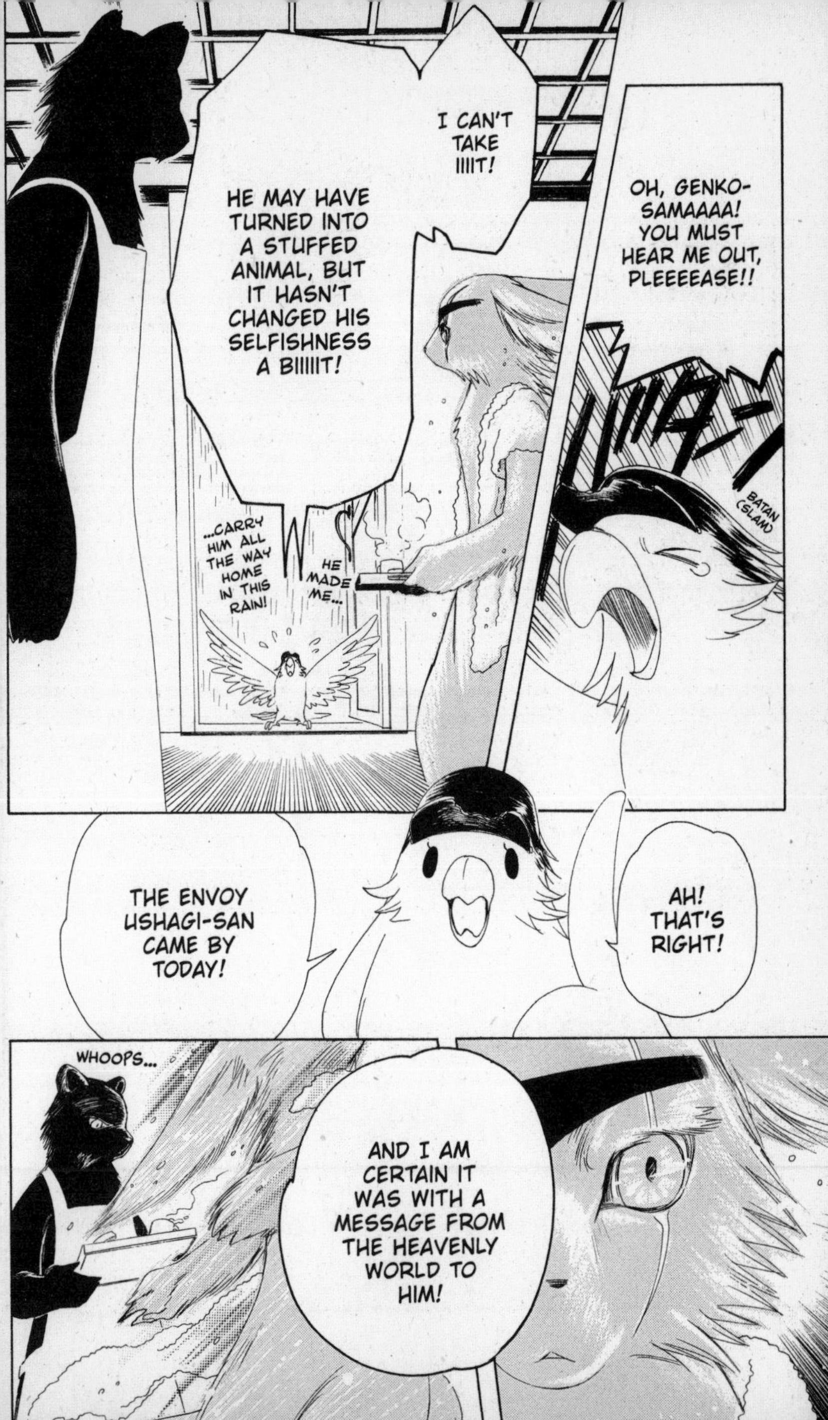
OH, GENKO-SAMAAAAA! YOU MUST HEAR ME OUT, PLEEEEASE!!
BATAN (SLAM)
I CAN'T TAKE IIIIT!
HE MAY HAVE TURNED INTO A STUFFED ANIMAL, BUT IT HASN'T CHANGED HIS SELFISHNESS A BIIIIIT!
HE MADE ME...
...CARRY HIM ALL THE WAY HOME IN THIS RAIN!
AH! THAT'S RIGHT!
THE ENVOY USHAGI-SAN CAME BY TODAY!
AND I AM CERTAIN IT WAS WITH A MESSAGE FROM THE HEAVENLY WORLD TO HIM!
WHOOPS...

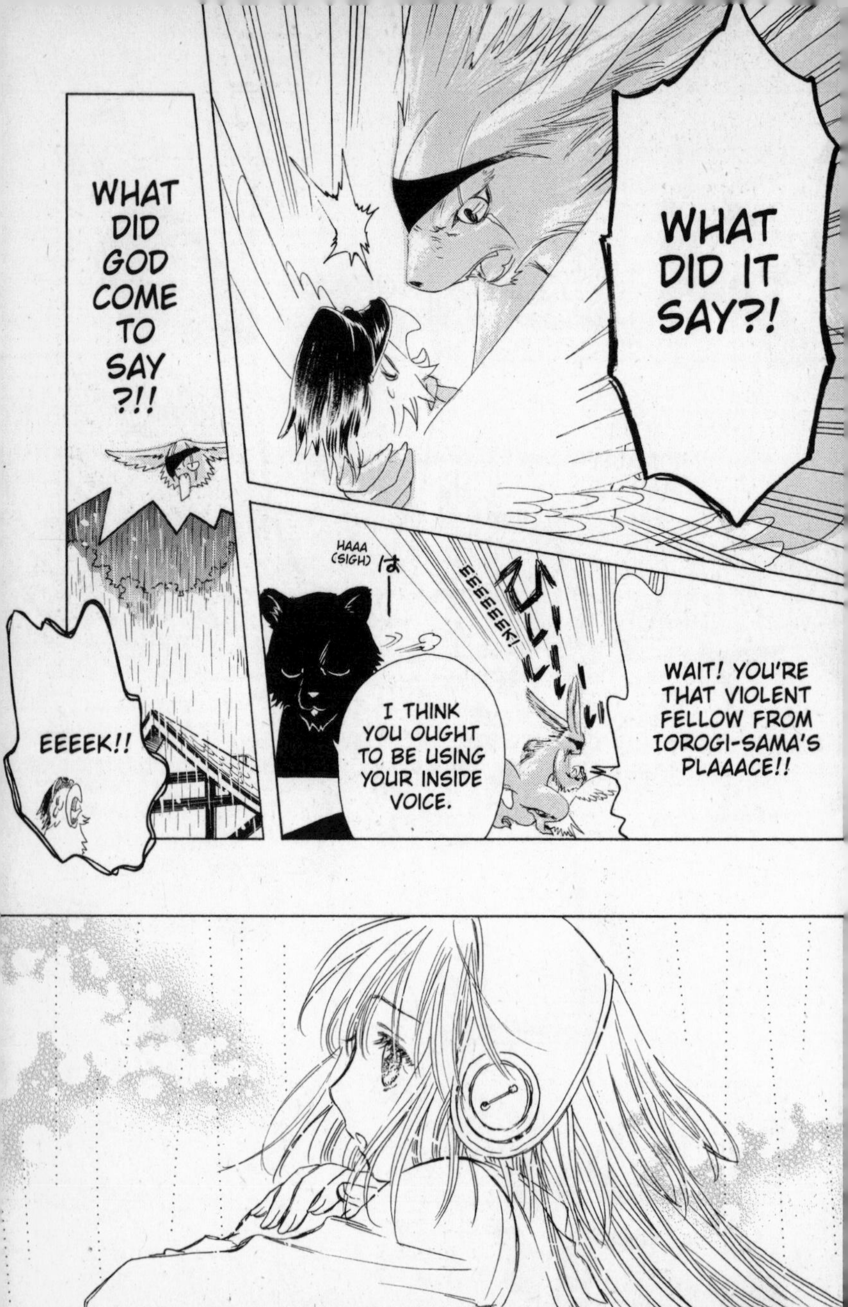
WHAT DID IT SAY?!
WAIT! YOU'RE THAT VIOLENT FELLOW FROM IOROGI-SAMA'S PLAAACE!!
EEEEEEEK!
HAAA (SIGH)
I THINK YOU OUGHT TO BE USING YOUR INSIDE VOICE.
WHAT DID GOD COME TO SAY?!!
EEEEK!!

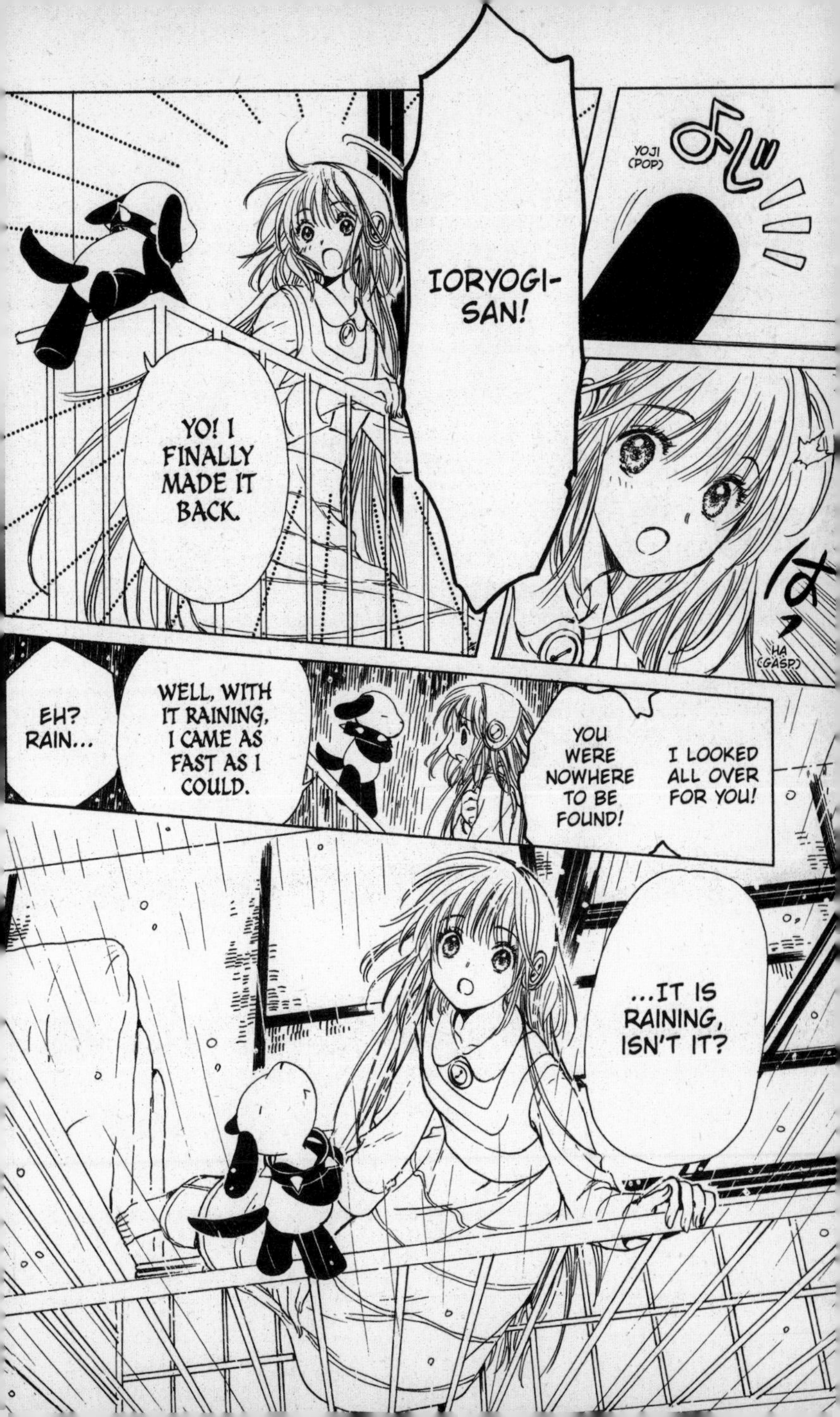
YOJI (POP)
IORYOGI-SAN!
HA (GASP)
YO! I FINALLY MADE IT BACK.
I LOOKED ALL OVER FOR YOU!
YOU WERE NOWHERE TO BE FOUND!
WELL, WITH IT RAINING, I CAME AS FAST AS I COULD.
EH? RAIN...
...IT IS RAINING, ISN'T IT?

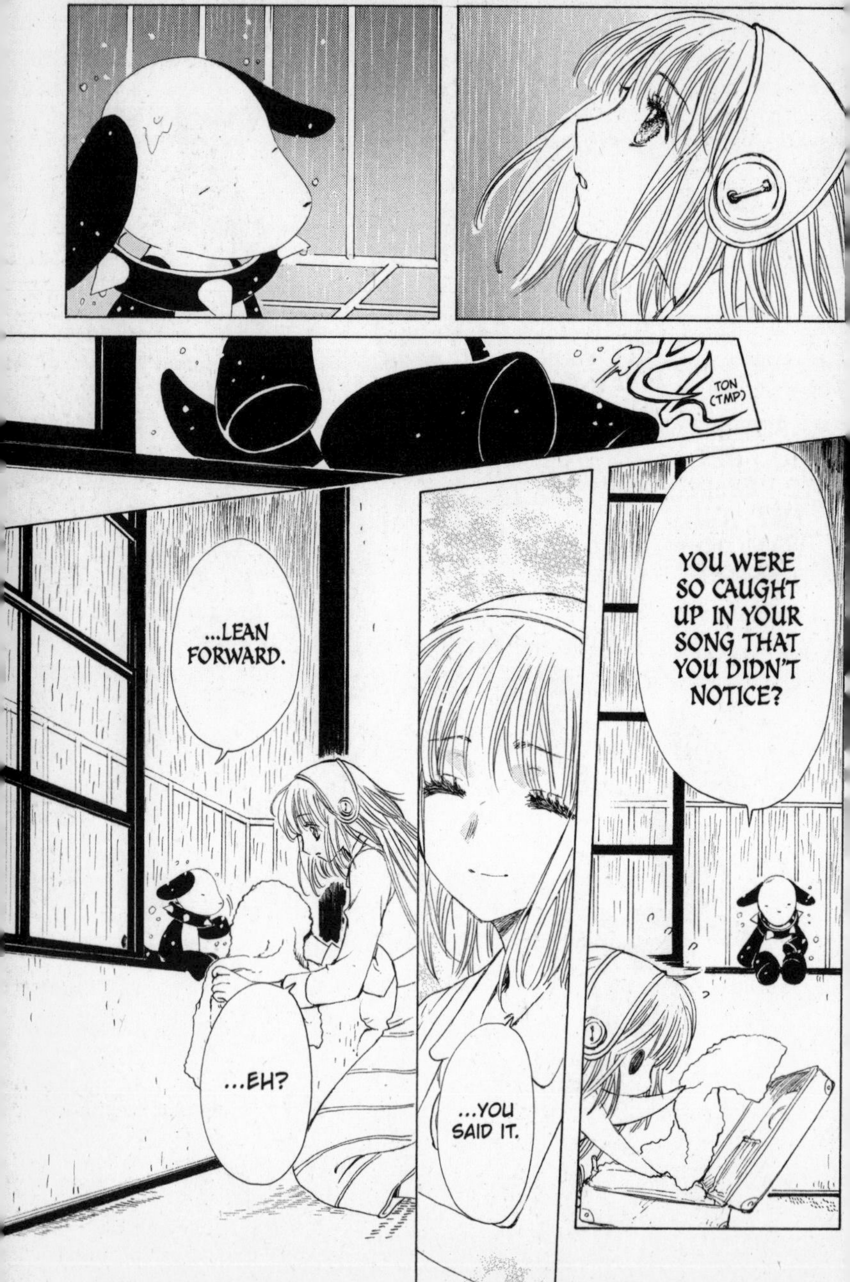
TON (TMP)
YOU WERE SO CAUGHT UP IN YOUR SONG THAT YOU DIDN'T NOTICE?
...YOU SAID IT.
...LEAN FORWARD.
...EH?

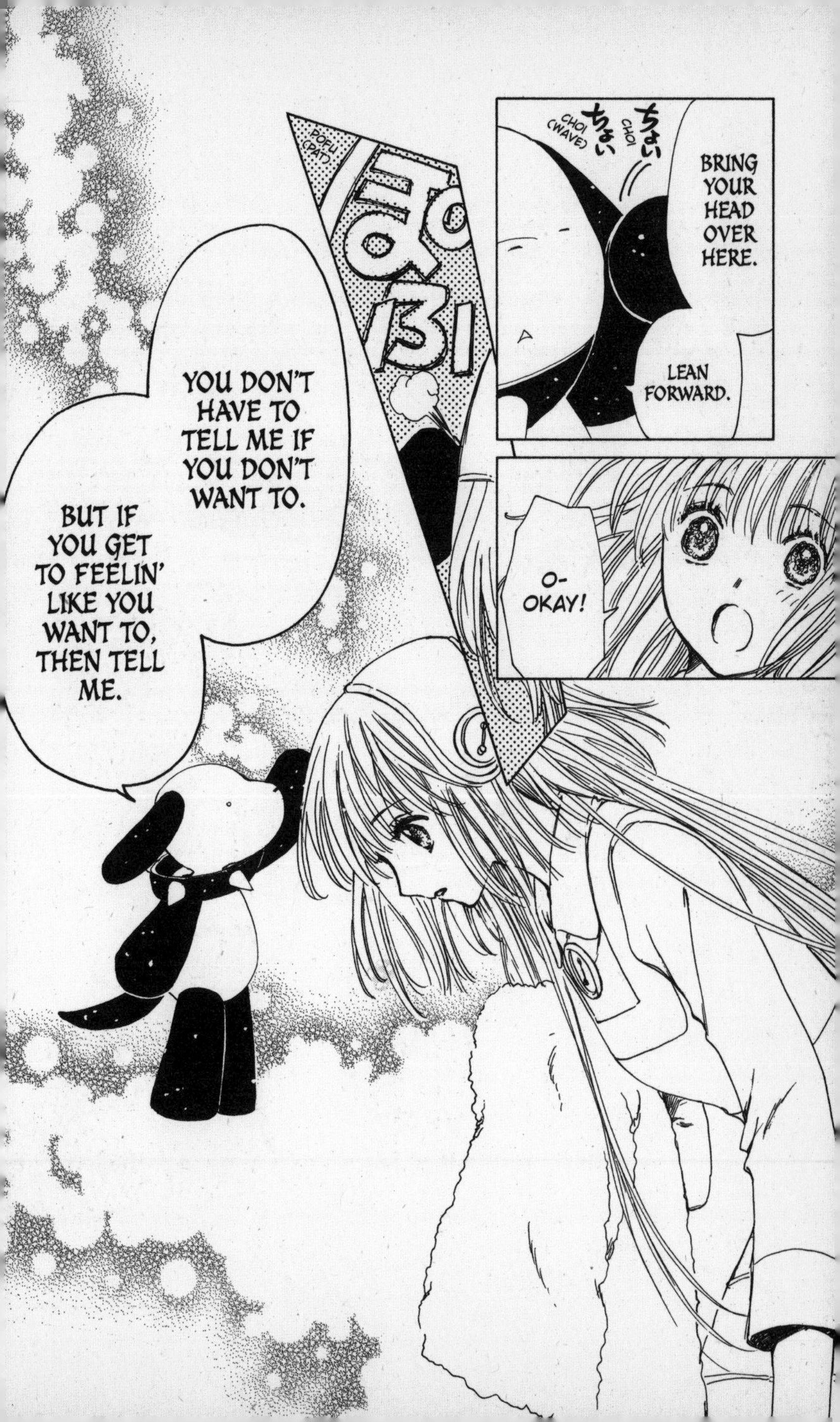
BRING YOUR HEAD OVER HERE.
ちょいちょい
CHOI CHOI (WAVE)
LEAN FORWARD.
O-OKAY!
POFU (PAT)
YOU DON'T HAVE TO TELL ME IF YOU DON'T WANT TO.
BUT IF YOU GET TO FEELIN' LIKE YOU WANT TO, THEN TELL ME.

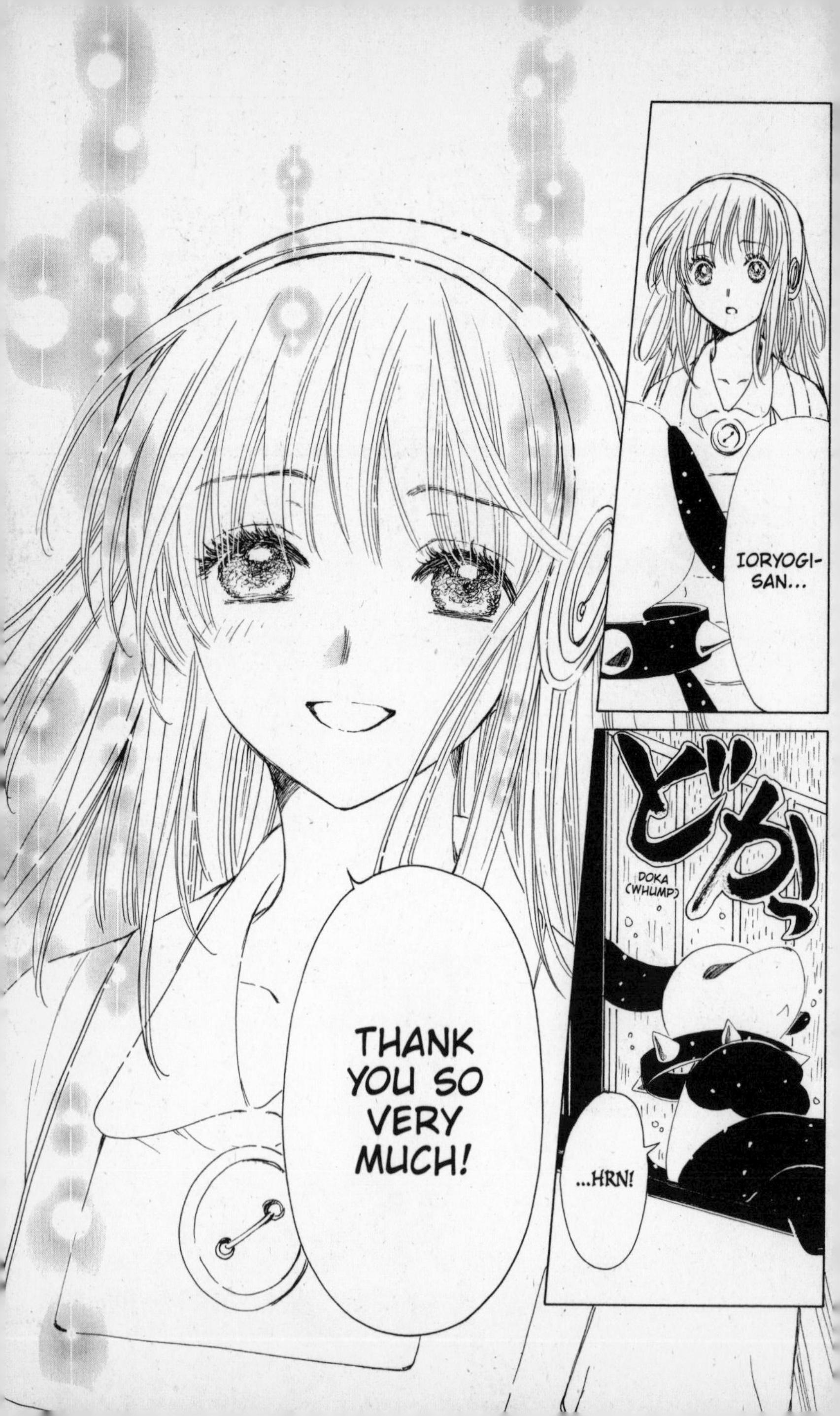
IORYOGI-SAN...
どか
DOKA (WHUMP)
...HRN!
THANK YOU SO VERY MUCH!

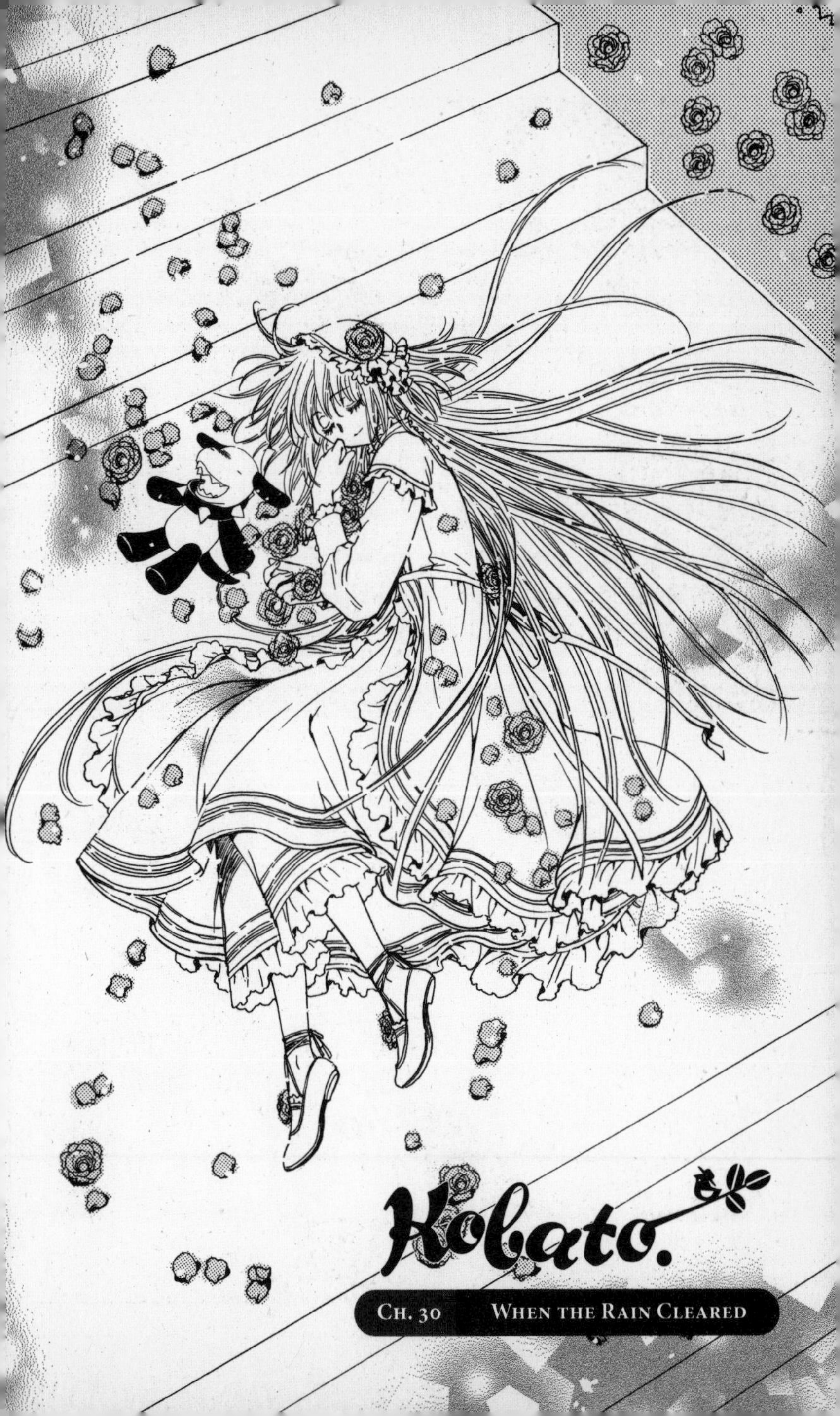
Kobato.
Ch. 30 When the Rain Cleared

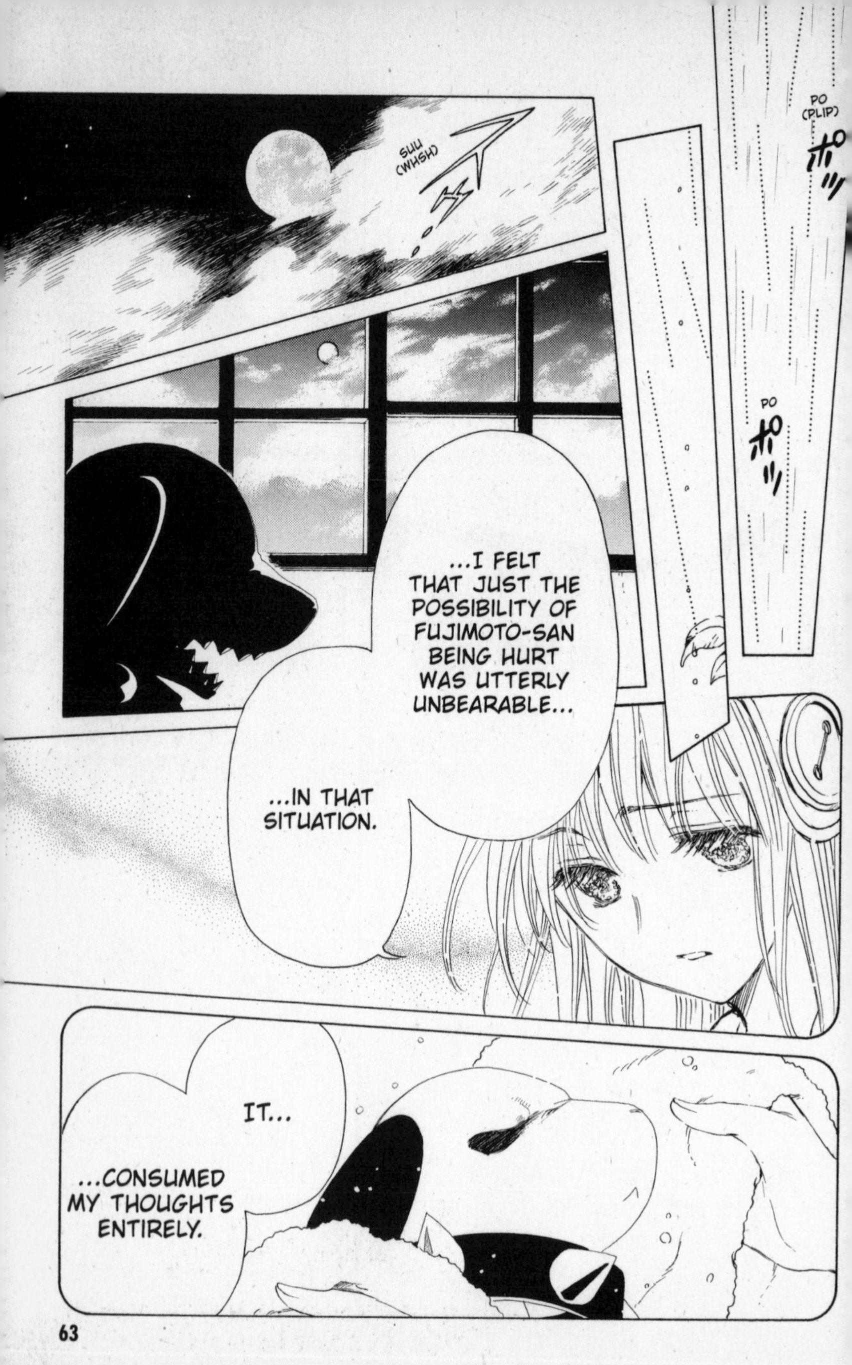
PO
(PLIP)
SUU
(WHSH)
PO
...I FELT THAT JUST THE POSSIBILITY OF FUJIMOTO-SAN BEING HURT WAS UTTERLY UNBEARABLE...
...IN THAT SITUATION.
IT...
...CONSUMED MY THOUGHTS ENTIRELY.

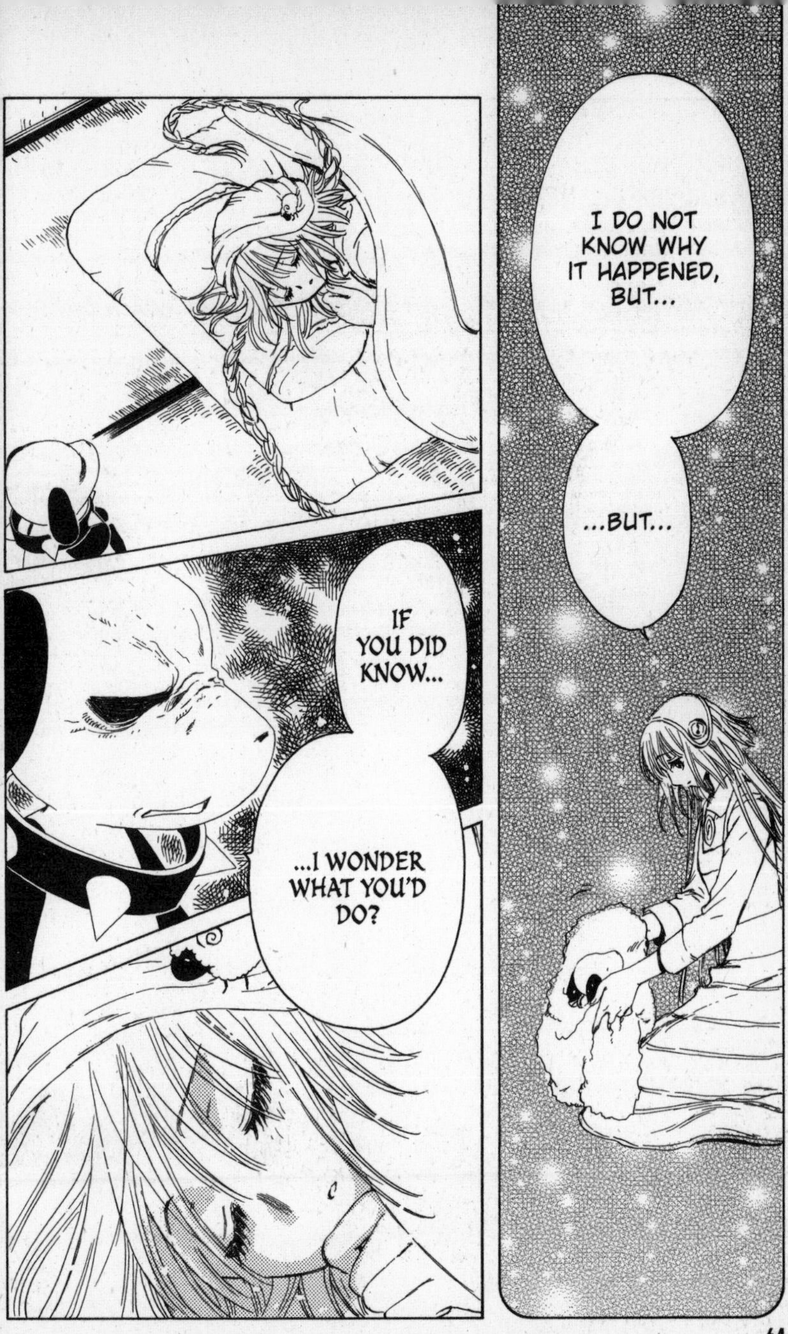
I DO NOT KNOW WHY IT HAPPENED, BUT...
...BUT...
IF YOU DID KNOW...
...I WONDER WHAT YOU'D DO?

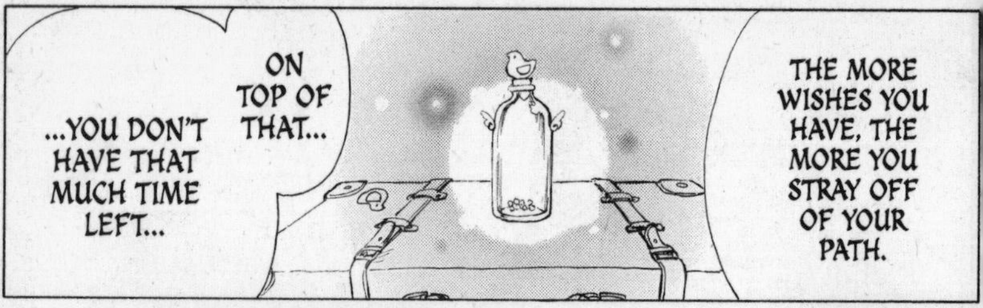
THE MORE WISHES YOU HAVE, THE MORE YOU STRAY OFF OF YOUR PATH.
ON TOP OF THAT...
...YOU DON'T HAVE THAT MUCH TIME LEFT...

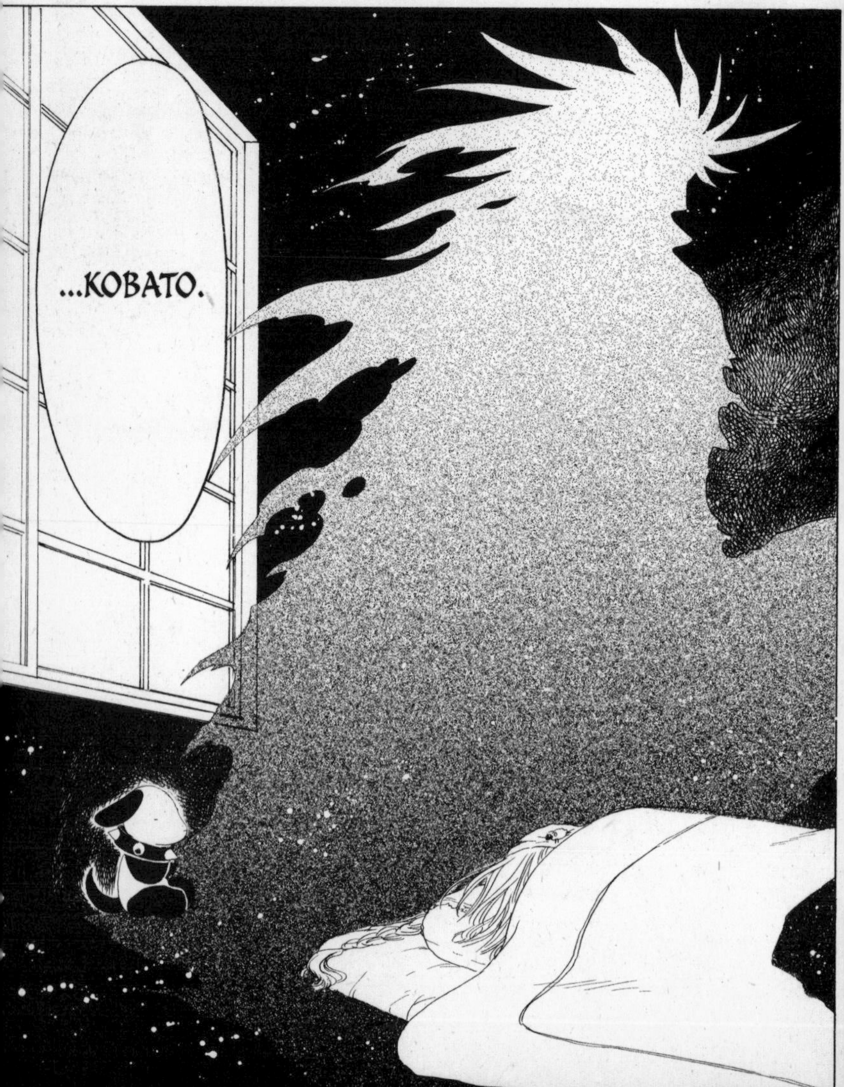
...KOBATO.

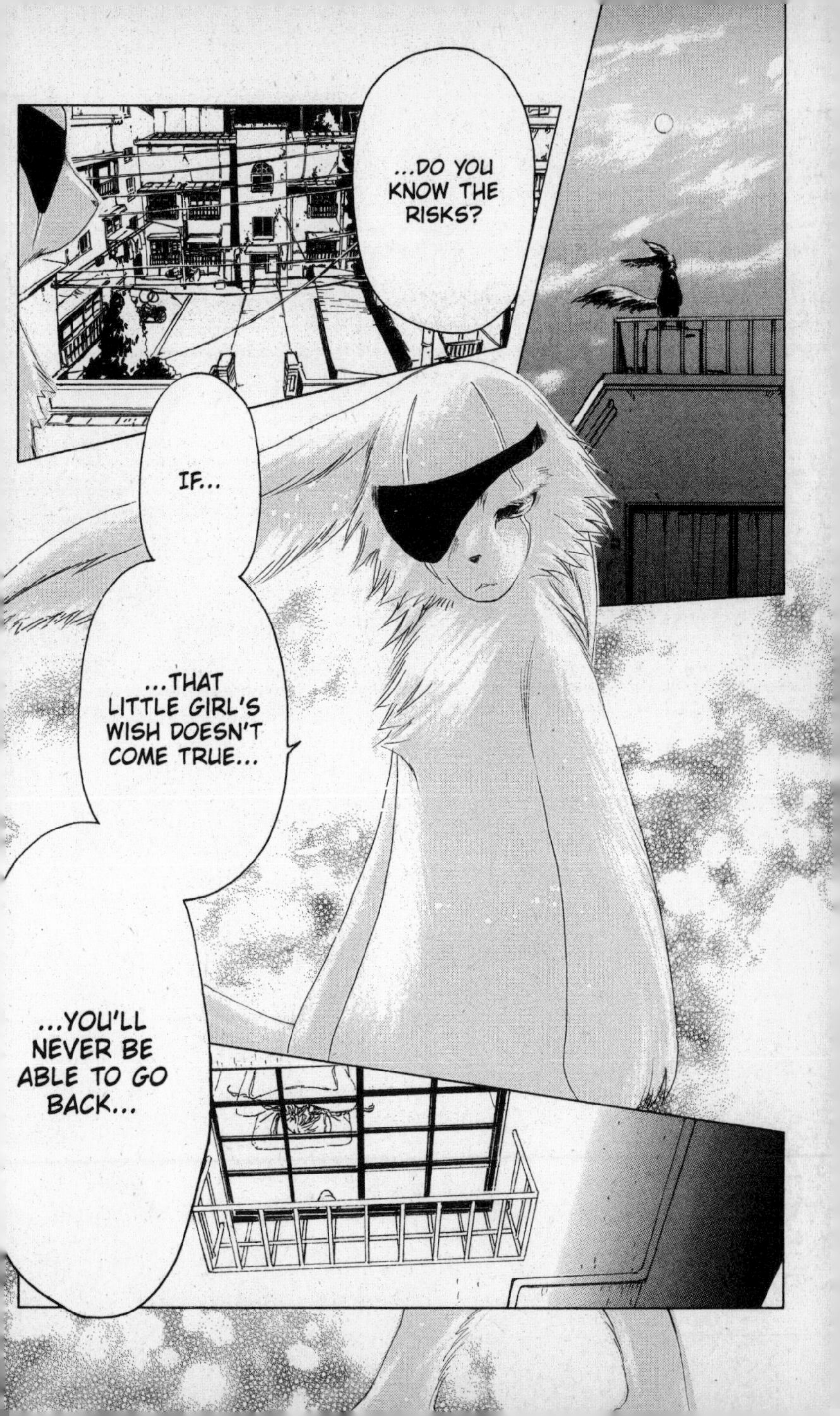
...DO YOU KNOW THE RISKS?
IF...
...THAT LITTLE GIRL'S WISH DOESN'T COME TRUE...
...YOU'LL NEVER BE ABLE TO GO BACK...

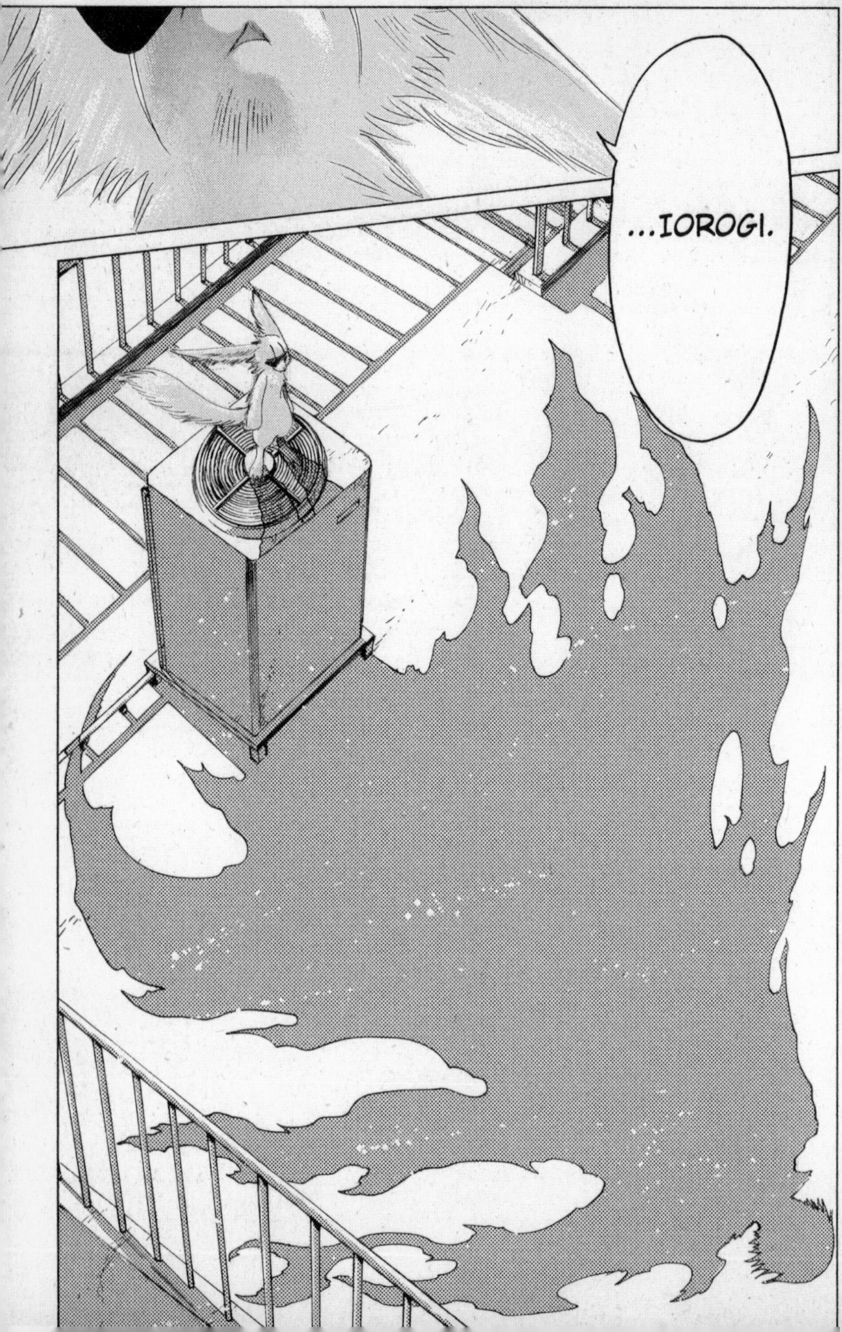
...IOROGI.

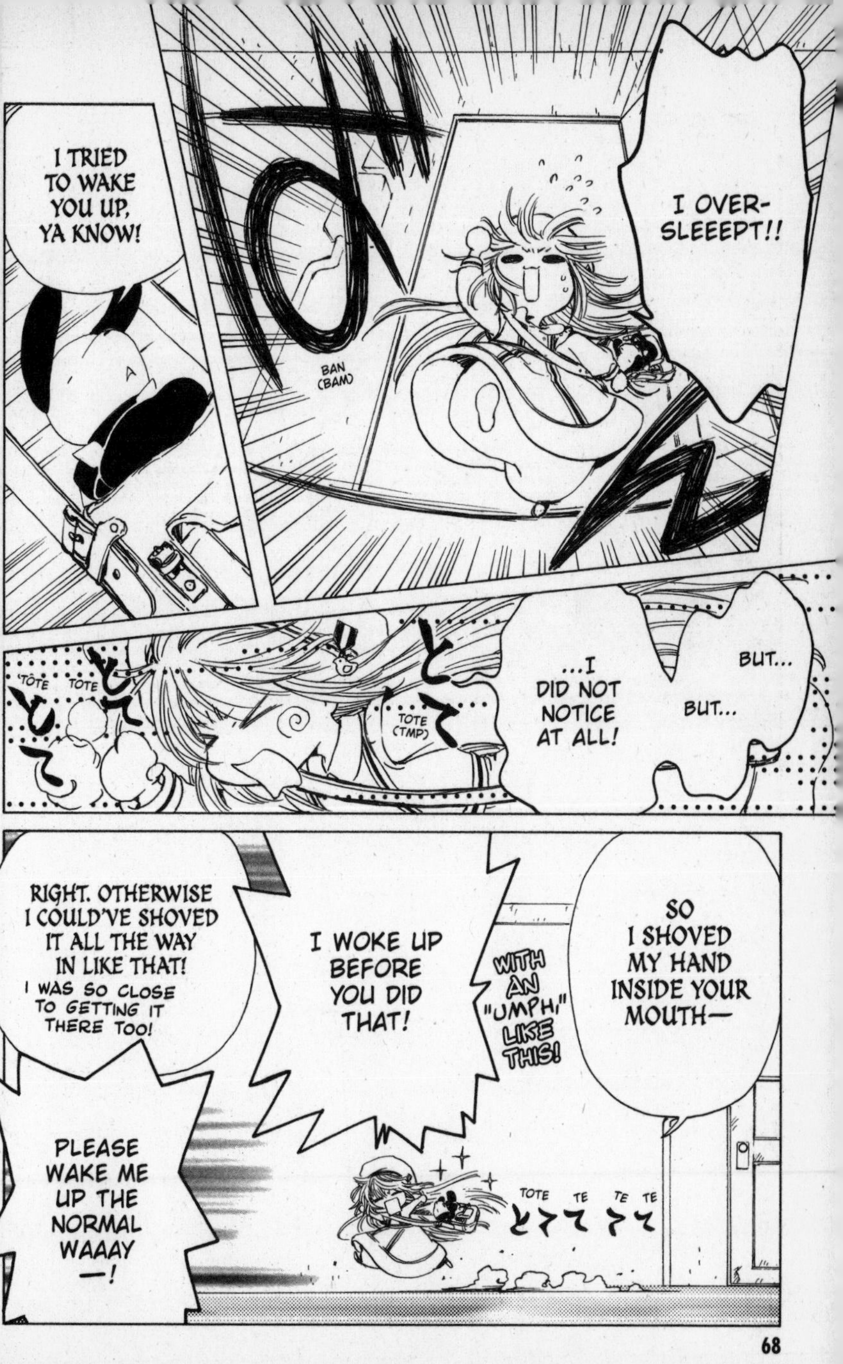
I OVER-SLEEEPT!!
BAN (BAM)
I TRIED TO WAKE YOU UP, YA KNOW!
BUT...
BUT...
...I DID NOT NOTICE AT ALL!
TOTE (TMP)
TOTE
TOTE
SO I SHOVED MY HAND INSIDE YOUR MOUTH—
WITH AN "UMPH" LIKE THIS!
I WOKE UP BEFORE YOU DID THAT!
RIGHT. OTHERWISE I COULD'VE SHOVED IT ALL THE WAY IN LIKE THAT!
I WAS SO CLOSE TO GETTING IT THERE TOO!
TOTE TE TE TE
PLEASE WAKE ME UP THE NORMAL WAAAY—!

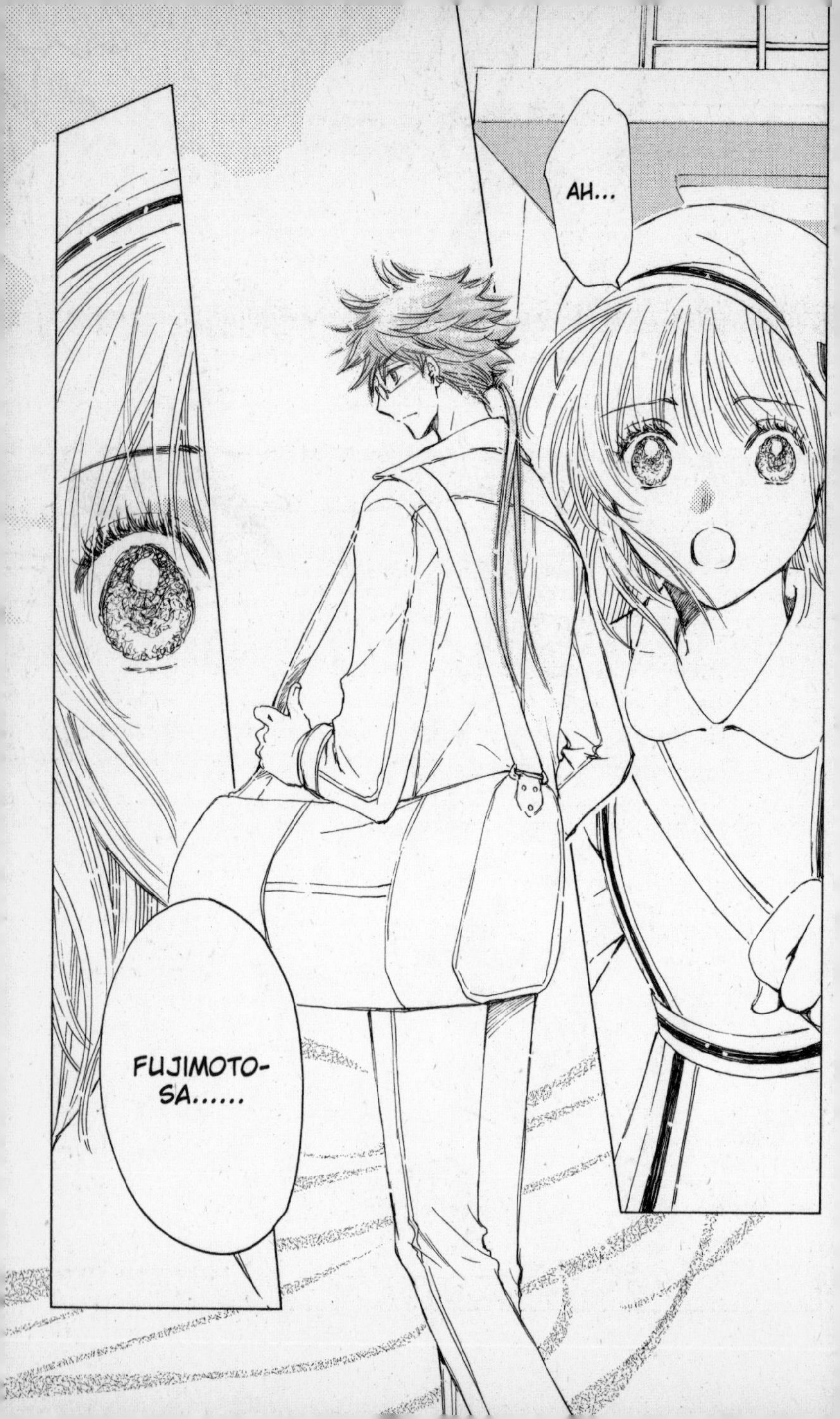
AH...
FUJIMOTO-SA......

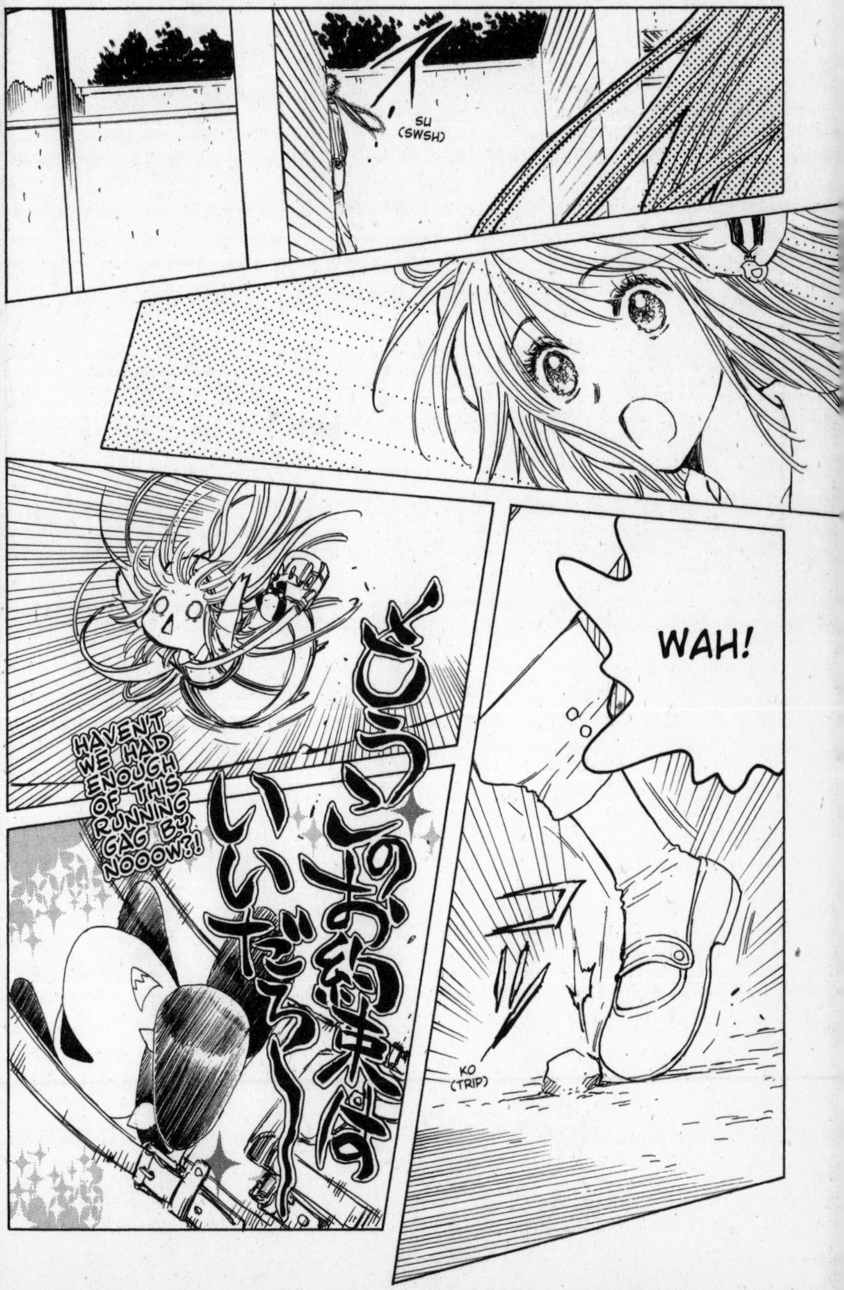
SU (SWSH)
WAH!
KO (TRIP)
どうこのお約束はいいだろ〜
HAVEN'T WE HAD ENOUGH OF THIS RUNNING GAG BY NOOOW?!

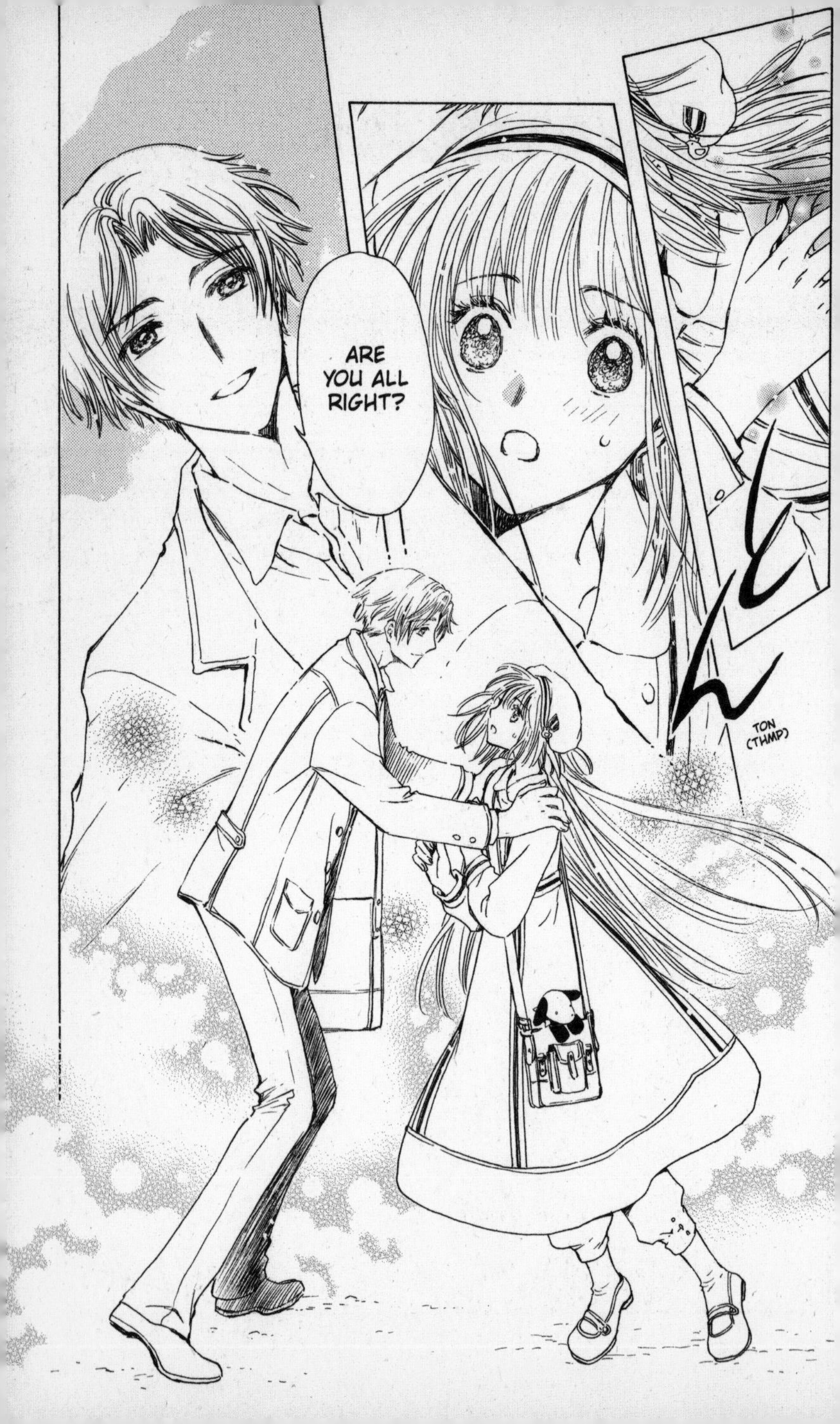
ARE YOU ALL RIGHT?
TON (THMP)

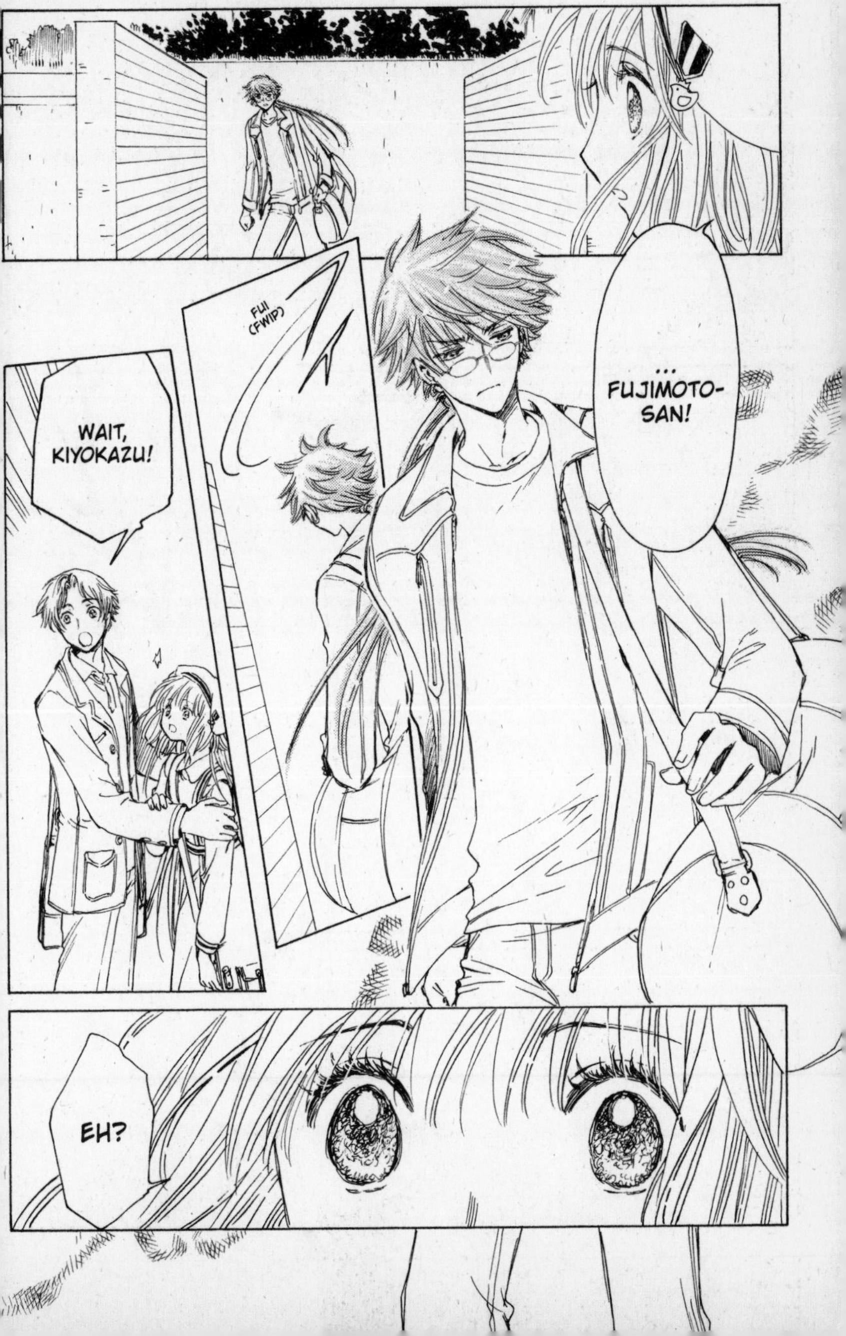
...FUJIMOTO-SAN!
FUI (FWIP)
WAIT, KIYOKAZU!
EH?

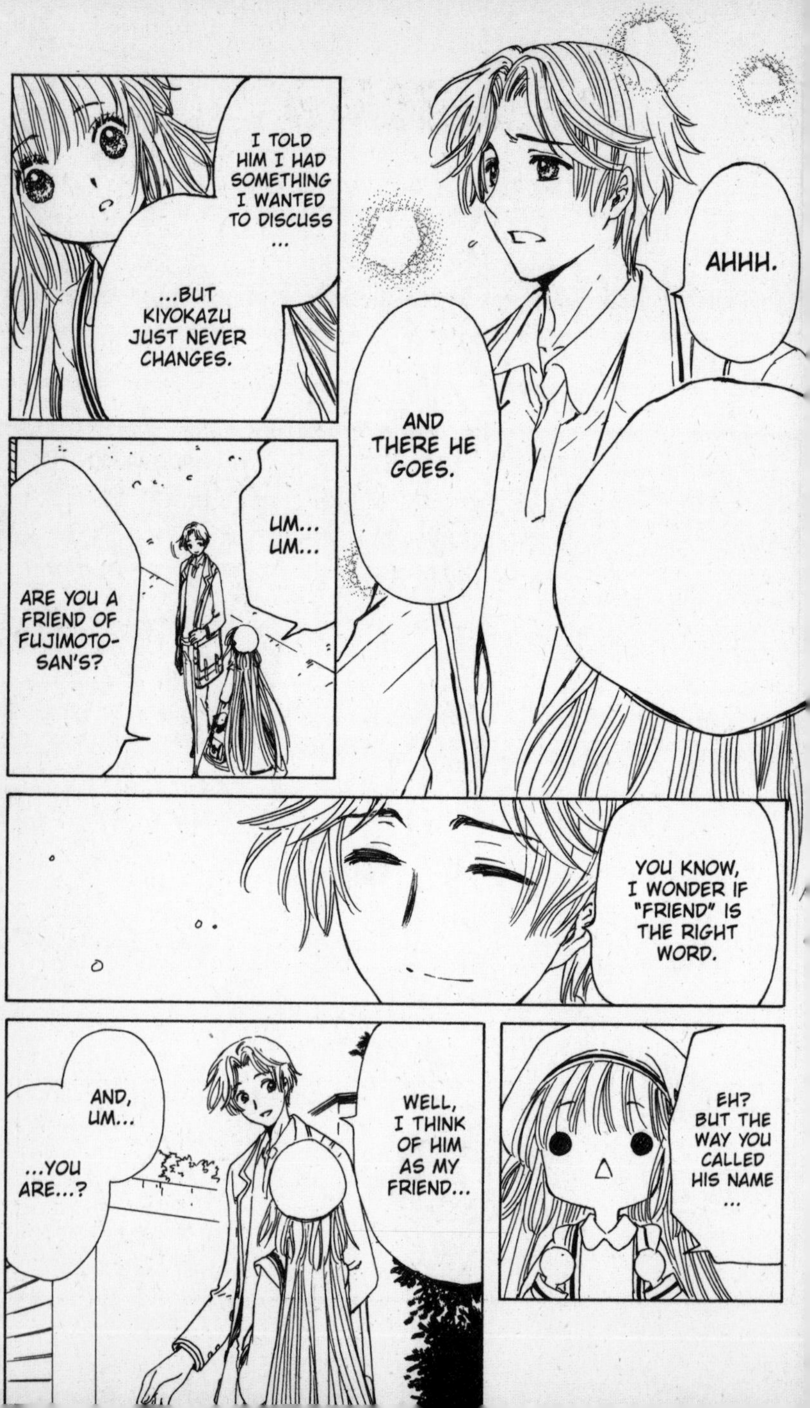
AHHH.
AND THERE HE GOES.
I TOLD HIM I HAD SOMETHING I WANTED TO DISCUSS ...
...BUT KIYOKAZU JUST NEVER CHANGES.
UM... UM...
ARE YOU A FRIEND OF FUJIMOTO-SAN'S?
YOU KNOW, I WONDER IF "FRIEND" IS THE RIGHT WORD.
EH? BUT THE WAY YOU CALLED HIS NAME ...
WELL, I THINK OF HIM AS MY FRIEND...
AND, UM...
...YOU ARE...?

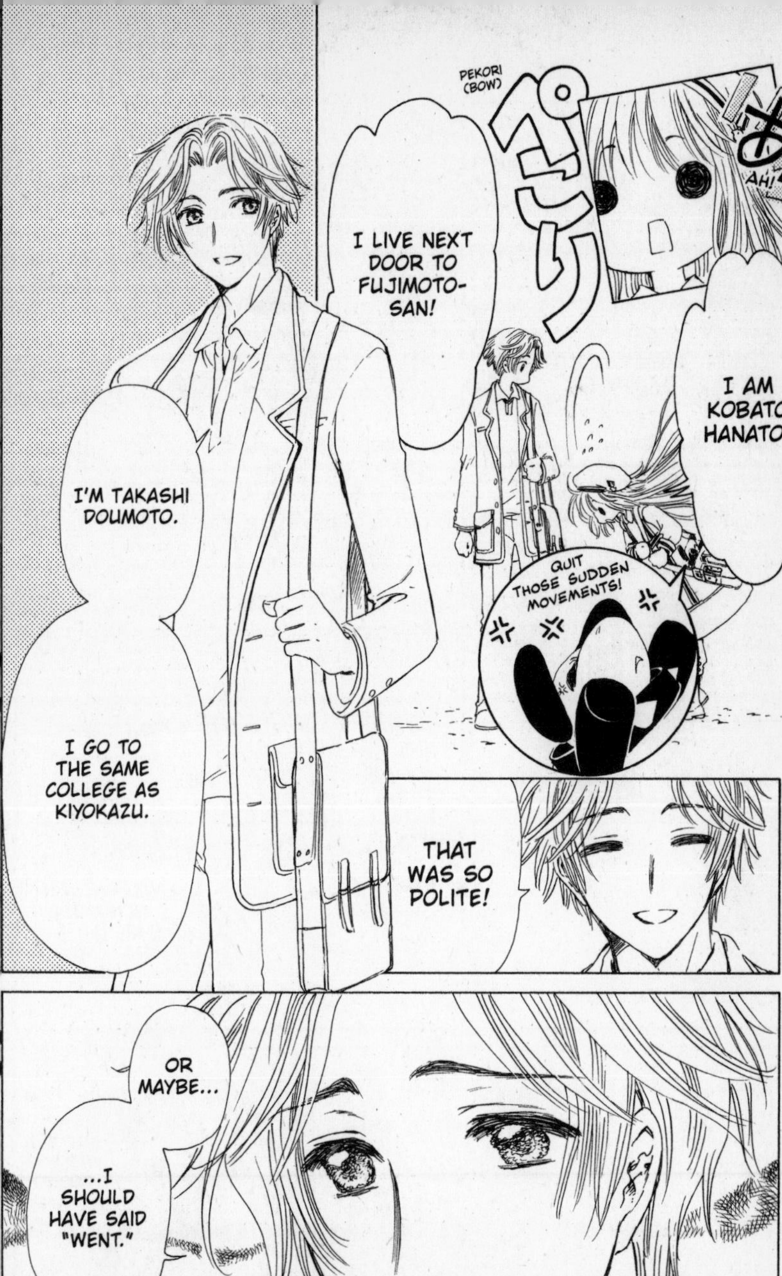
あ
AH!
ペこり
PEKORI (BOW)
I AM KOBATO HANATO!
I LIVE NEXT DOOR TO FUJIMOTO-SAN!
QUIT THOSE SUDDEN MOVEMENTS!
THAT WAS SO POLITE!
I'M TAKASHI DOUMOTO.
I GO TO THE SAME COLLEGE AS KIYOKAZU.
OR MAYBE...
...I SHOULD HAVE SAID "WENT."

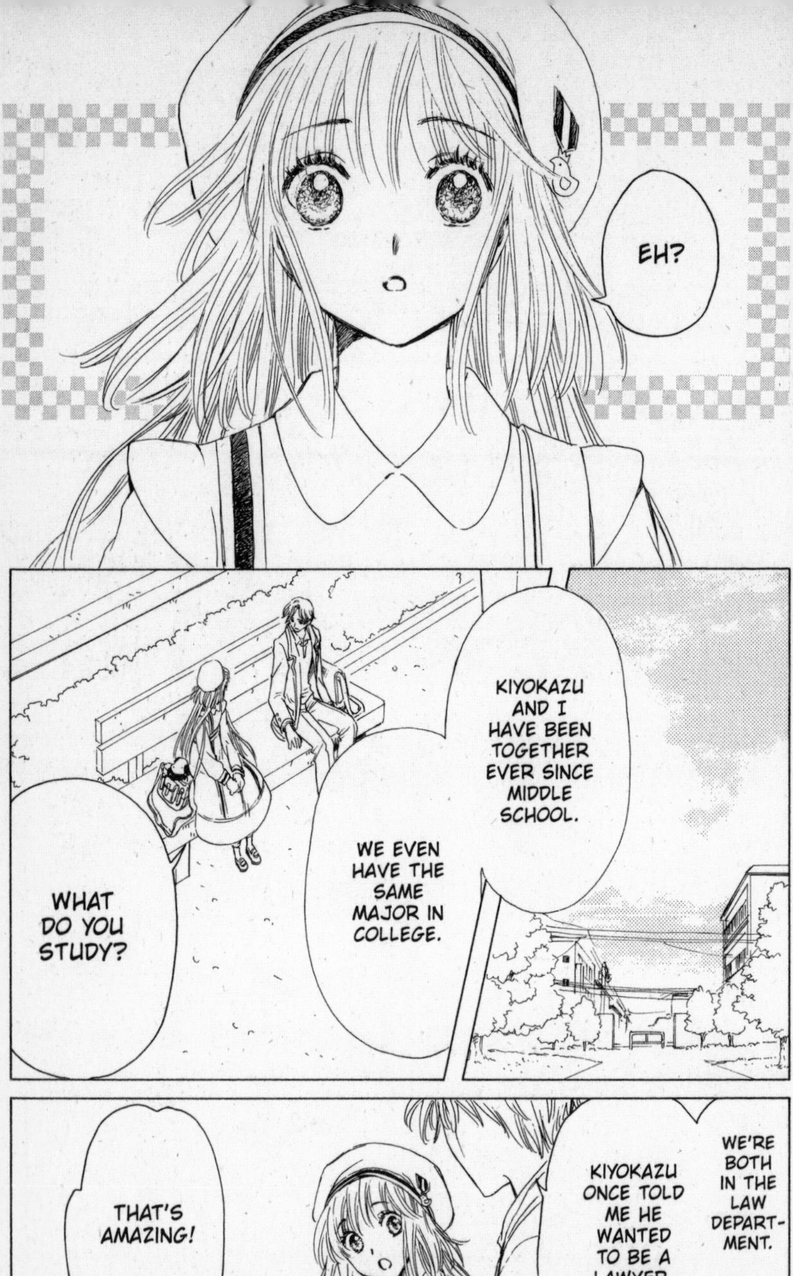
EH?
KIYOKAZU AND I HAVE BEEN TOGETHER EVER SINCE MIDDLE SCHOOL.
WE EVEN HAVE THE SAME MAJOR IN COLLEGE.
WHAT DO YOU STUDY?
WE'RE BOTH IN THE LAW DEPART-MENT.
KIYOKAZU ONCE TOLD ME HE WANTED TO BE A LAWYER.
THAT'S AMAZING!

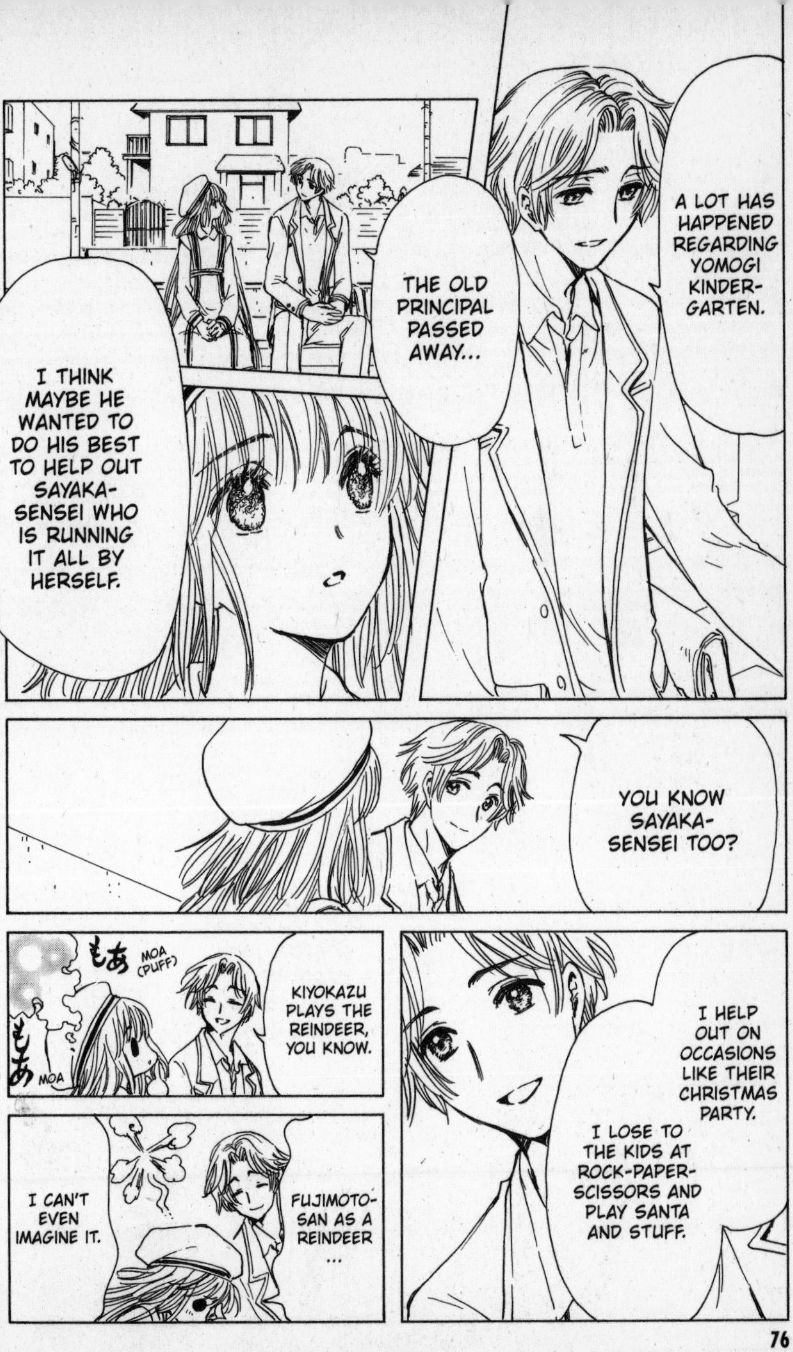
A LOT HAS HAPPENED REGARDING YOMOGI KINDERGARTEN.
THE OLD PRINCIPAL PASSED AWAY...
I THINK MAYBE HE WANTED TO DO HIS BEST TO HELP OUT SAYAKA-SENSEI WHO IS RUNNING IT ALL BY HERSELF.
YOU KNOW SAYAKA-SENSEI TOO?
I HELP OUT ON OCCASIONS LIKE THEIR CHRISTMAS PARTY.
I LOSE TO THE KIDS AT ROCK-PAPER-SCISSORS AND PLAY SANTA AND STUFF.
KIYOKAZU PLAYS THE REINDEER, YOU KNOW.
もあ MOA (PUFF)
もあ MOA
FUJIMOTO-SAN AS A REINDEER...
I CAN'T EVEN IMAGINE IT.

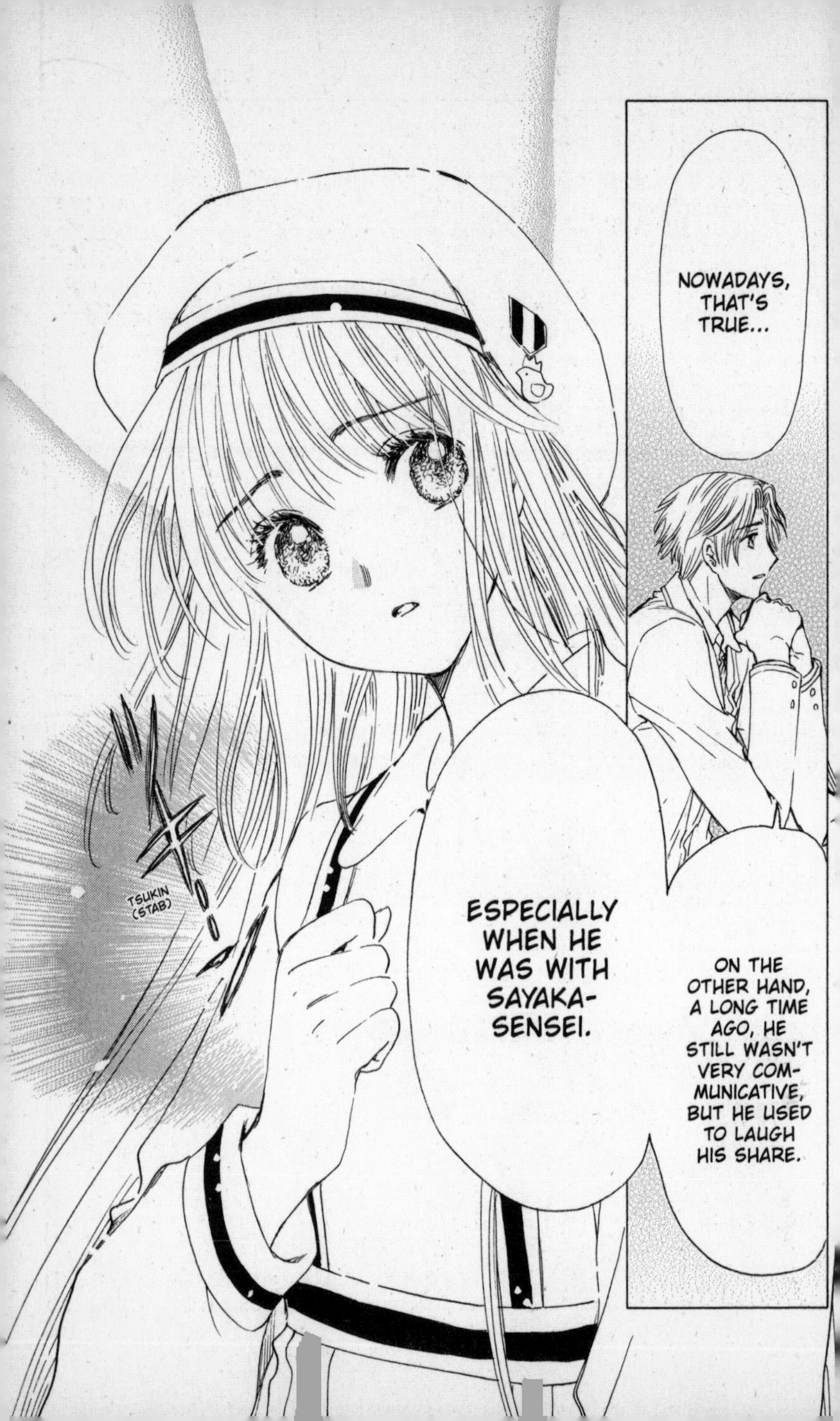
NOWADAYS, THAT'S TRUE...
ON THE OTHER HAND, A LONG TIME AGO, HE STILL WASN'T VERY COM-MUNICATIVE, BUT HE USED TO LAUGH HIS SHARE.
ESPECIALLY WHEN HE WAS WITH SAYAKA-SENSEI.
TSUKIN (STAB)

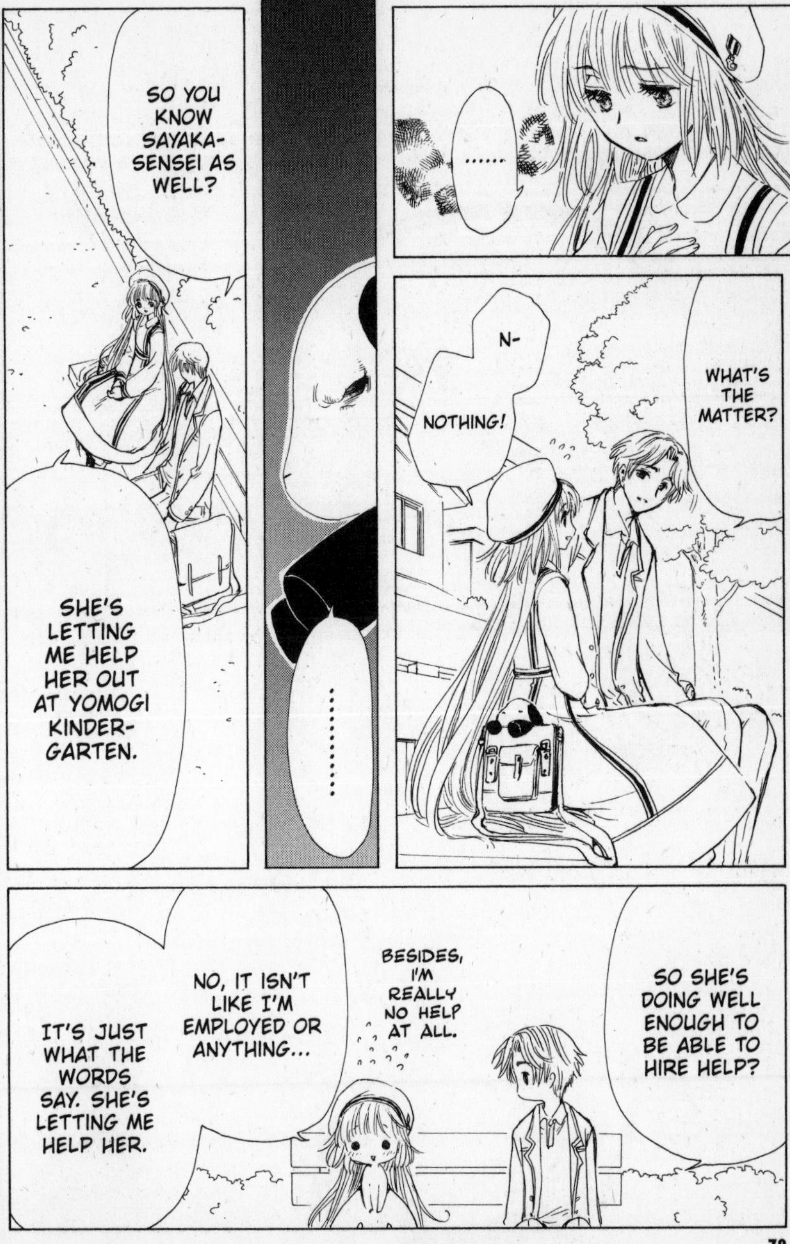
......
WHAT'S THE MATTER?
N-
NOTHING!
......
SO YOU KNOW SAYAKA-SENSEI AS WELL?
SHE'S LETTING ME HELP HER OUT AT YOMOGI KINDERGARTEN.
SO SHE'S DOING WELL ENOUGH TO BE ABLE TO HIRE HELP?
BESIDES, I'M REALLY NO HELP AT ALL.
NO, IT ISN'T LIKE I'M EMPLOYED OR ANYTHING...
IT'S JUST WHAT THE WORDS SAY. SHE'S LETTING ME HELP HER.

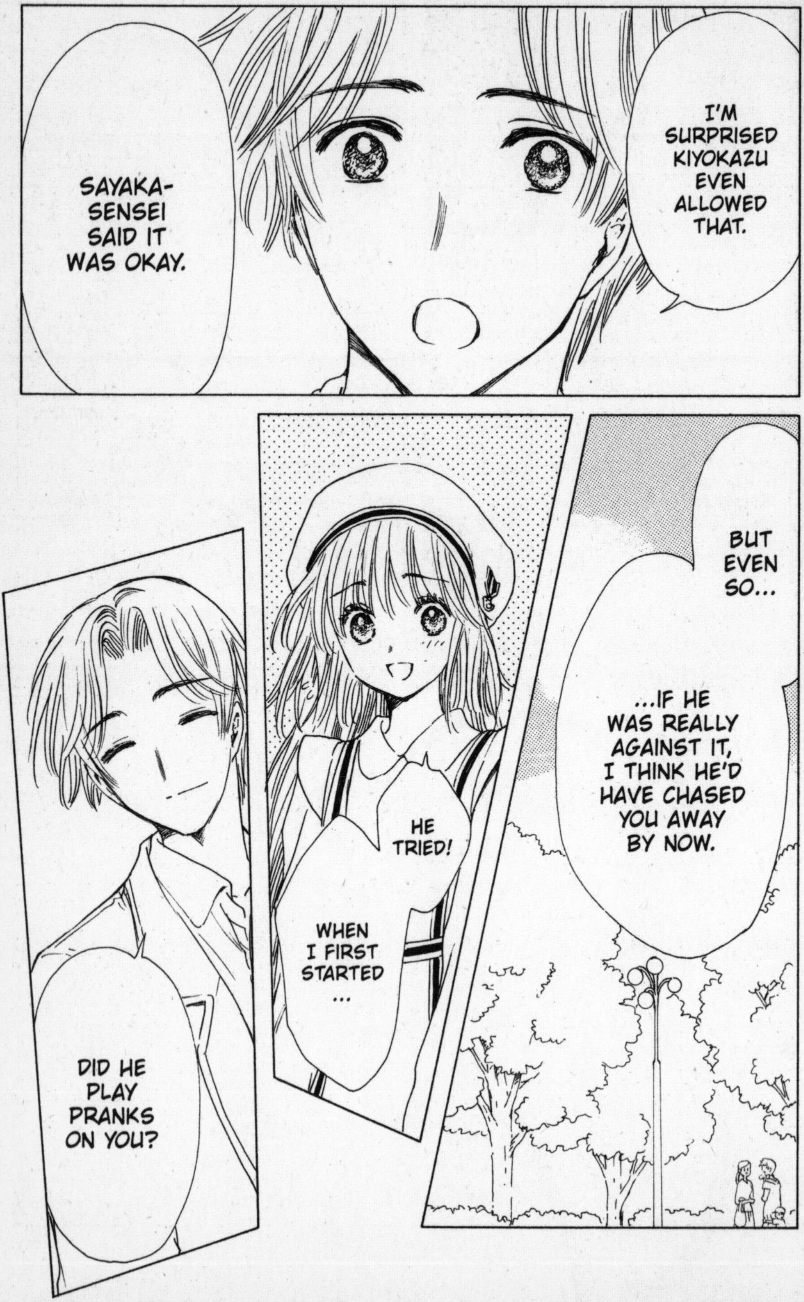
I'M SURPRISED KIYOKAZU EVEN ALLOWED THAT.
SAYAKA-SENSEI SAID IT WAS OKAY.
BUT EVEN SO...
...IF HE WAS REALLY AGAINST IT, I THINK HE'D HAVE CHASED YOU AWAY BY NOW.
HE TRIED!
WHEN I FIRST STARTED ...
DID HE PLAY PRANKS ON YOU?

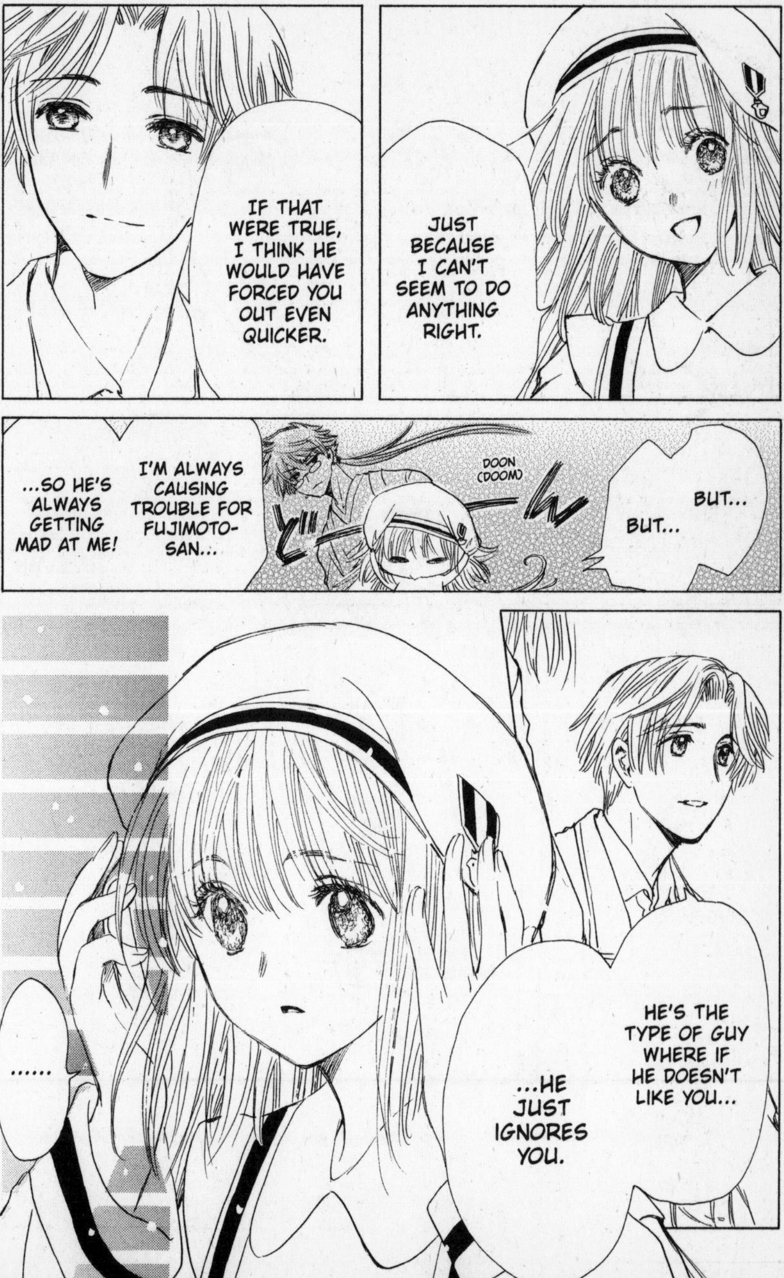
JUST BECAUSE I CAN'T SEEM TO DO ANYTHING RIGHT.
IF THAT WERE TRUE, I THINK HE WOULD HAVE FORCED YOU OUT EVEN QUICKER.
BUT...
BUT...
DOON (DOOM)
I'M ALWAYS CAUSING TROUBLE FOR FUJIMOTO-SAN...
...SO HE'S ALWAYS GETTING MAD AT ME!
HE'S THE TYPE OF GUY WHERE IF HE DOESN'T LIKE YOU...
...HE JUST IGNORES YOU.
......

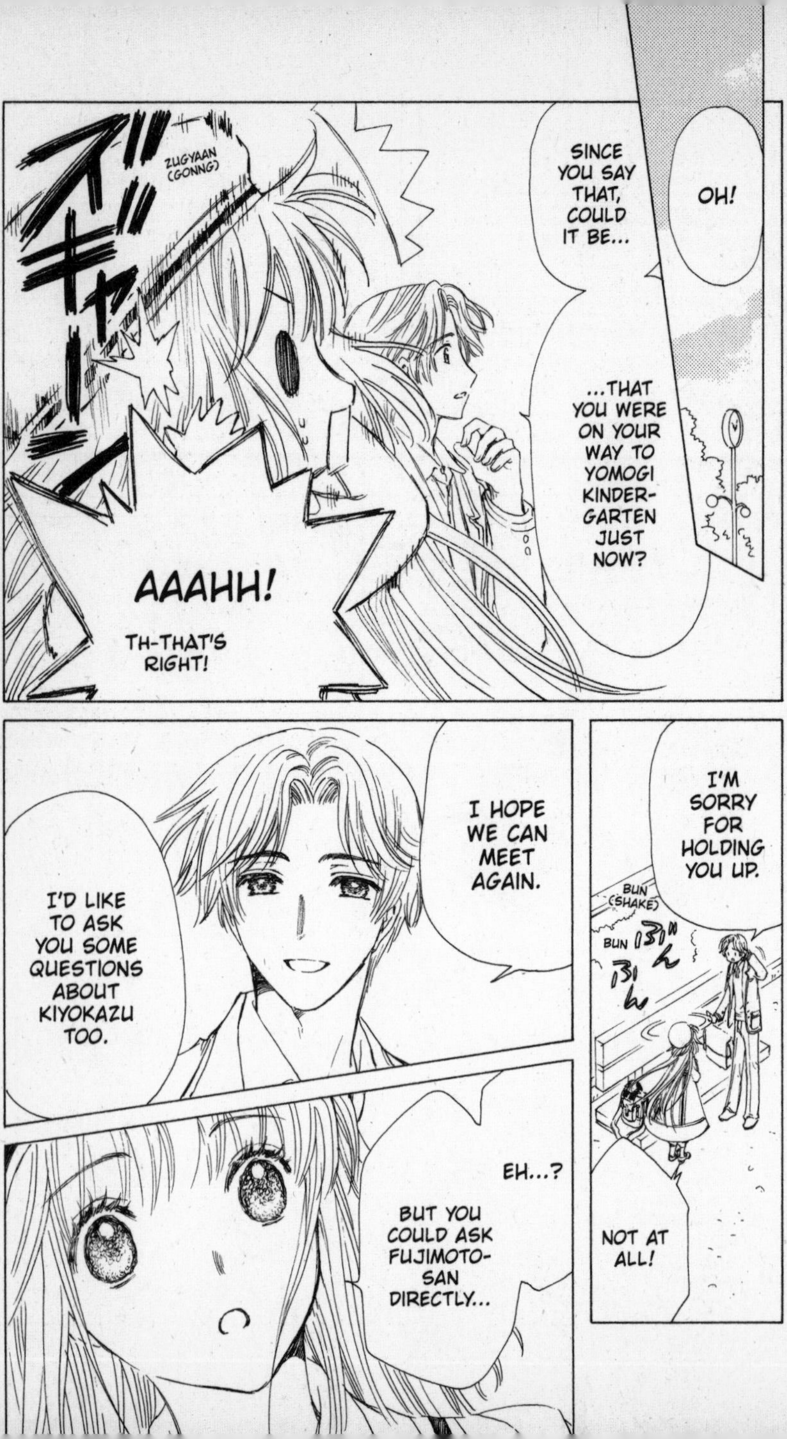
OH!
SINCE YOU SAY THAT, COULD IT BE...
...THAT YOU WERE ON YOUR WAY TO YOMOGI KINDER-GARTEN JUST NOW?
ZUGYAAN (GONNG)
AAAHH!
TH-THAT'S RIGHT!
I'M SORRY FOR HOLDING YOU UP.
BUN (SHAKE)
BUN
NOT AT ALL!
I HOPE WE CAN MEET AGAIN.
I'D LIKE TO ASK YOU SOME QUESTIONS ABOUT KIYOKAZU TOO.
EH...?
BUT YOU COULD ASK FUJIMOTO-SAN DIRECTLY...

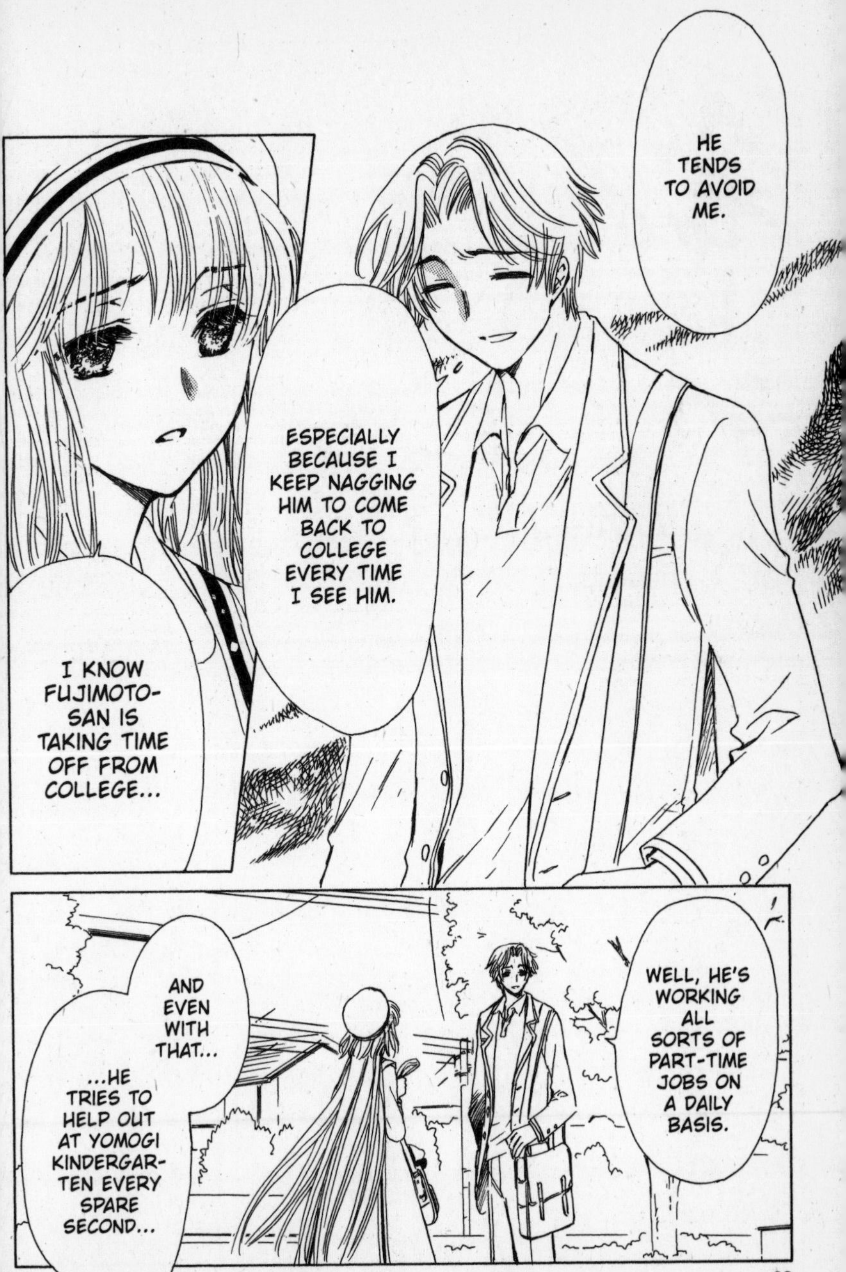
HE TENDS TO AVOID ME.
ESPECIALLY BECAUSE I KEEP NAGGING HIM TO COME BACK TO COLLEGE EVERY TIME I SEE HIM.
I KNOW FUJIMOTO-SAN IS TAKING TIME OFF FROM COLLEGE...
WELL, HE'S WORKING ALL SORTS OF PART-TIME JOBS ON A DAILY BASIS.
AND EVEN WITH THAT...
...HE TRIES TO HELP OUT AT YOMOGI KINDERGAR-TEN EVERY SPARE SECOND...

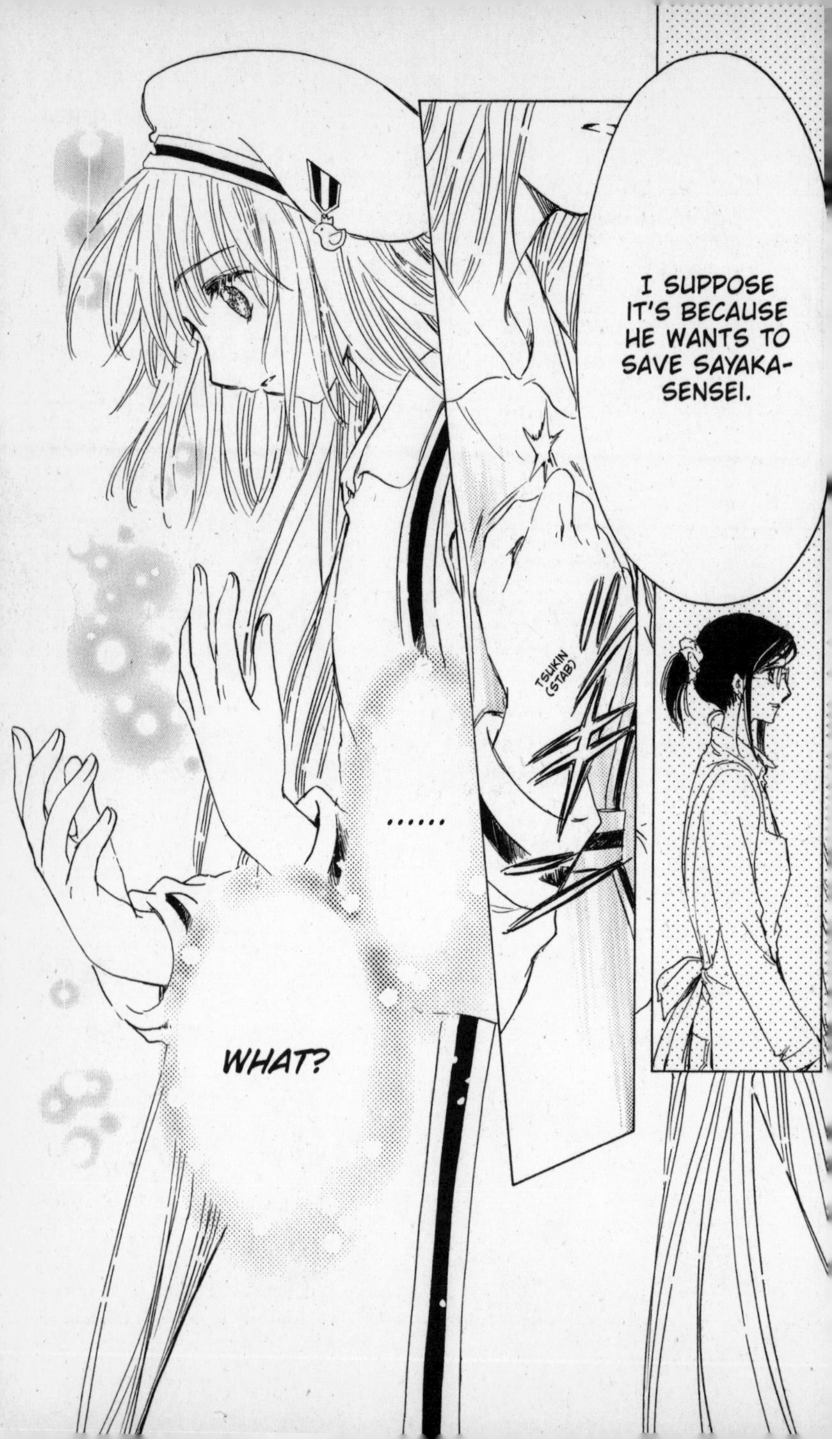
I SUPPOSE IT'S BECAUSE HE WANTS TO SAVE SAYAKA-SENSEI.
TSUKIN (STAB)
......
WHAT?

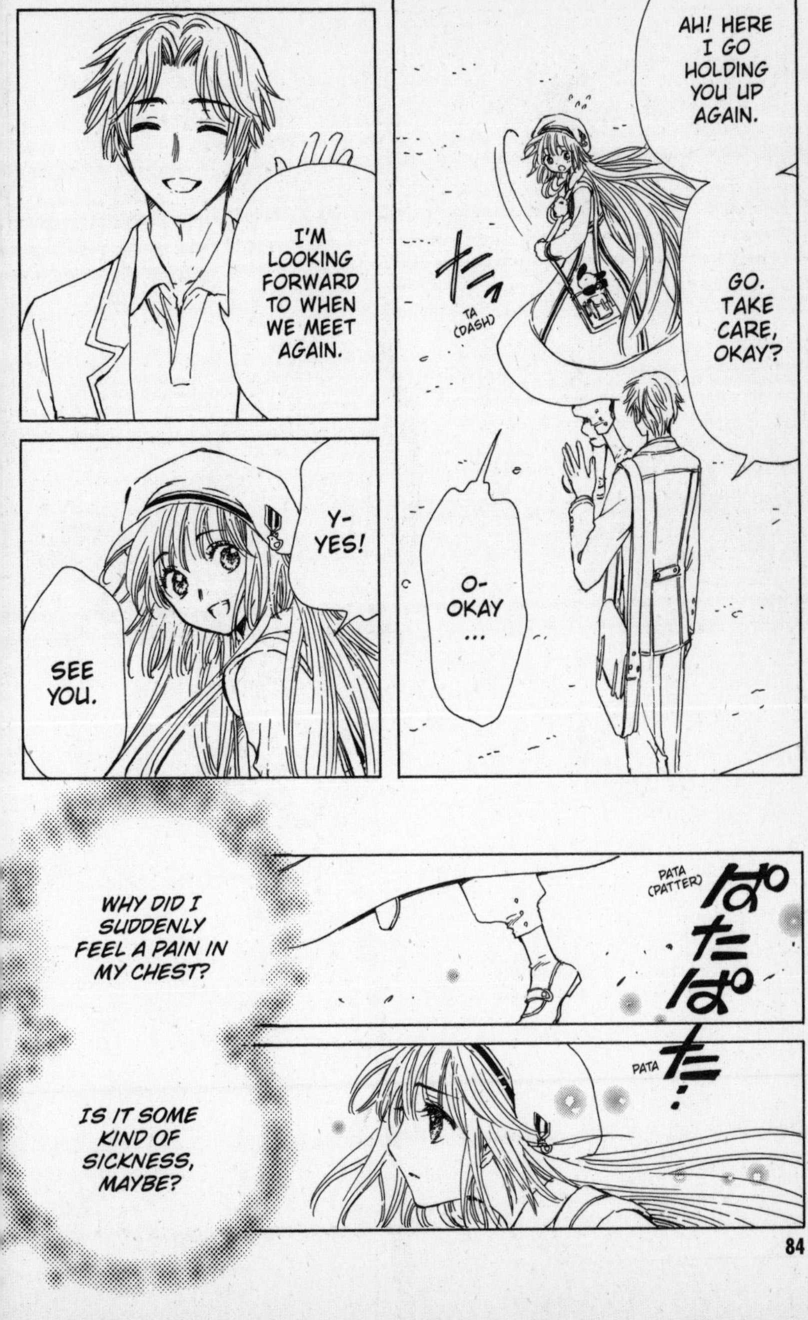

AH! HERE I GO HOLDING YOU UP AGAIN.
TA (DASH)
GO. TAKE CARE, OKAY?
O-OKAY ...
I'M LOOKING FORWARD TO WHEN WE MEET AGAIN.
Y-YES!
SEE YOU.
PATA (PATTER)
WHY DID I SUDDENLY FEEL A PAIN IN MY CHEST?
PATA
IS IT SOME KIND OF SICKNESS, MAYBE?

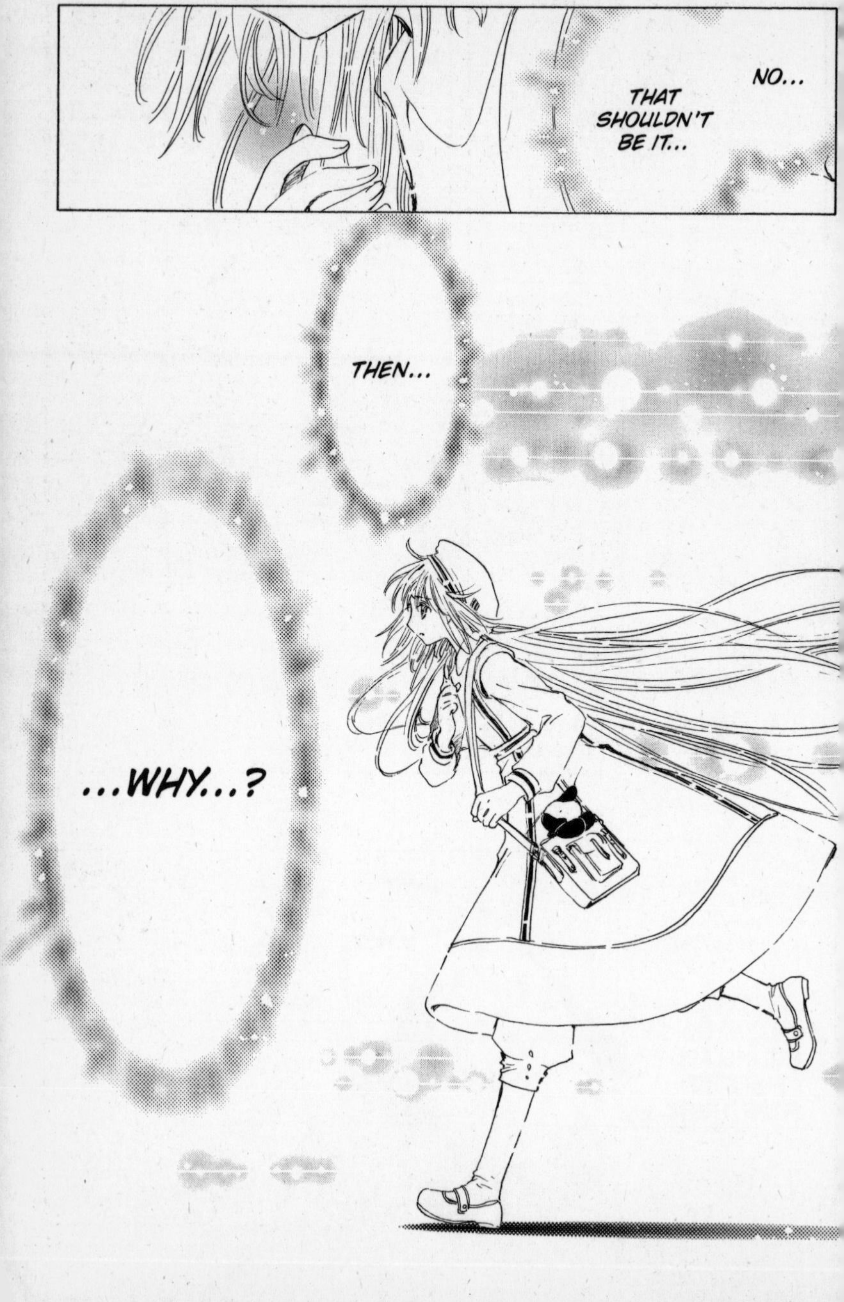
NO...
THAT SHOULDN'T BE IT...
THEN...
...WHY...?

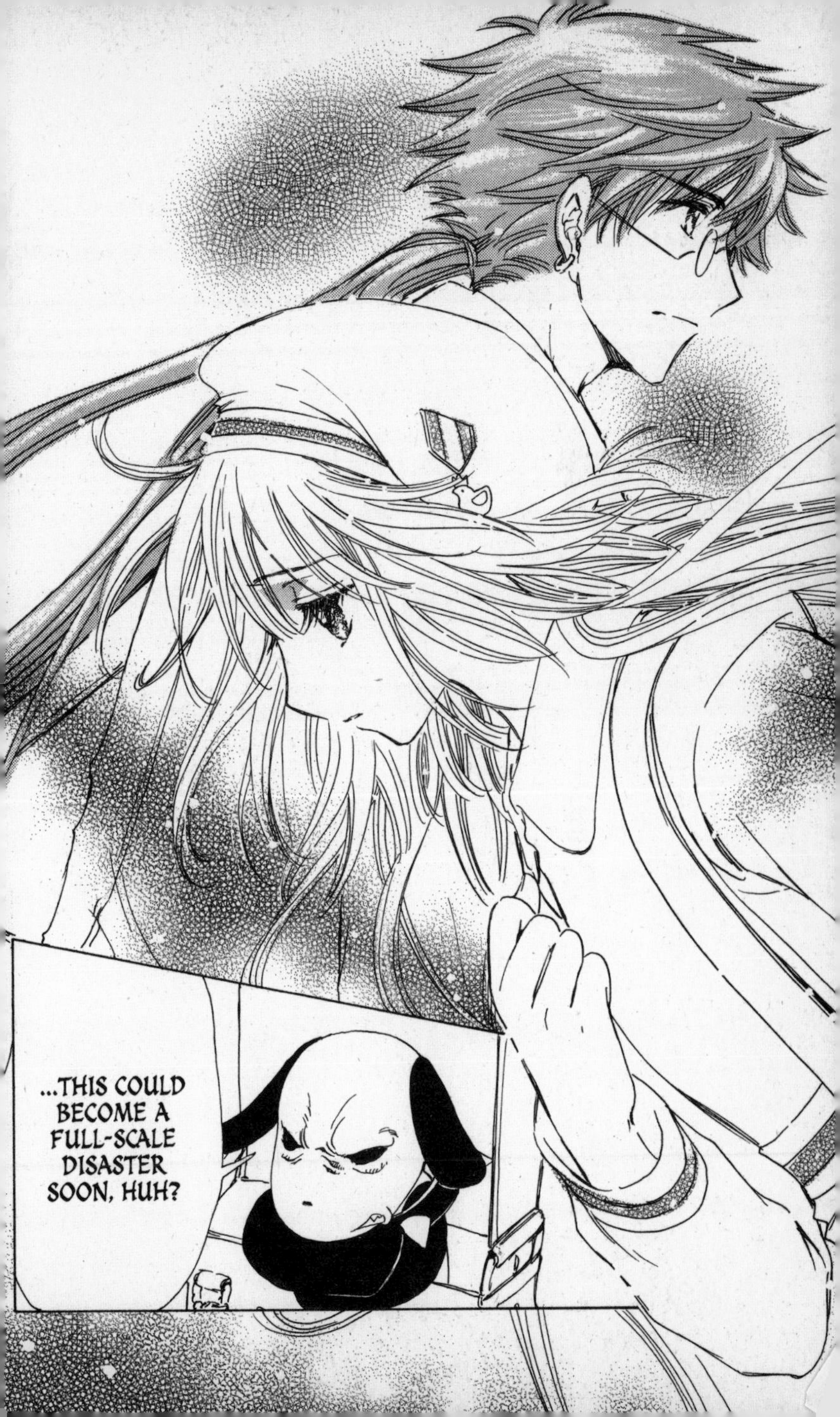
...THIS COULD BECOME A FULL-SCALE DISASTER SOON, HUH?

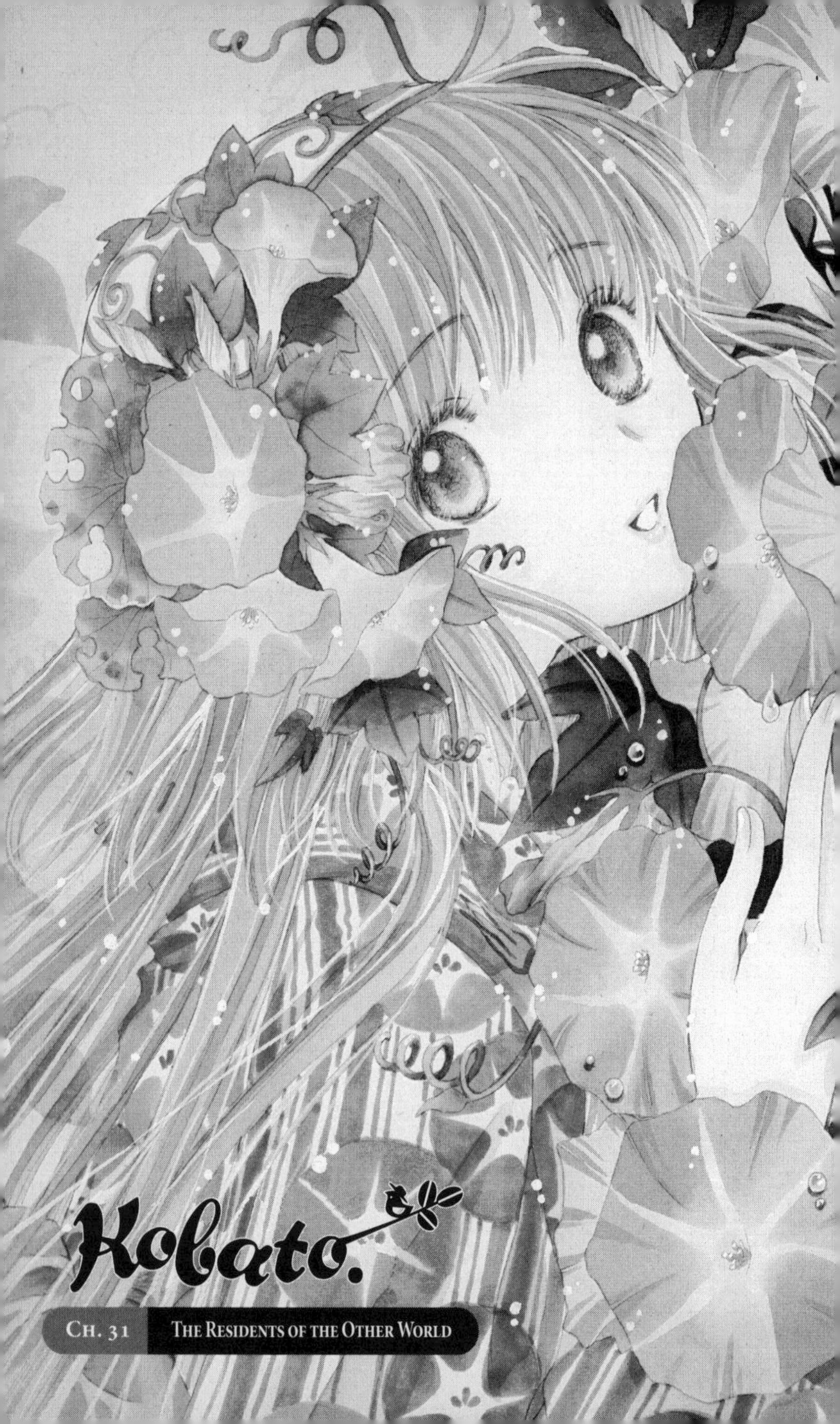
Kobato.
Ch. 31
The Residents of the Other World

SIGN: THE BEAR'S BAUMKUCHEN SHOP

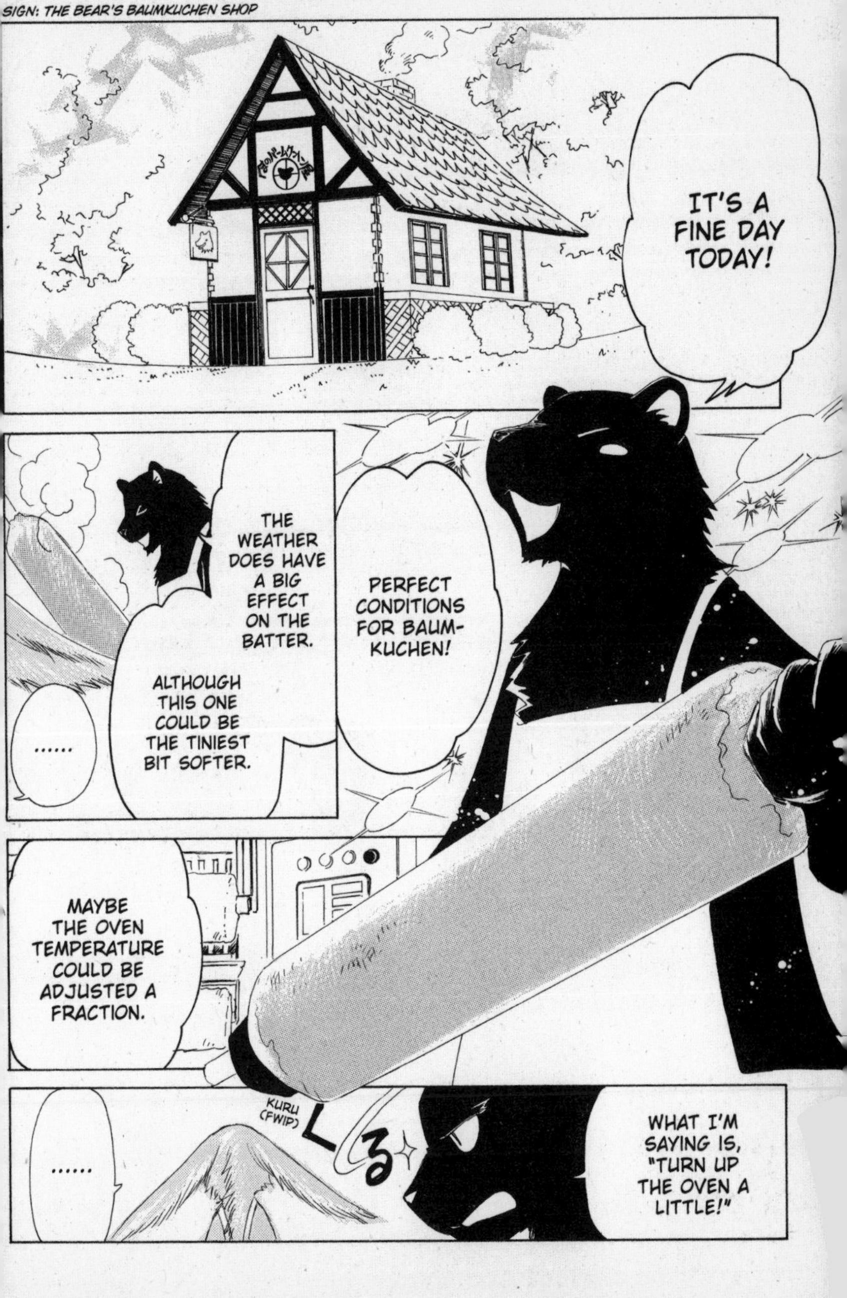

IT'S A FINE DAY TODAY!
PERFECT CONDITIONS FOR BAUMKUCHEN!
THE WEATHER DOES HAVE A BIG EFFECT ON THE BATTER.
ALTHOUGH THIS ONE COULD BE THE TINIEST BIT SOFTER.
......
MAYBE THE OVEN TEMPERATURE COULD BE ADJUSTED A FRACTION.
WHAT I'M SAYING IS, "TURN UP THE OVEN A LITTLE!"
KURU (FWIP)
......

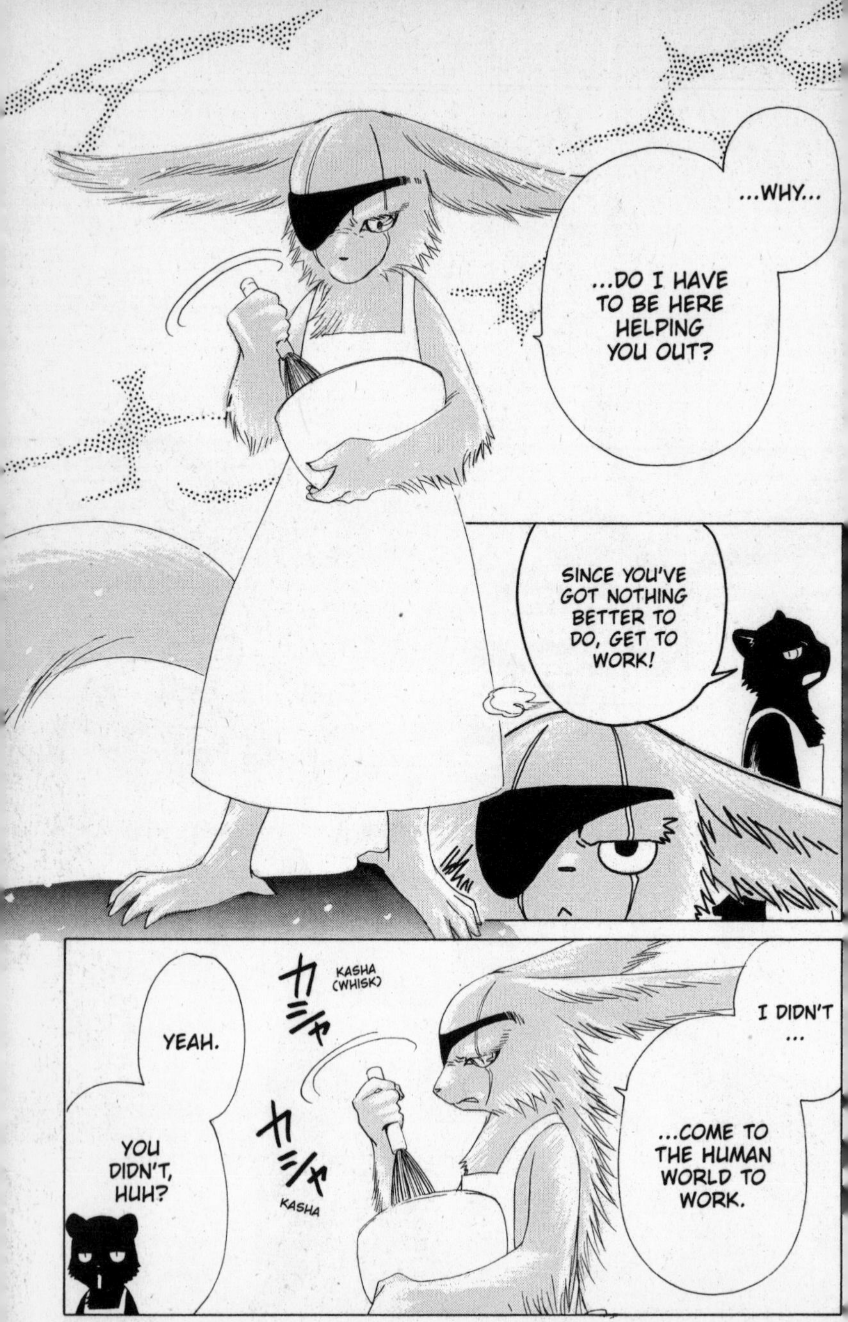
...WHY...
...DO I HAVE TO BE HERE HELPING YOU OUT?
SINCE YOU'VE GOT NOTHING BETTER TO DO, GET TO WORK!
I DIDN'T ...
...COME TO THE HUMAN WORLD TO WORK.
カシャ
KASHA (WHISK)
カシャ
KASHA
YEAH.
YOU DIDN'T, HUH?

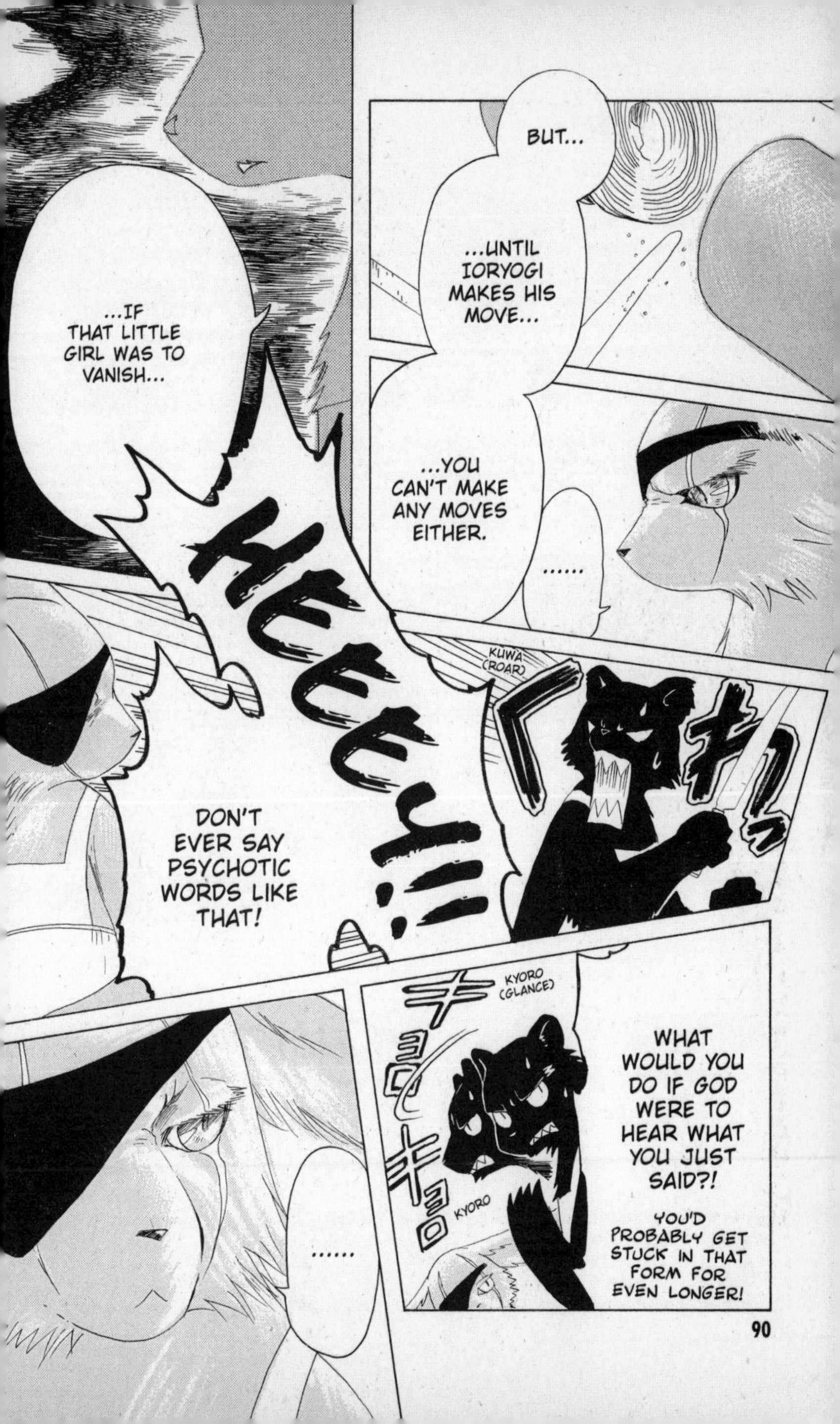
BUT...
...UNTIL IORYOGI MAKES HIS MOVE...
...YOU CAN'T MAKE ANY MOVES EITHER.
......
...IF THAT LITTLE GIRL WAS TO VANISH...
KUWA (ROAR)
HEEEY!!!
DON'T EVER SAY PSYCHOTIC WORDS LIKE THAT!
KYORO (GLANCE)
KYORO
WHAT WOULD YOU DO IF GOD WERE TO HEAR WHAT YOU JUST SAID?!
YOU'D PROBABLY GET STUCK IN THAT FORM FOR EVEN LONGER!
......

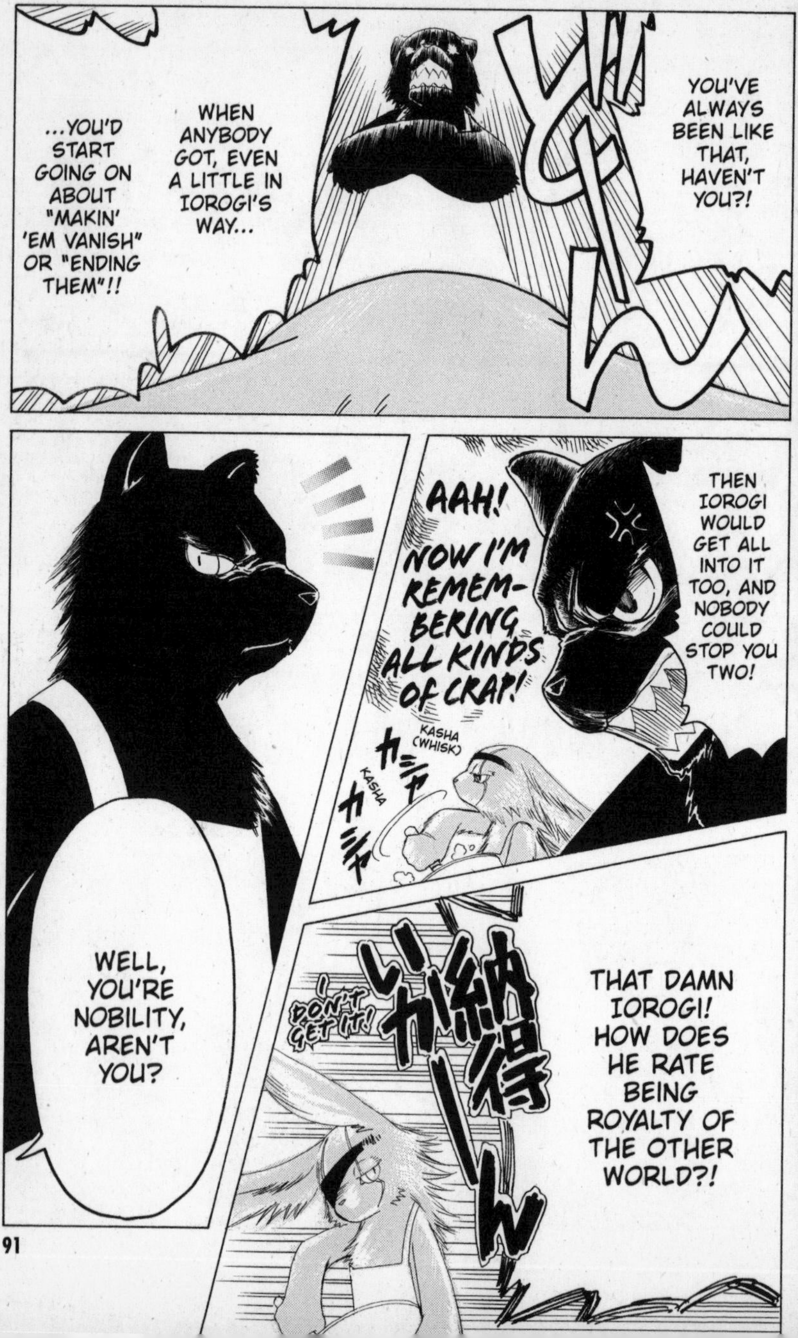

YOU'VE ALWAYS BEEN LIKE THAT, HAVEN'T YOU?!
WHEN ANYBODY GOT, EVEN A LITTLE IN IOROGI'S WAY...
...YOU'D START GOING ON ABOUT "MAKIN' 'EM VANISH" OR "ENDING THEM"!!
THEN IOROGI WOULD GET ALL INTO IT TOO, AND NOBODY COULD STOP YOU TWO!
AAH! NOW I'M REMEMBERING ALL KINDS OF CRAP!
KASHA (WHISK)
KASHA
カシャ
カシャ
THAT DAMN IOROGI! HOW DOES HE RATE BEING ROYALTY OF THE OTHER WORLD?!
納得いかーーん
I DON'T GET IT!
WELL, YOU'RE NOBILITY, AREN'T YOU?

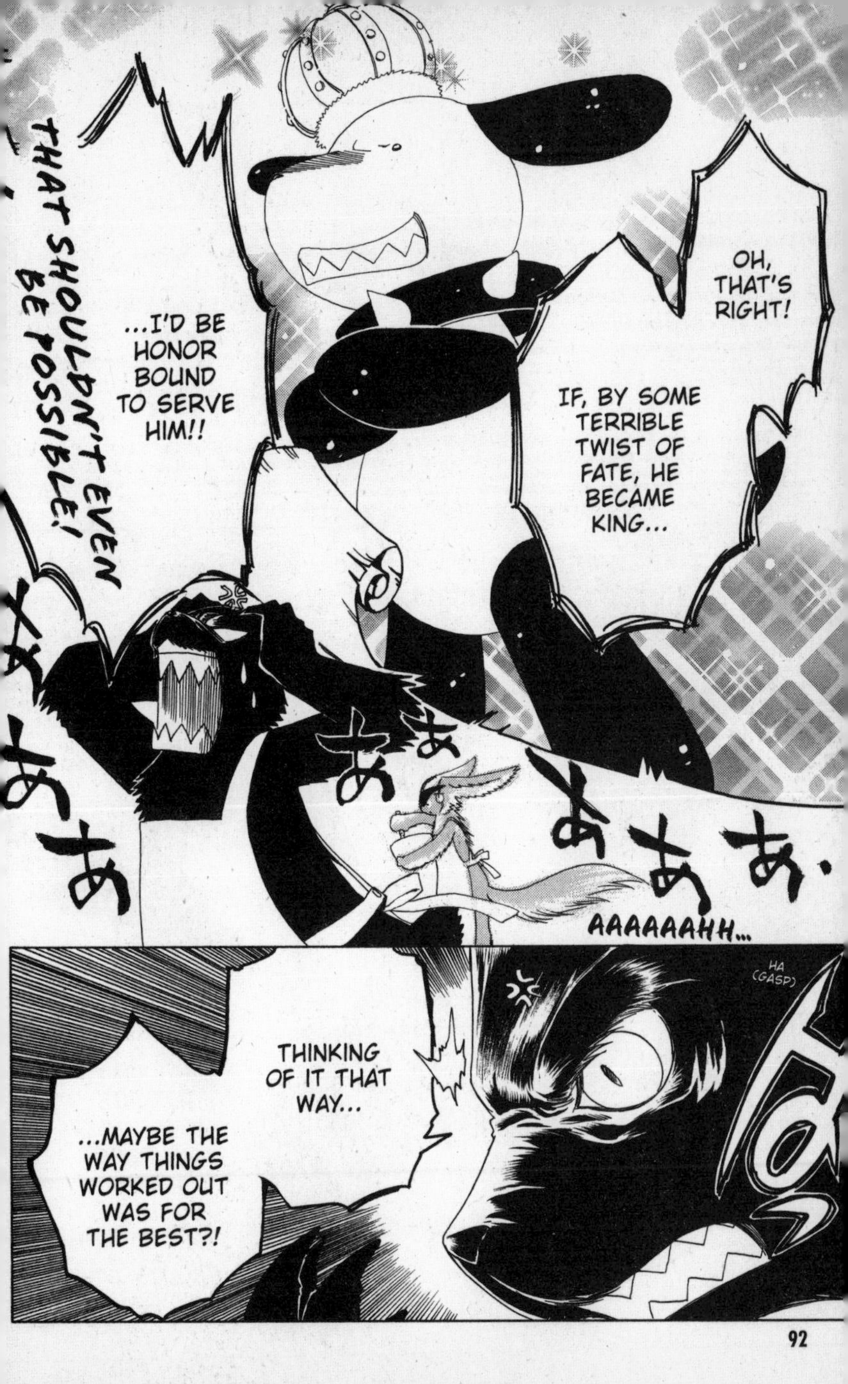
OH, THAT'S RIGHT!
IF, BY SOME TERRIBLE TWIST OF FATE, HE BECAME KING...
...I'D BE HONOR BOUND TO SERVE HIM!!
THAT SHOULDN'T EVEN BE POSSIBLE!
AAAAAAHH...
HA (GASP)
THINKING OF IT THAT WAY...
...MAYBE THE WAY THINGS WORKED OUT WAS FOR THE BEST?!

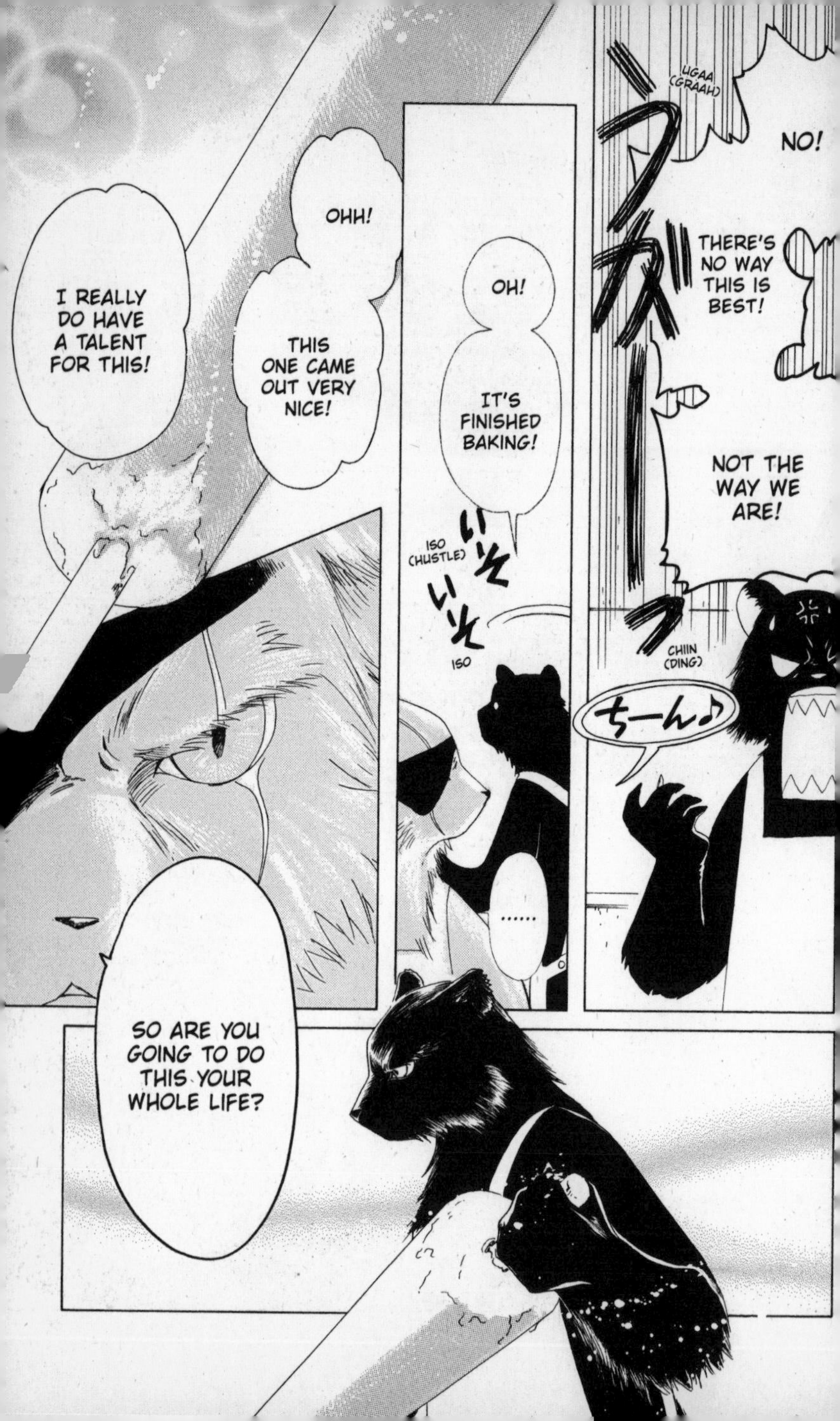
UGAA (GRAAH)
ウガーッ
NO!
THERE'S NO WAY THIS IS BEST!
NOT THE WAY WE ARE!
CHIIN (DING)
ちーん♪
OH!
IT'S FINISHED BAKING!
ISO (HUSTLE)
いそ
いそ
ISO
......
OHH!
THIS ONE CAME OUT VERY NICE!
I REALLY DO HAVE A TALENT FOR THIS!
SO ARE YOU GOING TO DO THIS YOUR WHOLE LIFE?

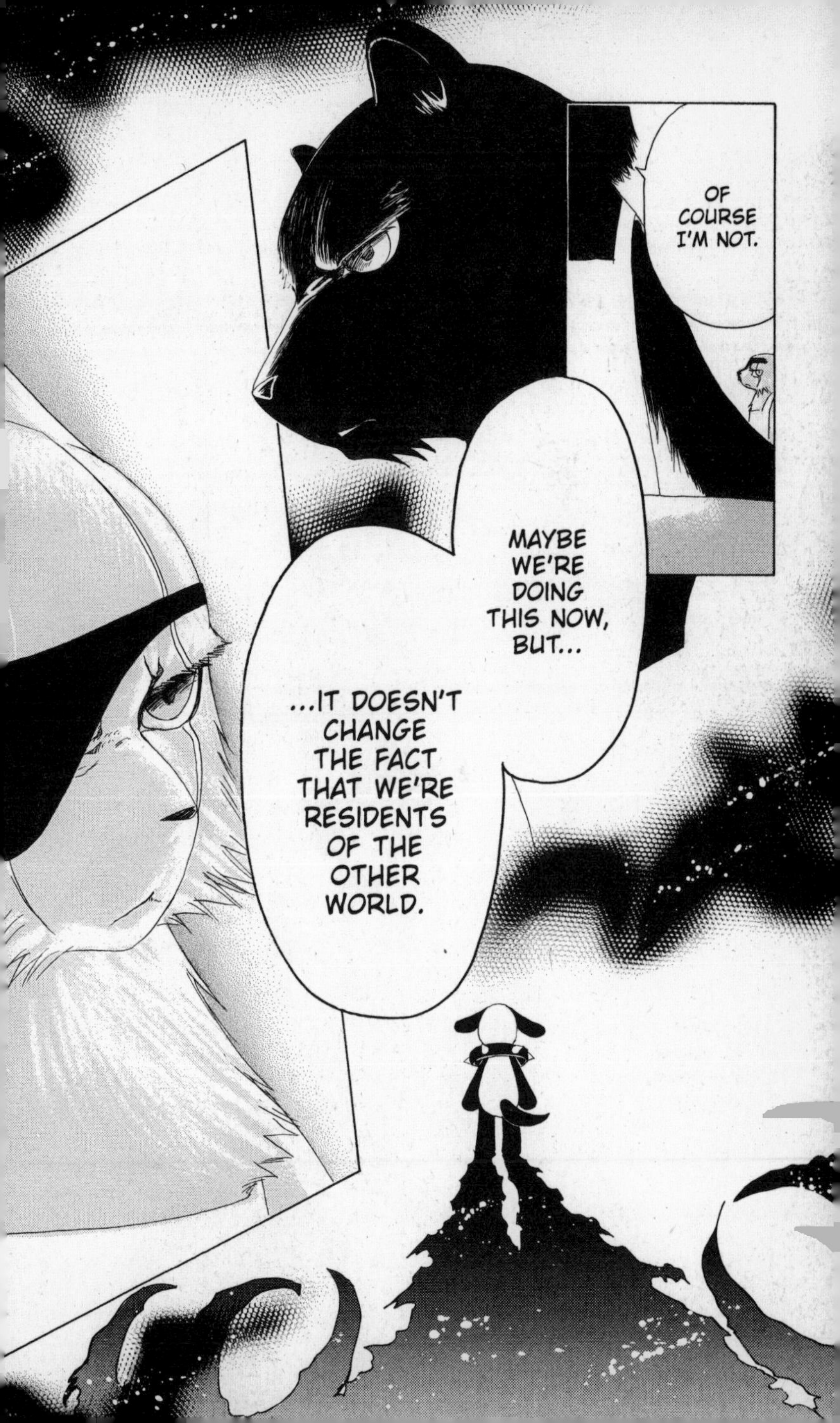
OF COURSE I'M NOT.
MAYBE WE'RE DOING THIS NOW, BUT...
...IT DOESN'T CHANGE THE FACT THAT WE'RE RESIDENTS OF THE OTHER WORLD.

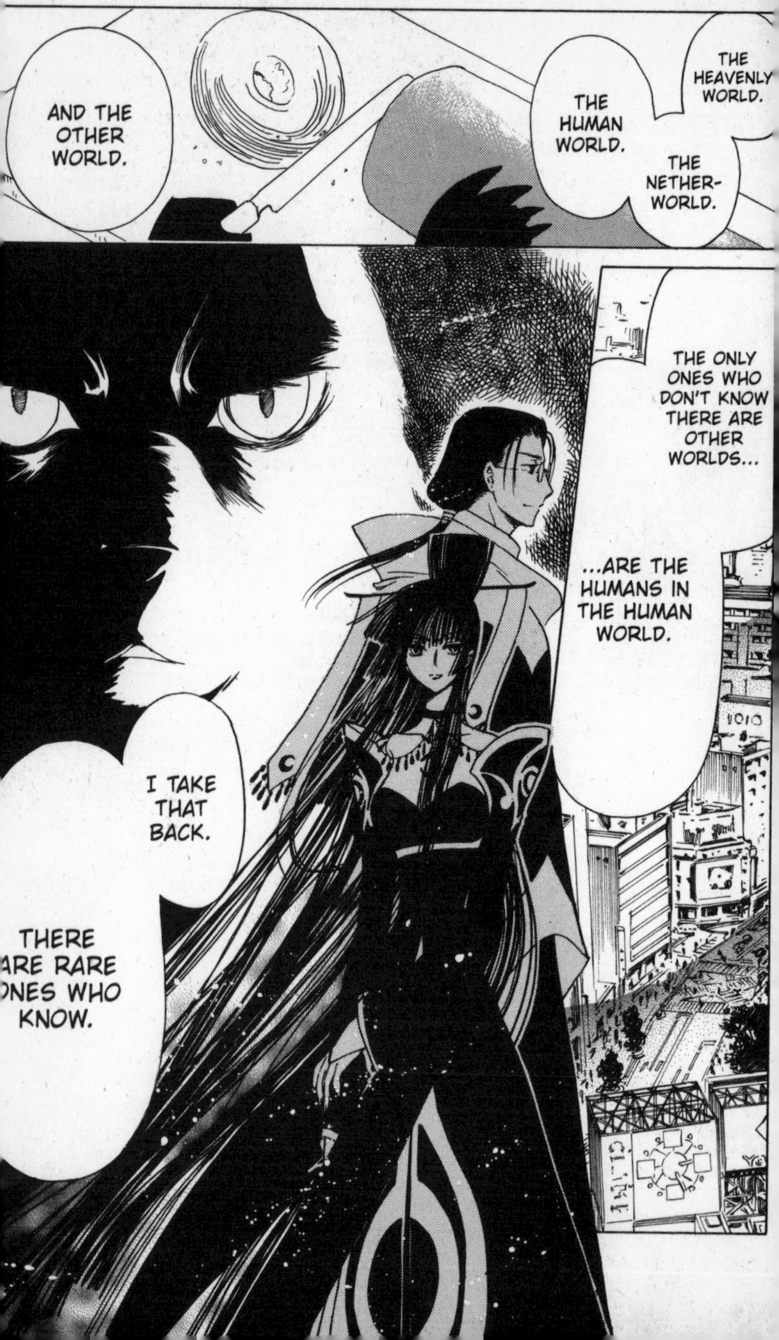
THE HEAVENLY WORLD.
THE HUMAN WORLD.
THE NETHER-WORLD.
AND THE OTHER WORLD.
THE ONLY ONES WHO DON'T KNOW THERE ARE OTHER WORLDS...
...ARE THE HUMANS IN THE HUMAN WORLD.
I TAKE THAT BACK.
THERE ARE RARE ONES WHO KNOW.

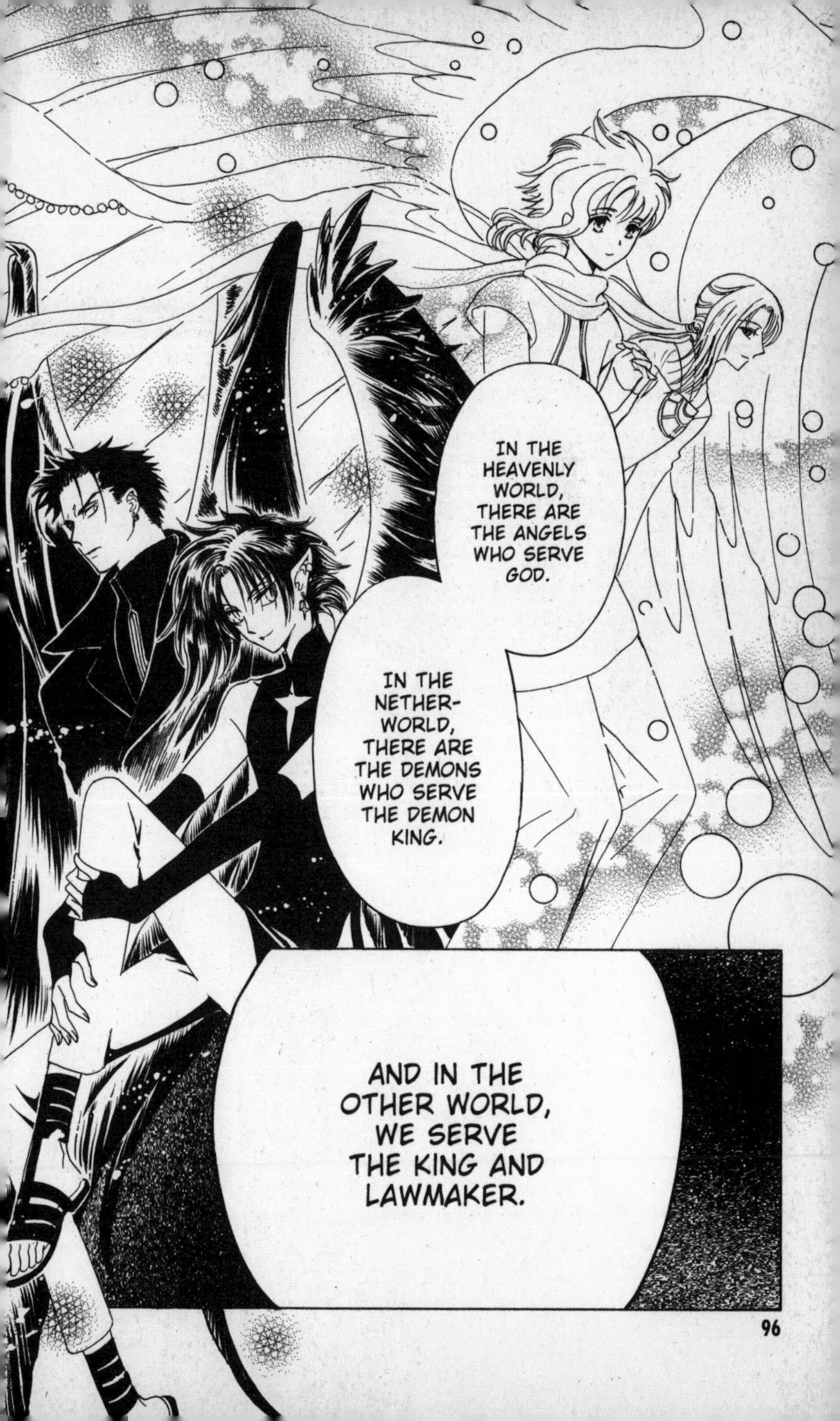
IN THE HEAVENLY WORLD, THERE ARE THE ANGELS WHO SERVE GOD.
IN THE NETHER-WORLD, THERE ARE THE DEMONS WHO SERVE THE DEMON KING.
AND IN THE OTHER WORLD, WE SERVE THE KING AND LAWMAKER.

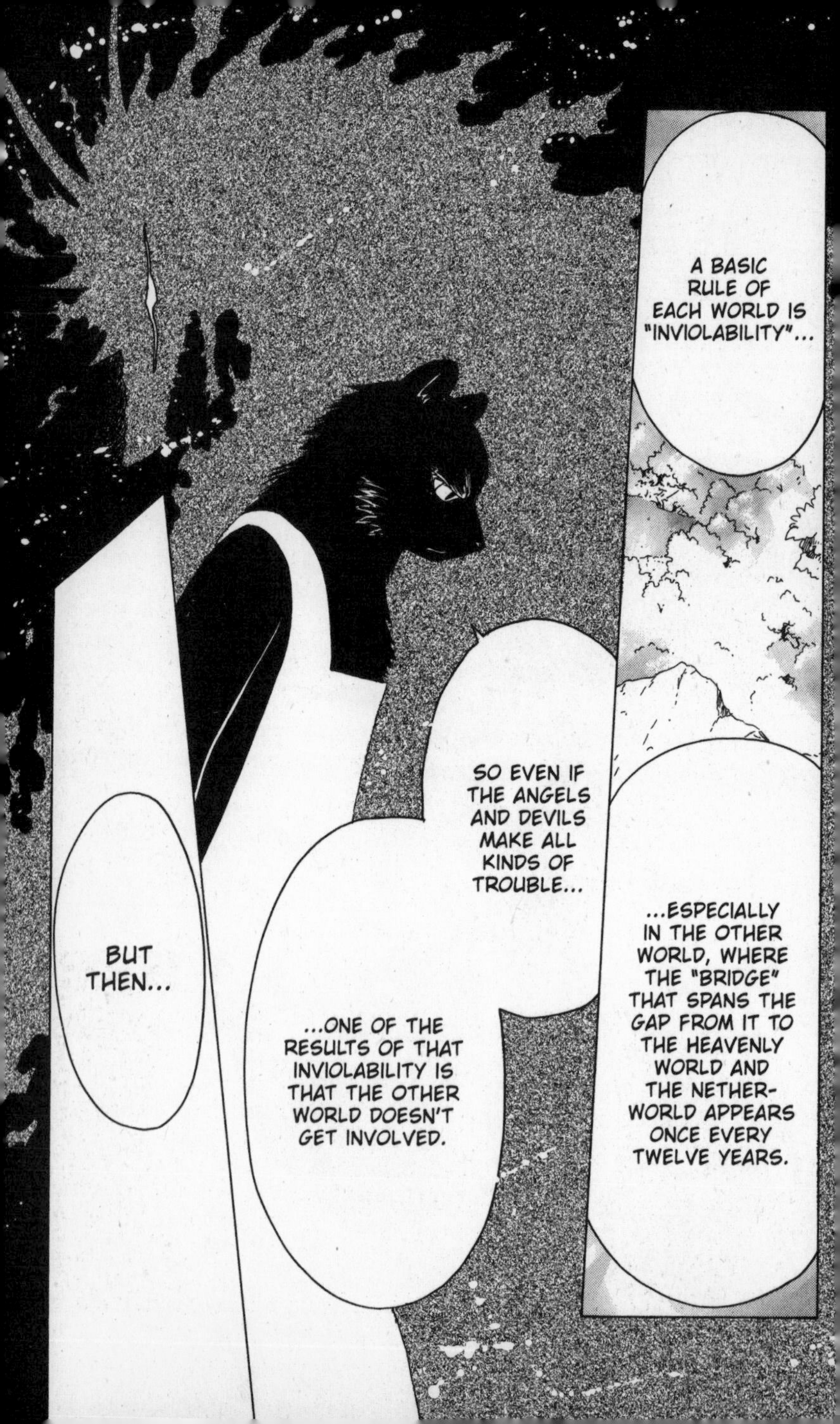
A BASIC RULE OF EACH WORLD IS "INVIOLABILITY"...
...ESPECIALLY IN THE OTHER WORLD, WHERE THE "BRIDGE" THAT SPANS THE GAP FROM IT TO THE HEAVENLY WORLD AND THE NETHER-WORLD APPEARS ONCE EVERY TWELVE YEARS.
SO EVEN IF THE ANGELS AND DEVILS MAKE ALL KINDS OF TROUBLE...
...ONE OF THE RESULTS OF THAT INVIOLABILITY IS THAT THE OTHER WORLD DOESN'T GET INVOLVED.
BUT THEN...

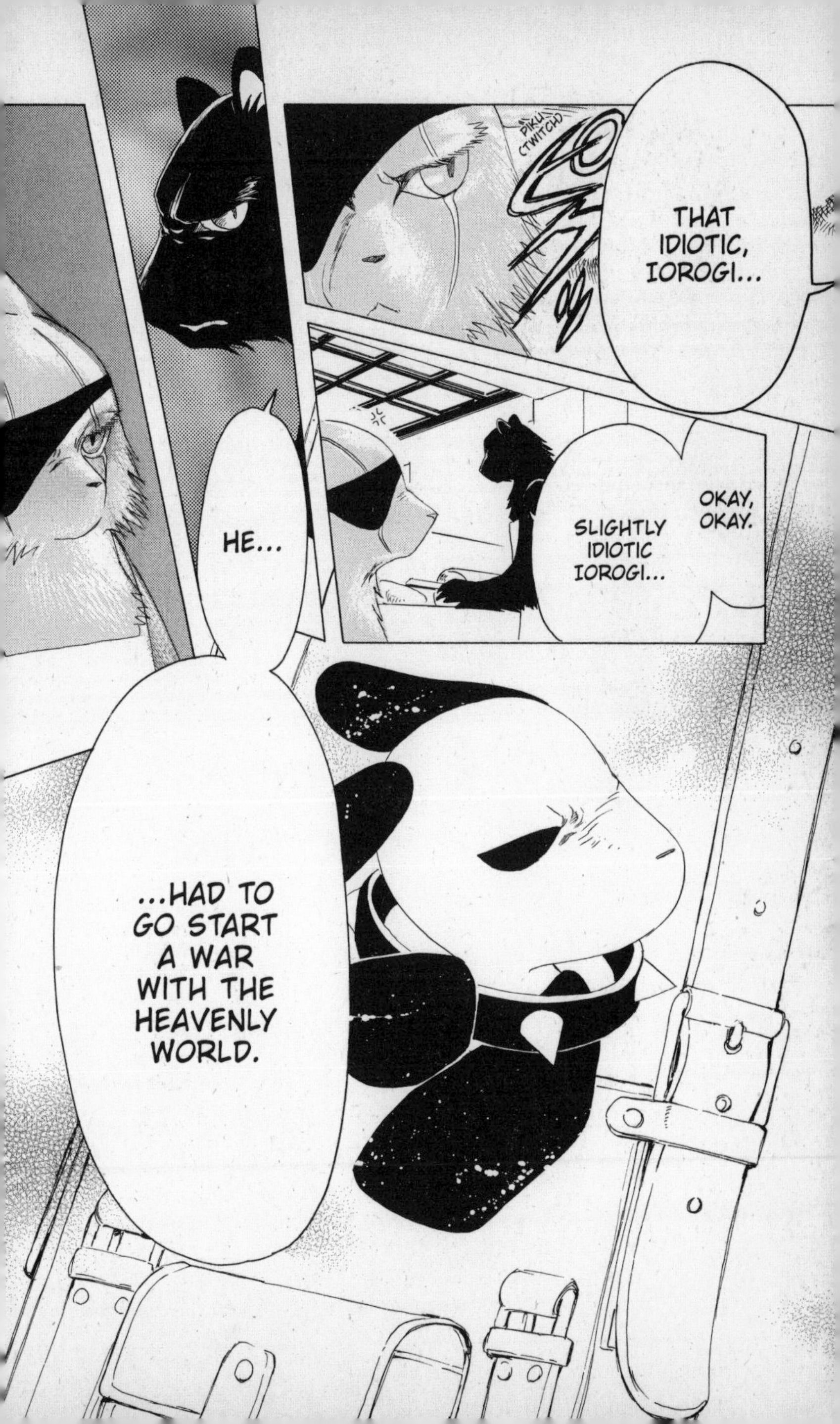
THAT IDIOTIC, IOROGI...
PIKU (TWITCH)
OKAY, OKAY.
SLIGHTLY IDIOTIC IOROGI...
HE...
...HAD TO GO START A WAR WITH THE HEAVENLY WORLD.

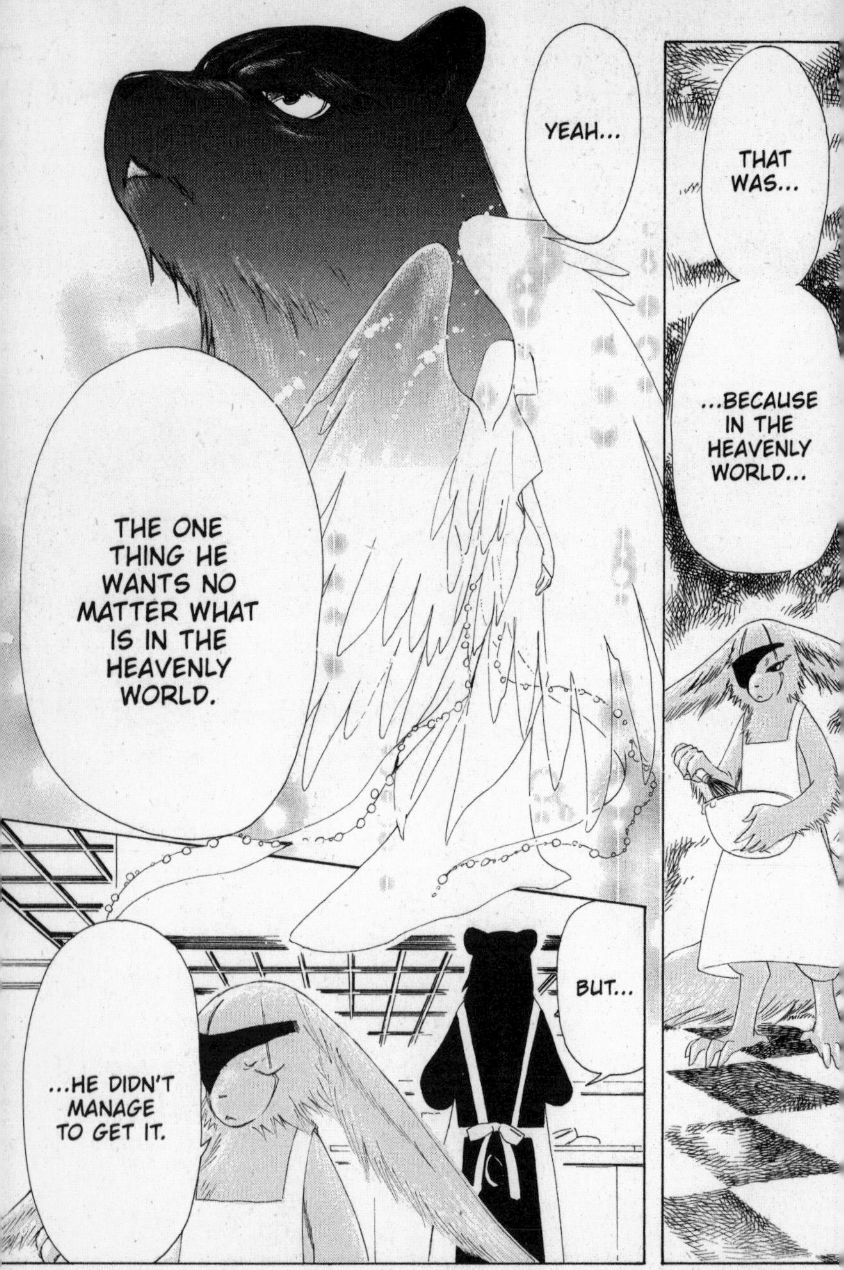
THAT WAS...
...BECAUSE IN THE HEAVENLY WORLD...
YEAH...
THE ONE THING HE WANTS NO MATTER WHAT IS IN THE HEAVENLY WORLD.
BUT...
...HE DIDN'T MANAGE TO GET IT.

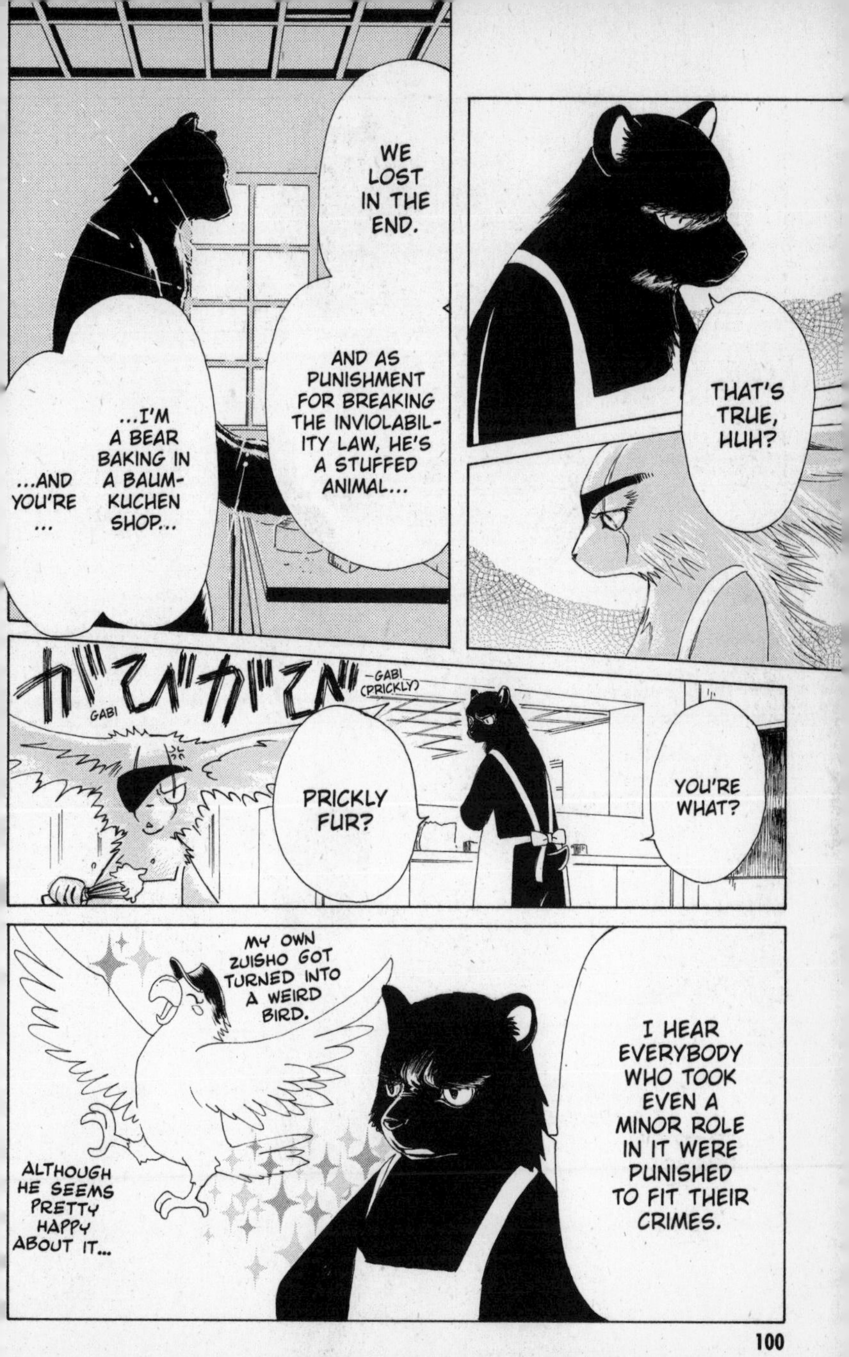
THAT'S TRUE, HUH?
WE LOST IN THE END.
AND AS PUNISHMENT FOR BREAKING THE INVIOLABILITY LAW, HE'S A STUFFED ANIMAL...
...I'M A BEAR BAKING IN A BAUMKUCHEN SHOP...
...AND YOU'RE ...
YOU'RE WHAT?
PRICKLY FUR?
GABI
—GABI (PRICKLY)
I HEAR EVERYBODY WHO TOOK EVEN A MINOR ROLE IN IT WERE PUNISHED TO FIT THEIR CRIMES.
MY OWN ZUISHO GOT TURNED INTO A WEIRD BIRD.
ALTHOUGH HE SEEMS PRETTY HAPPY ABOUT IT...

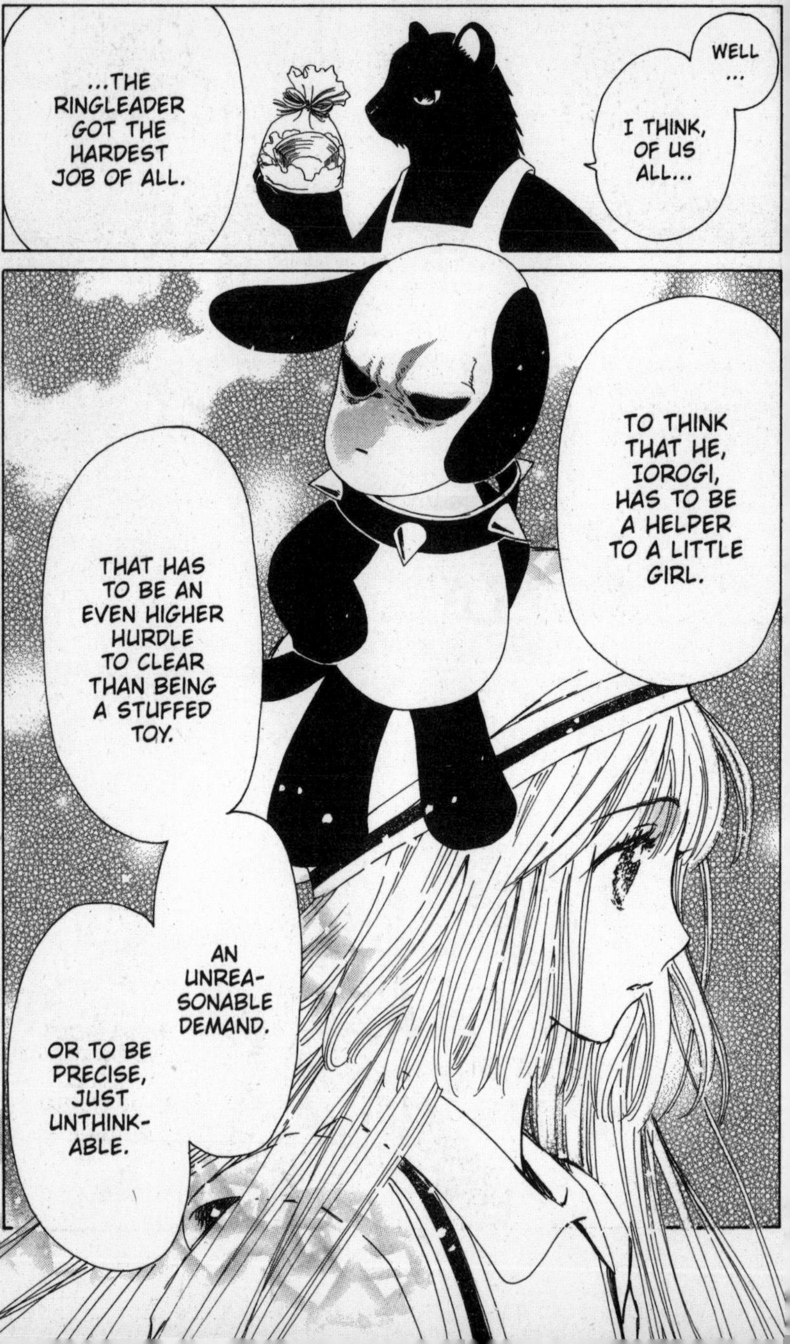
WELL ... I THINK, OF US ALL...
...THE RINGLEADER GOT THE HARDEST JOB OF ALL.
TO THINK THAT HE, IOROGI, HAS TO BE A HELPER TO A LITTLE GIRL.
THAT HAS TO BE AN EVEN HIGHER HURDLE TO CLEAR THAN BEING A STUFFED TOY.
AN UNREA-SONABLE DEMAND.
OR TO BE PRECISE, JUST UNTHINK-ABLE.

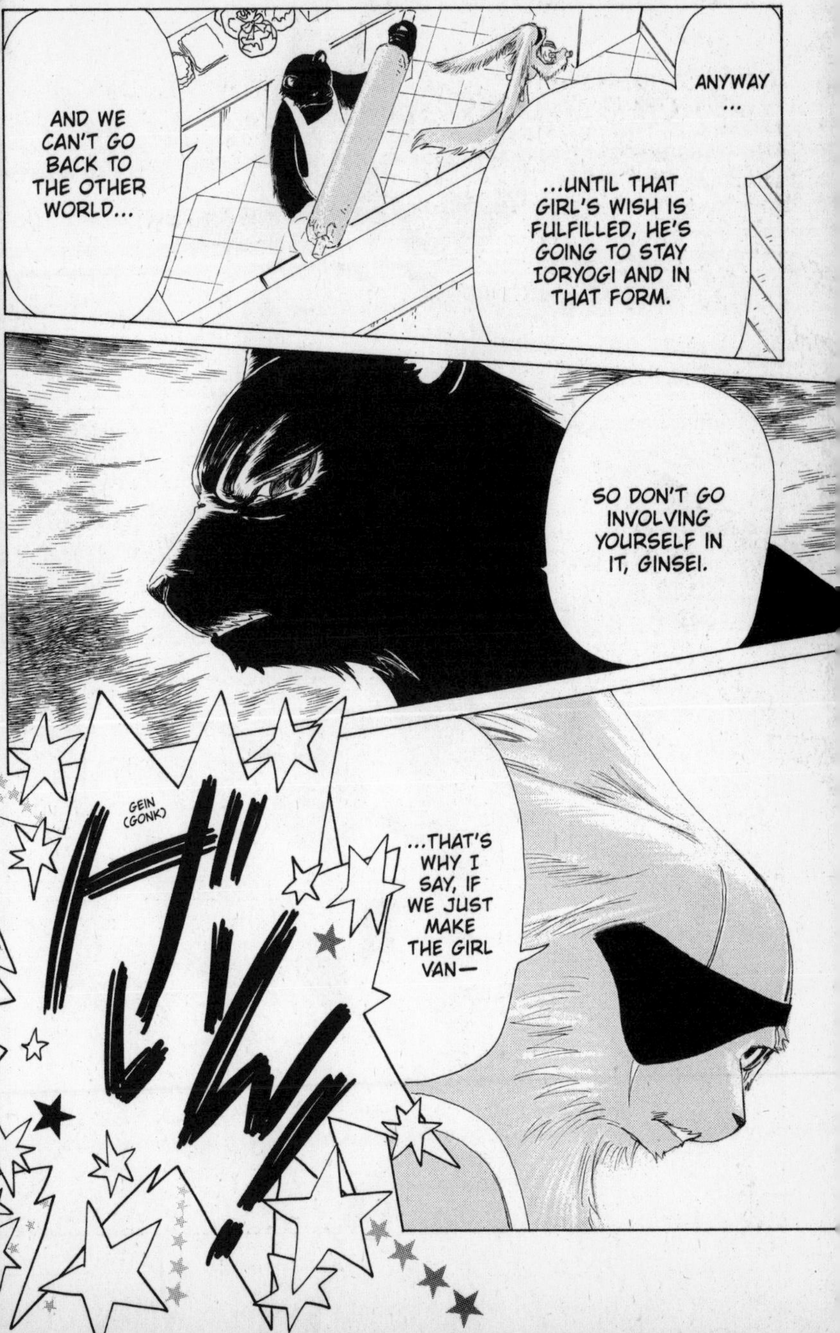
ANYWAY ...
...UNTIL THAT GIRL'S WISH IS FULFILLED, HE'S GOING TO STAY IORYOGI AND IN THAT FORM.
AND WE CAN'T GO BACK TO THE OTHER WORLD...
SO DON'T GO INVOLVING YOURSELF IN IT, GINSEI.
...THAT'S WHY I SAY, IF WE JUST MAKE THE GIRL VAN—
GEIN (GONK)

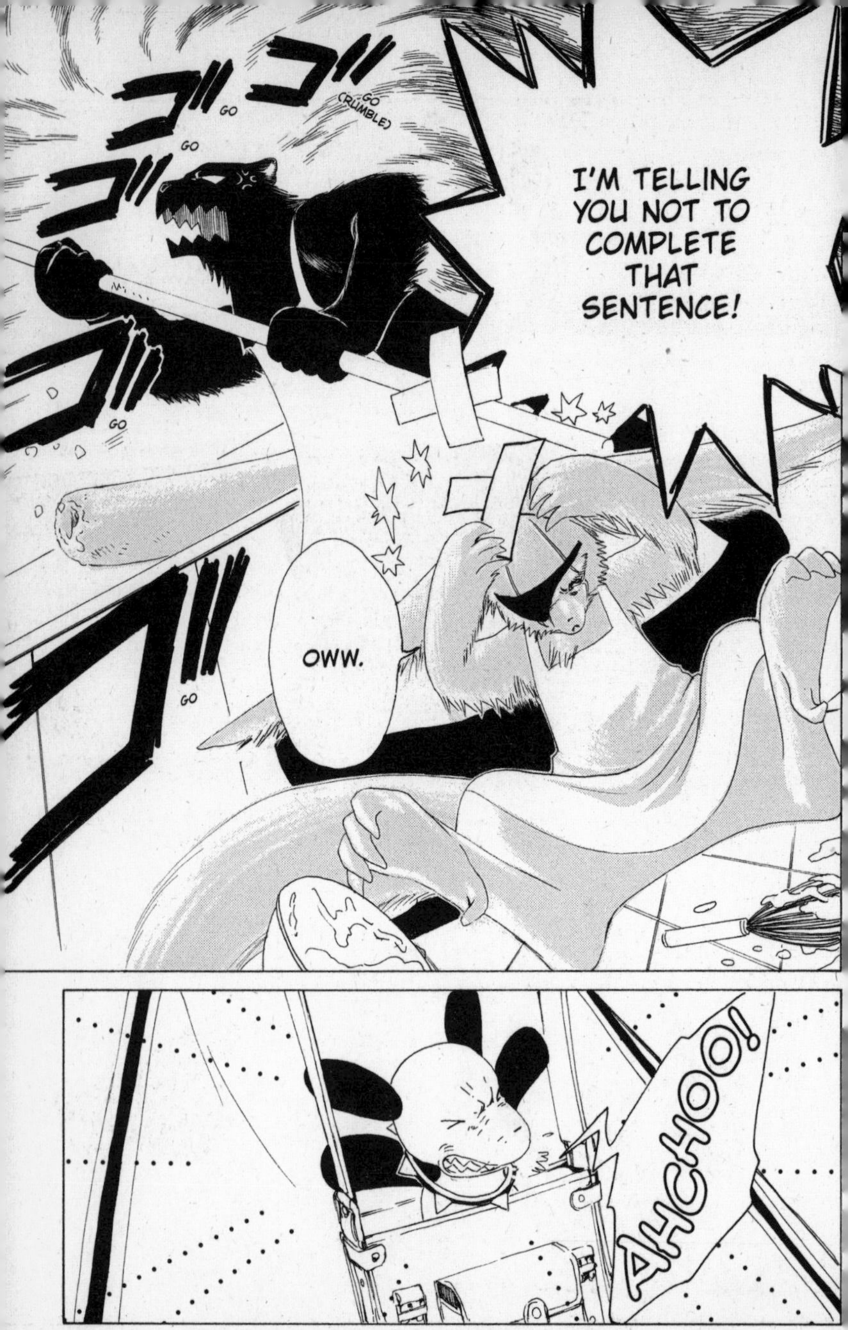
I'M TELLING YOU NOT TO COMPLETE THAT SENTENCE!
GO (RUMBLE)
GO
GO
GO
OWW.
GO
AHCHOO!

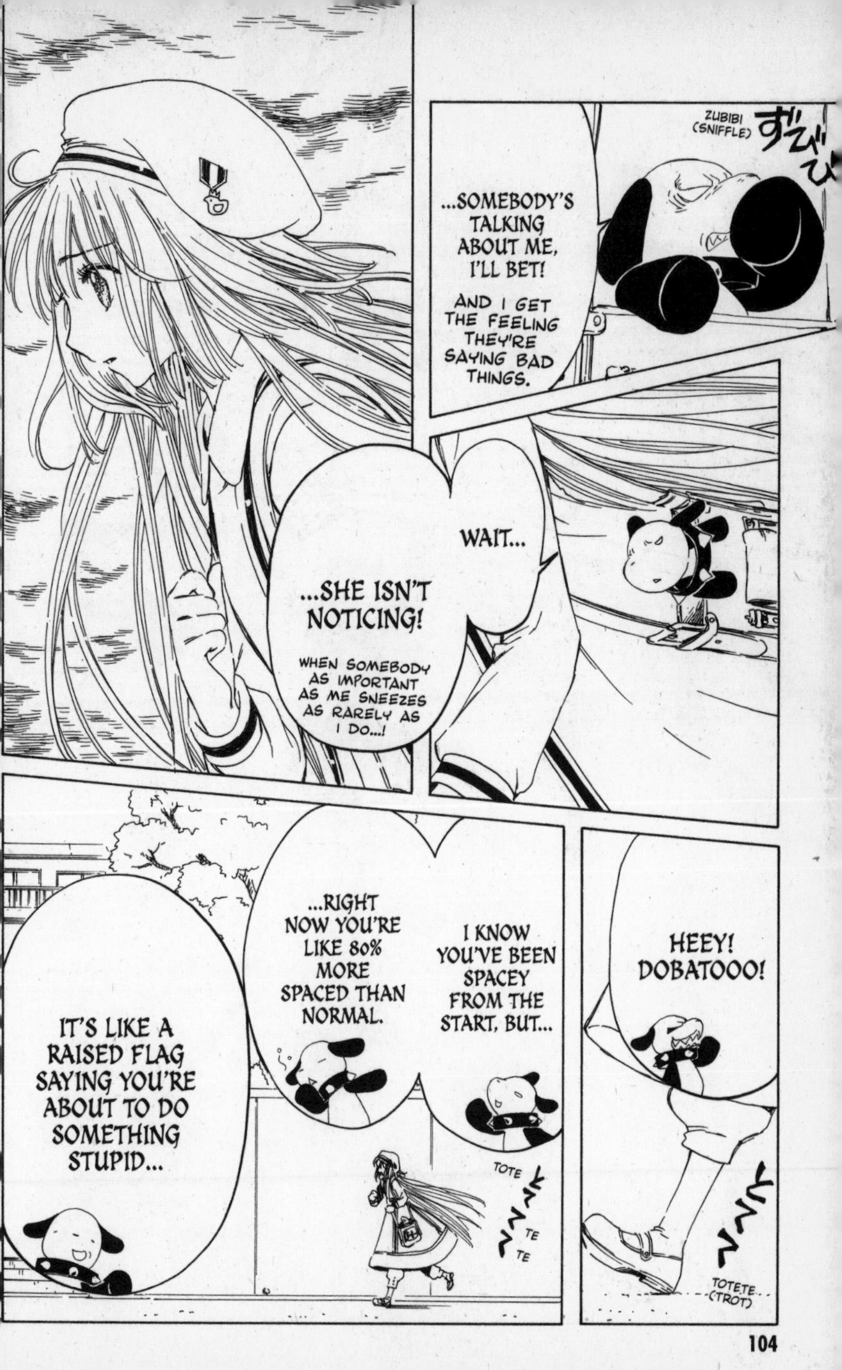
ZUBIBI (SNIFFLE) ずびび
...SOMEBODY'S TALKING ABOUT ME, I'LL BET!
AND I GET THE FEELING THEY'RE SAYING BAD THINGS.
WAIT...
...SHE ISN'T NOTICING!
WHEN SOMEBODY AS IMPORTANT AS ME SNEEZES AS RARELY AS I DO...!
HEEY! DOBATOOO!
TOTETE (TROT)
I KNOW YOU'VE BEEN SPACEY FROM THE START, BUT...
...RIGHT NOW YOU'RE LIKE 80% MORE SPACED THAN NORMAL.
IT'S LIKE A RAISED FLAG SAYING YOU'RE ABOUT TO DO SOMETHING STUPID...
TOTE TE TE

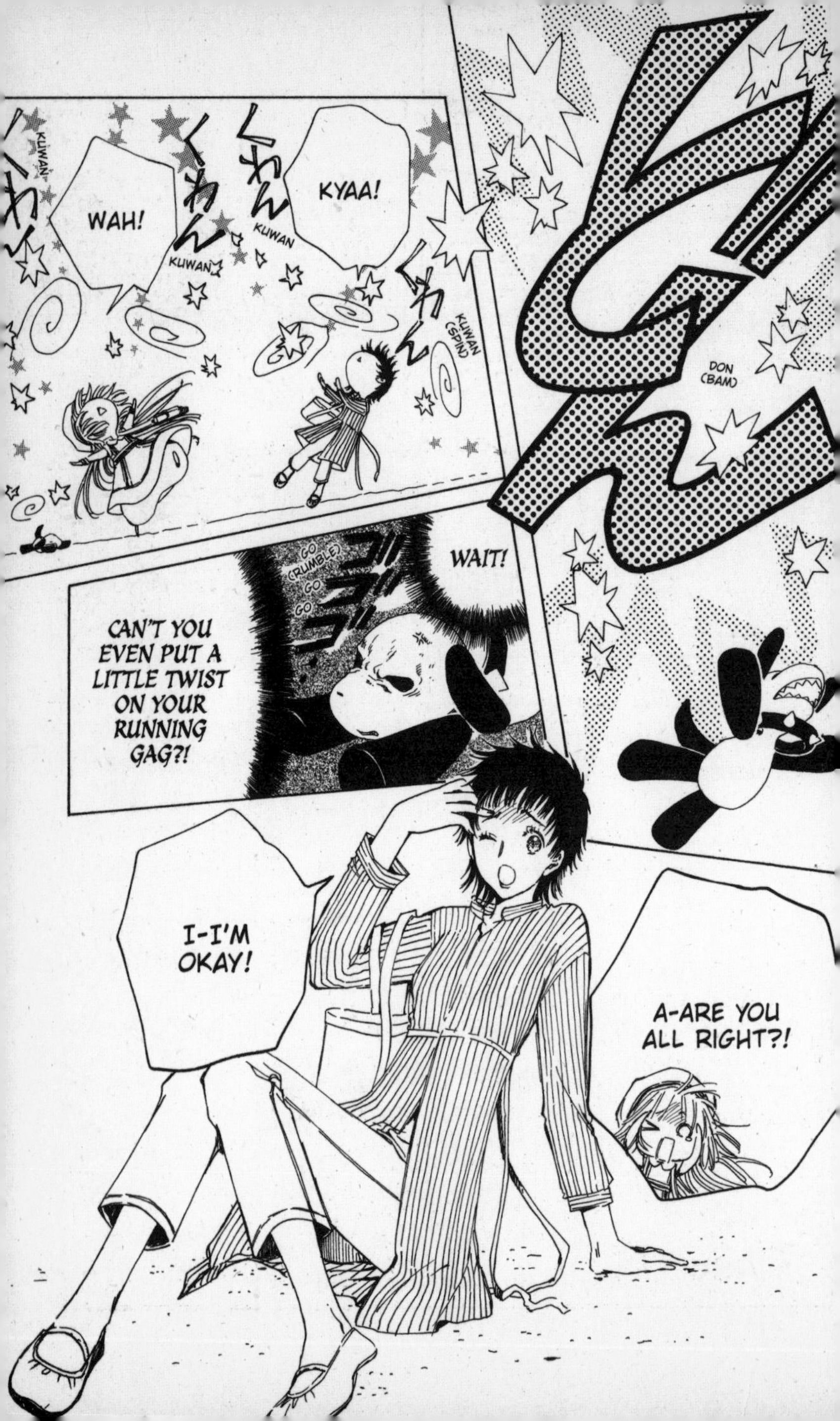
DON (BAM)
KYAA!
KUWAN
KUWAN (SPIN)
KUWAN
WAH!
KUWAN
WAIT!
GO (RUMBLE) GO GO
CAN'T YOU EVEN PUT A LITTLE TWIST ON YOUR RUNNING GAG?!
A-ARE YOU ALL RIGHT?!
I-I'M OKAY!

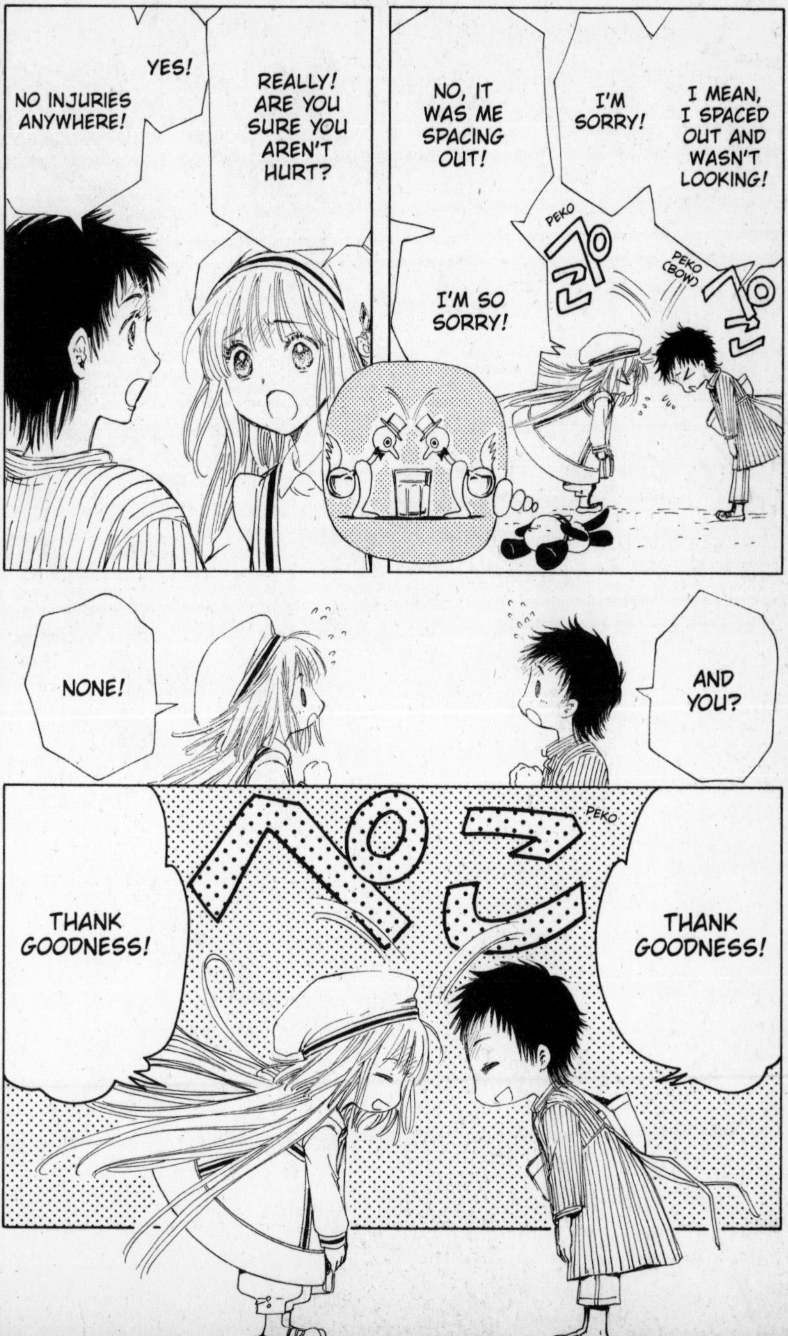
I MEAN, I SPACED OUT AND WASN'T LOOKING!
I'M SORRY!
PEKO (BOW)
PEKO
NO, IT WAS ME SPACING OUT!
I'M SO SORRY!
REALLY! ARE YOU SURE YOU AREN'T HURT?
YES!
NO INJURIES ANYWHERE!
AND YOU?
NONE!
THANK GOODNESS!
PEKO
THANK GOODNESS!

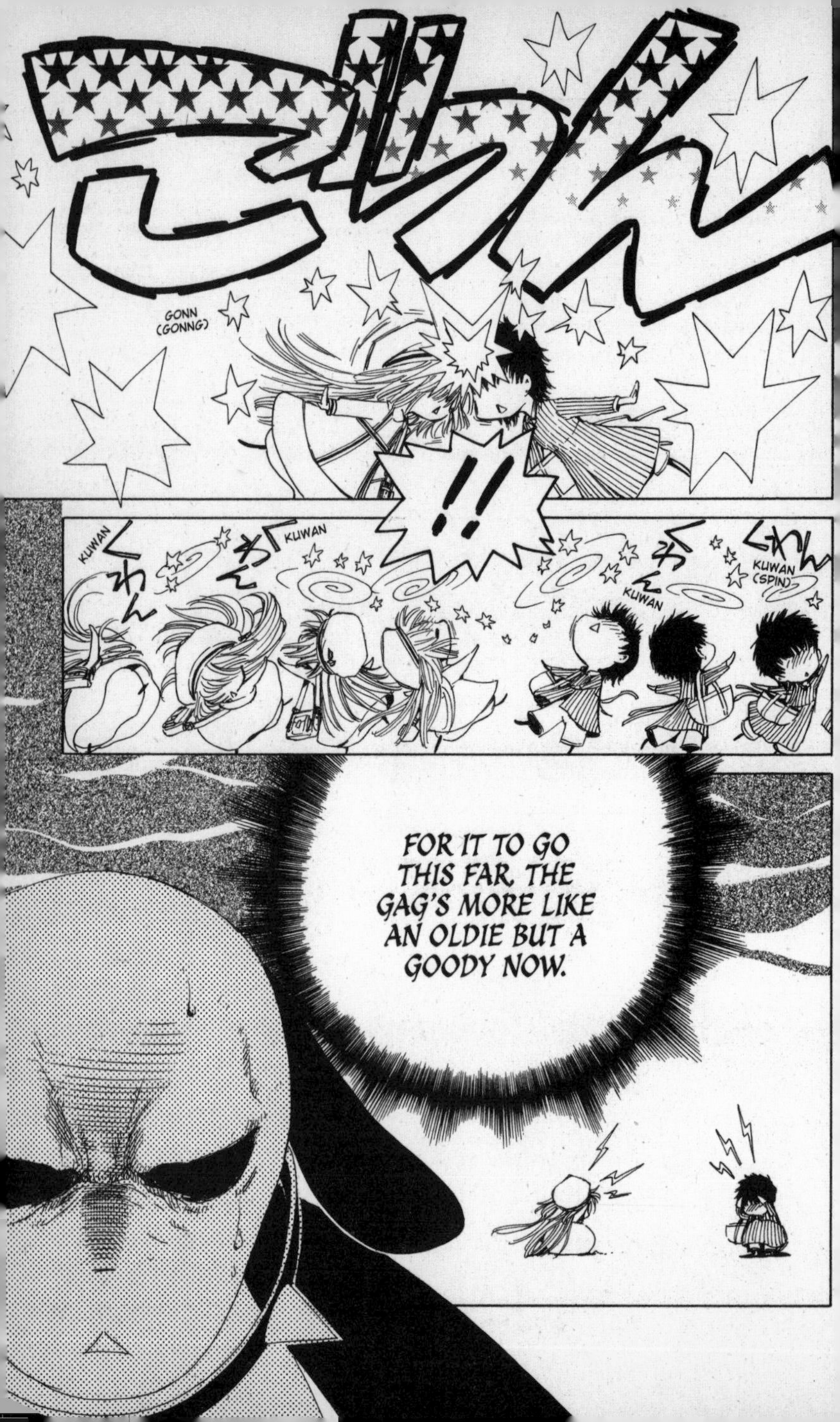
ごーん
GONN (GONNG)
!!
くわん
KUWAN (SPIN)
くわん
KUWAN
くわん
KUWAN
くわん
KUWAN
FOR IT TO GO THIS FAR, THE GAG'S MORE LIKE AN OLDIE BUT A GOODY NOW.

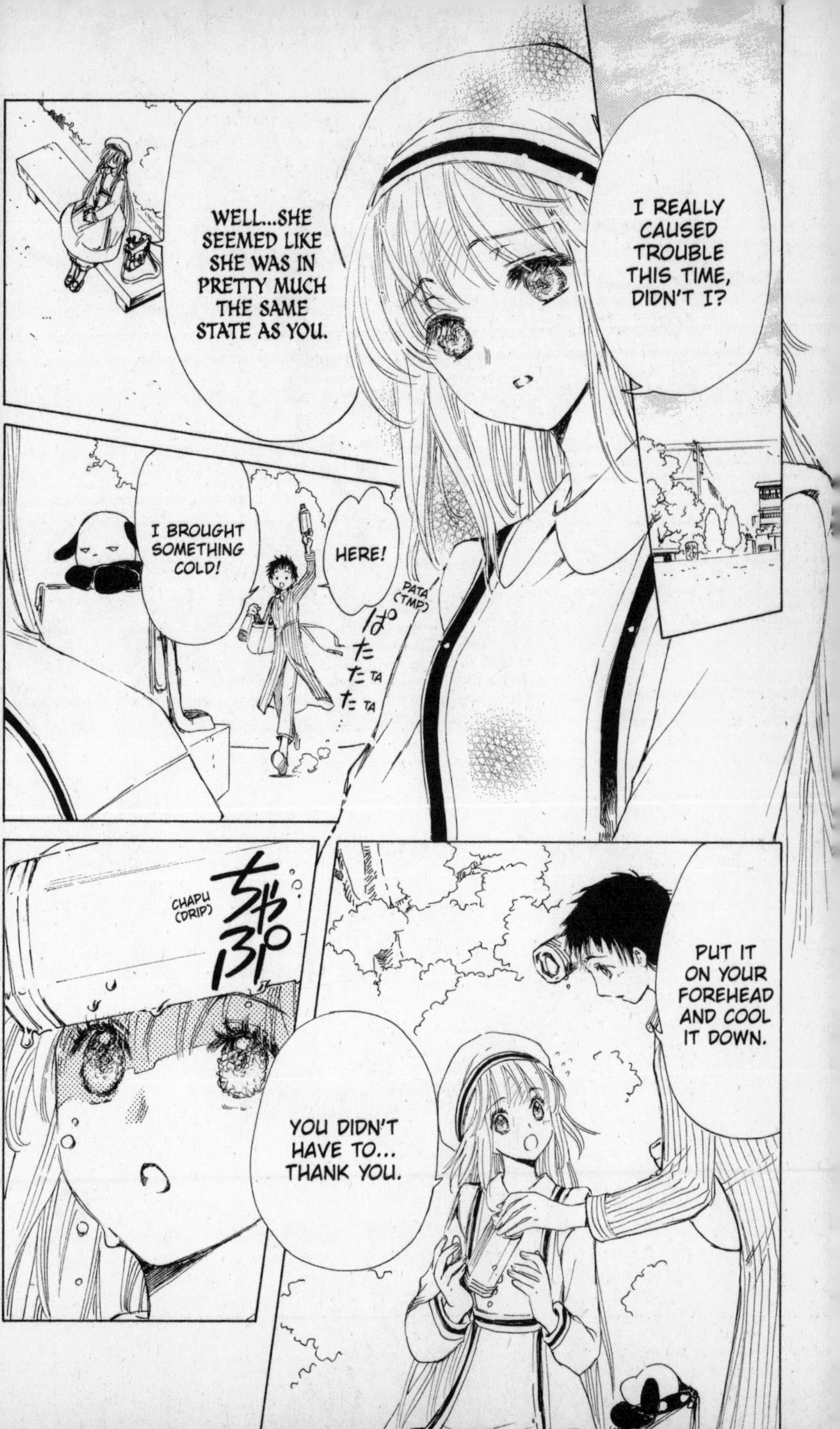
I REALLY CAUSED TROUBLE THIS TIME, DIDN'T I?
WELL...SHE SEEMED LIKE SHE WAS IN PRETTY MUCH THE SAME STATE AS YOU.
HERE!
I BROUGHT SOMETHING COLD!
ぱたたた
PATA (TMP) TA TA
PUT IT ON YOUR FOREHEAD AND COOL IT DOWN.
YOU DIDN'T HAVE TO... THANK YOU.
ちゃぷ
CHAPU (DRIP)

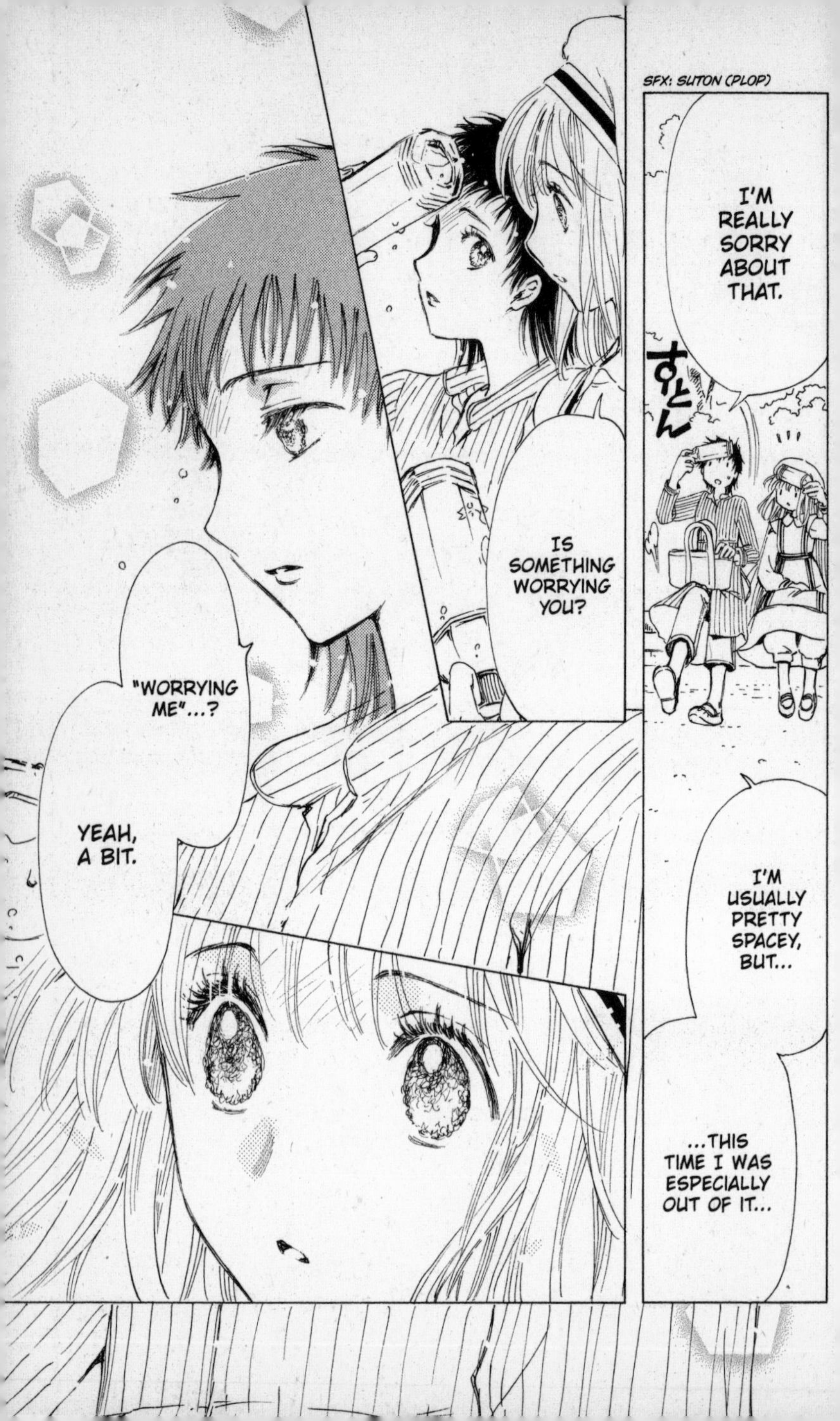

SFX: SUTON (PLOP)
I'M REALLY SORRY ABOUT THAT.
すとん
I'M USUALLY PRETTY SPACEY, BUT...
...THIS TIME I WAS ESPECIALLY OUT OF IT...
IS SOMETHING WORRYING YOU?
"WORRYING ME"...?
YEAH, A BIT.

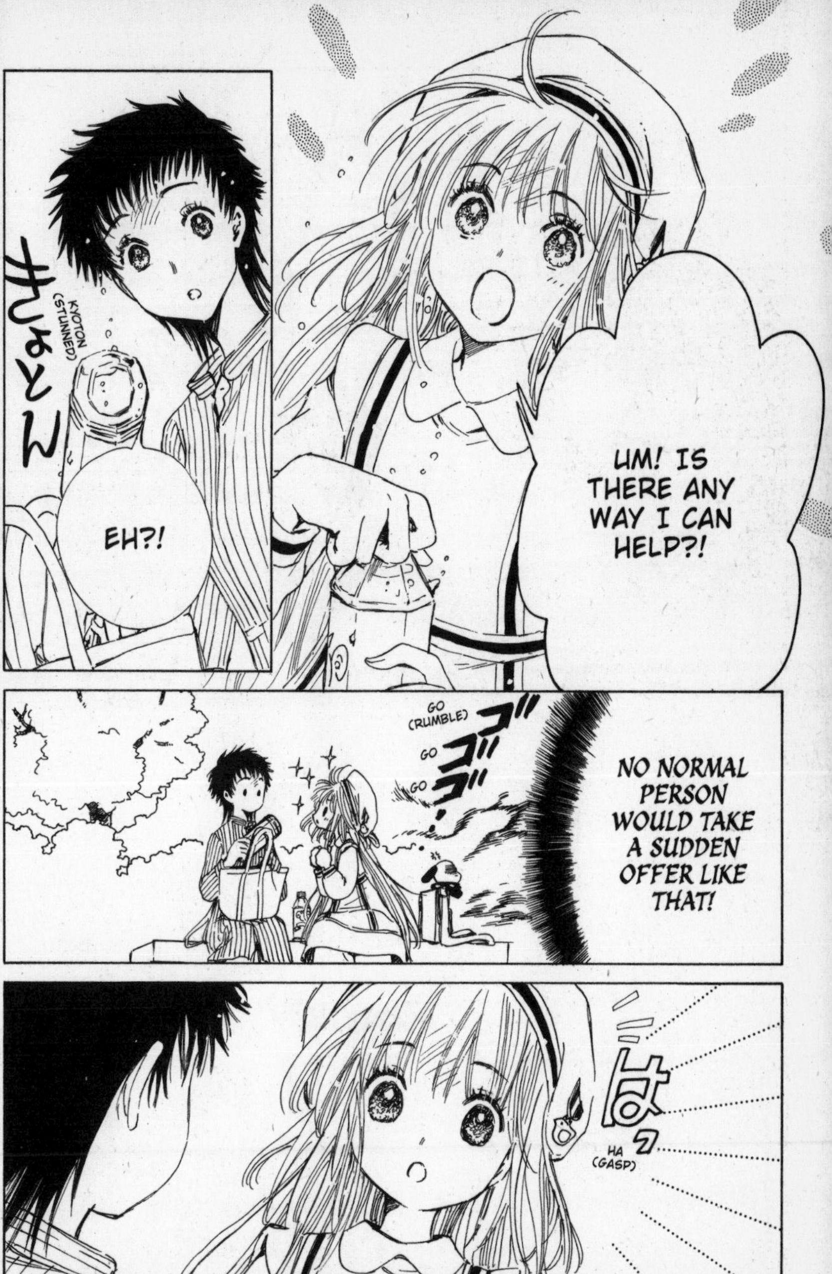
UM! IS THERE ANY WAY I CAN HELP?!
きょとん
KYOTON (STUNNED)
EH?!
NO NORMAL PERSON WOULD TAKE A SUDDEN OFFER LIKE THAT!
ゴゴゴ
GO (RUMBLE) GO GO
はっ
HA (GASP)

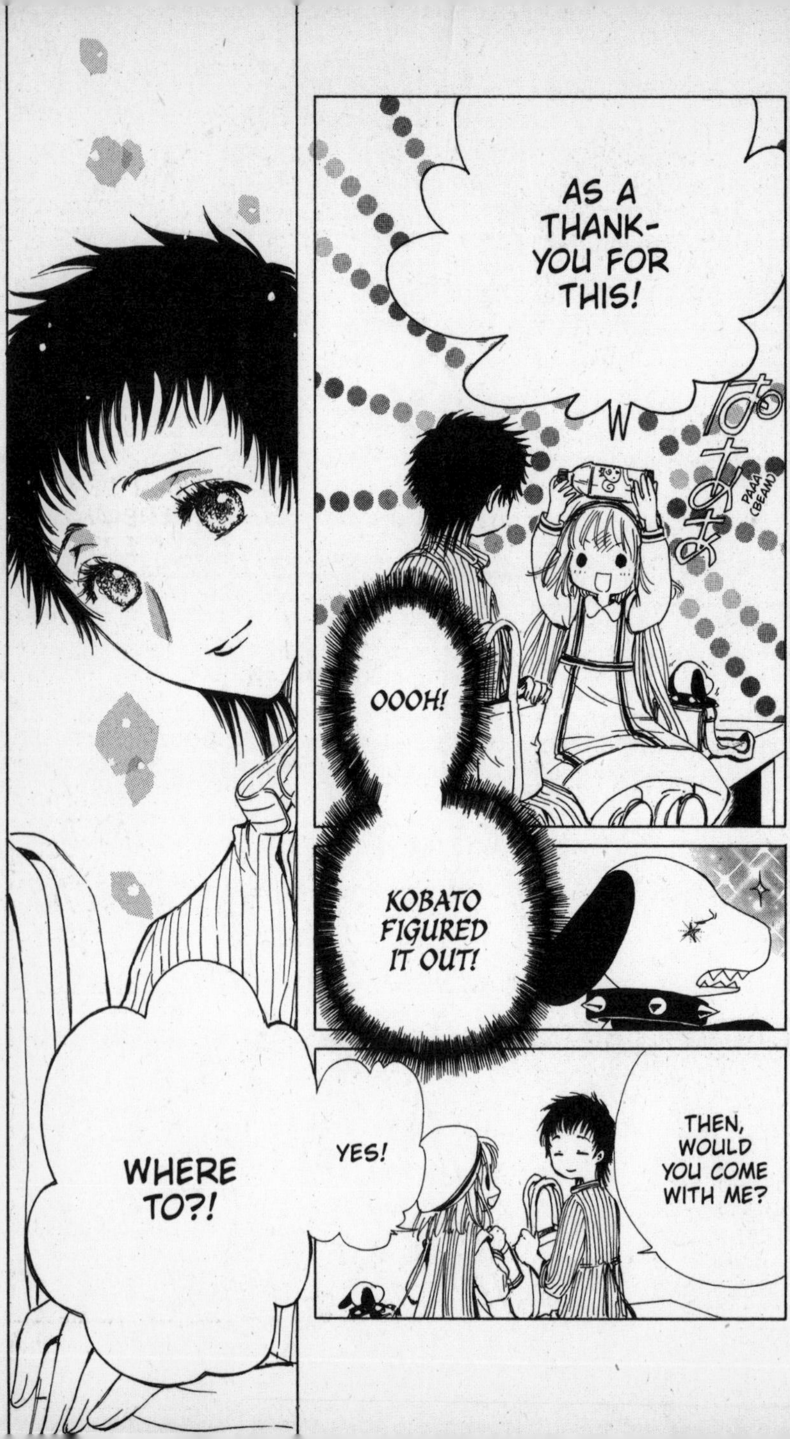
AS A THANK-YOU FOR THIS!
PAAA (BEAM)
OOOH!
KOBATO FIGURED IT OUT!
THEN, WOULD YOU COME WITH ME?
YES!
WHERE TO?!

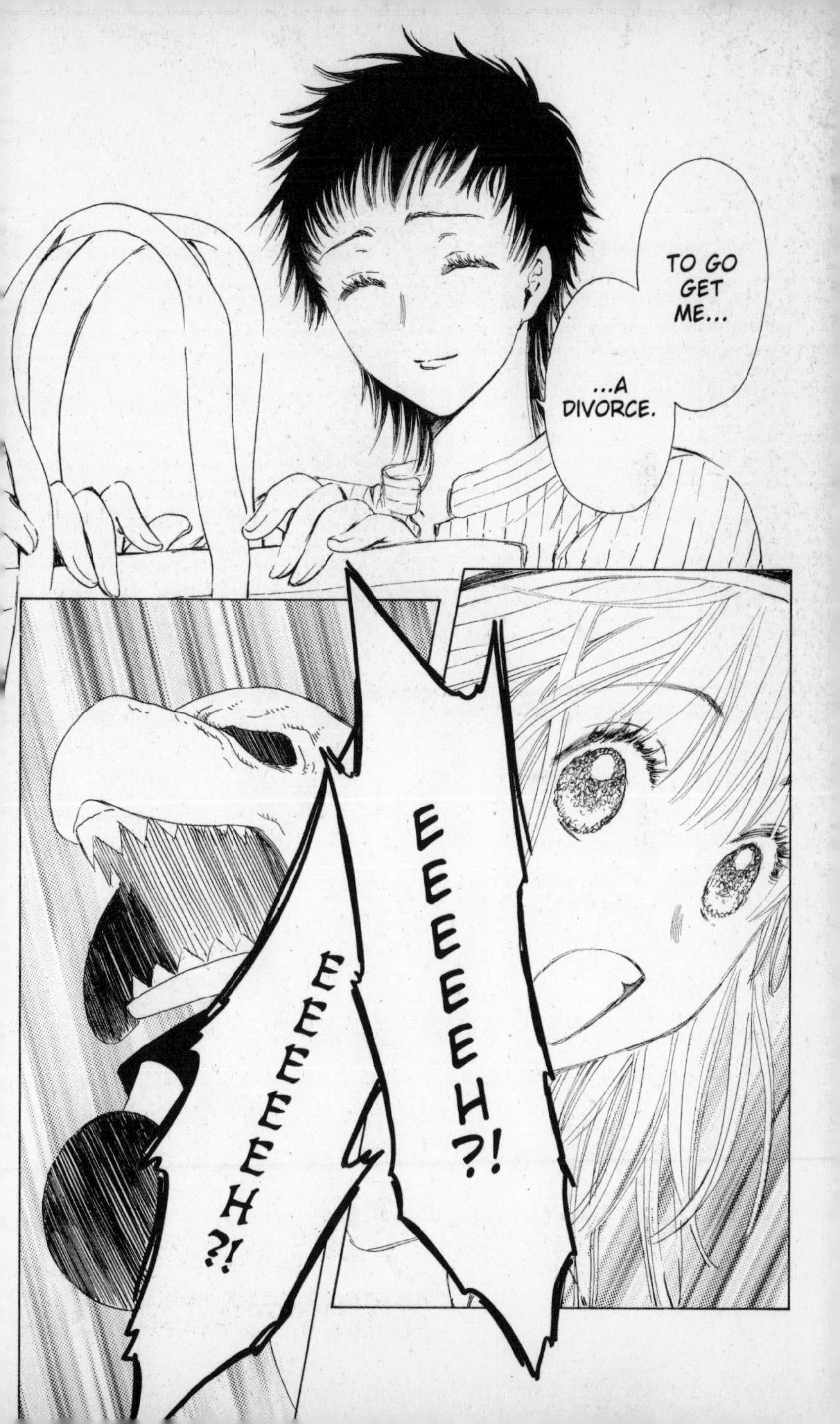
TO GO GET ME...
...A DIVORCE.
EEEEEH?!
EEEEEEH?!

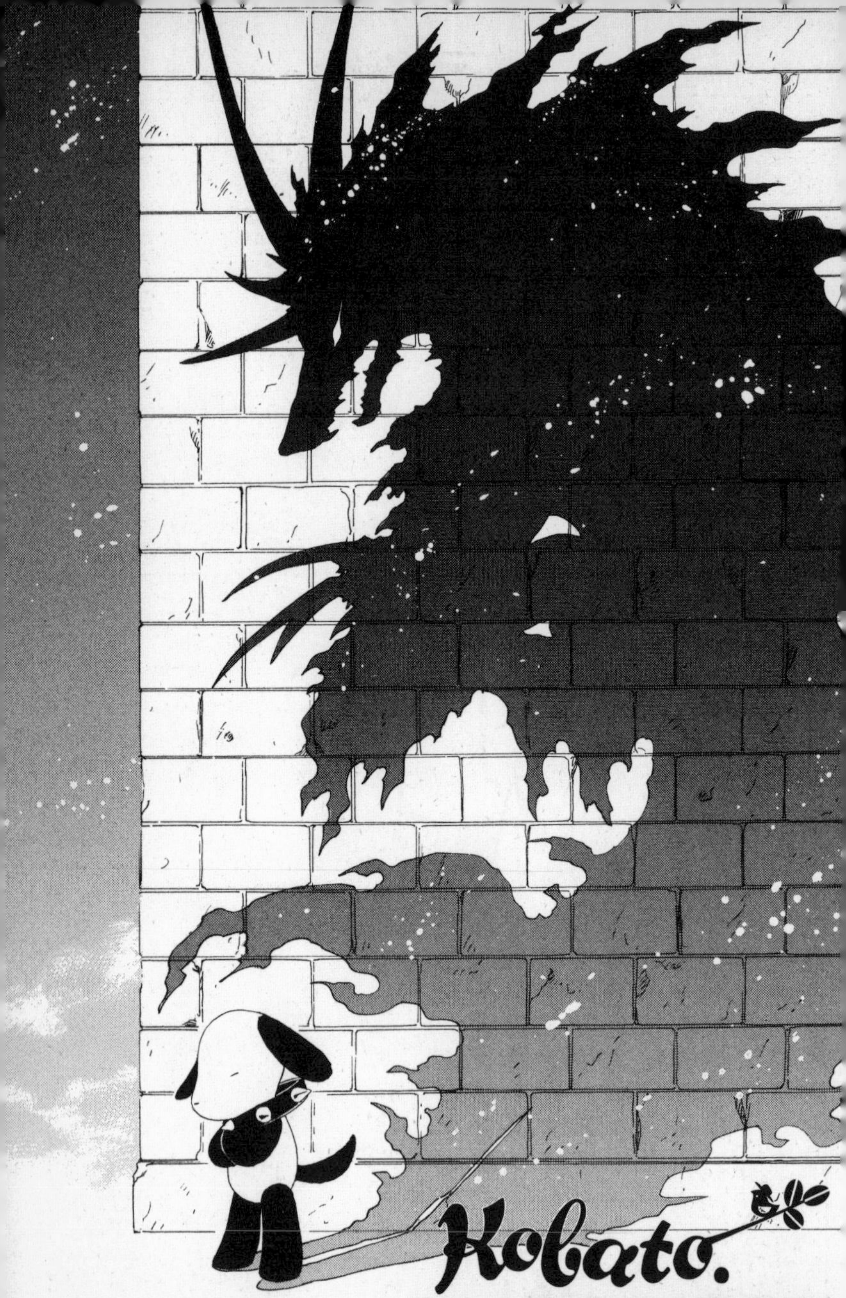
Kobato.

Ch. 32 Fujimoto's Worry

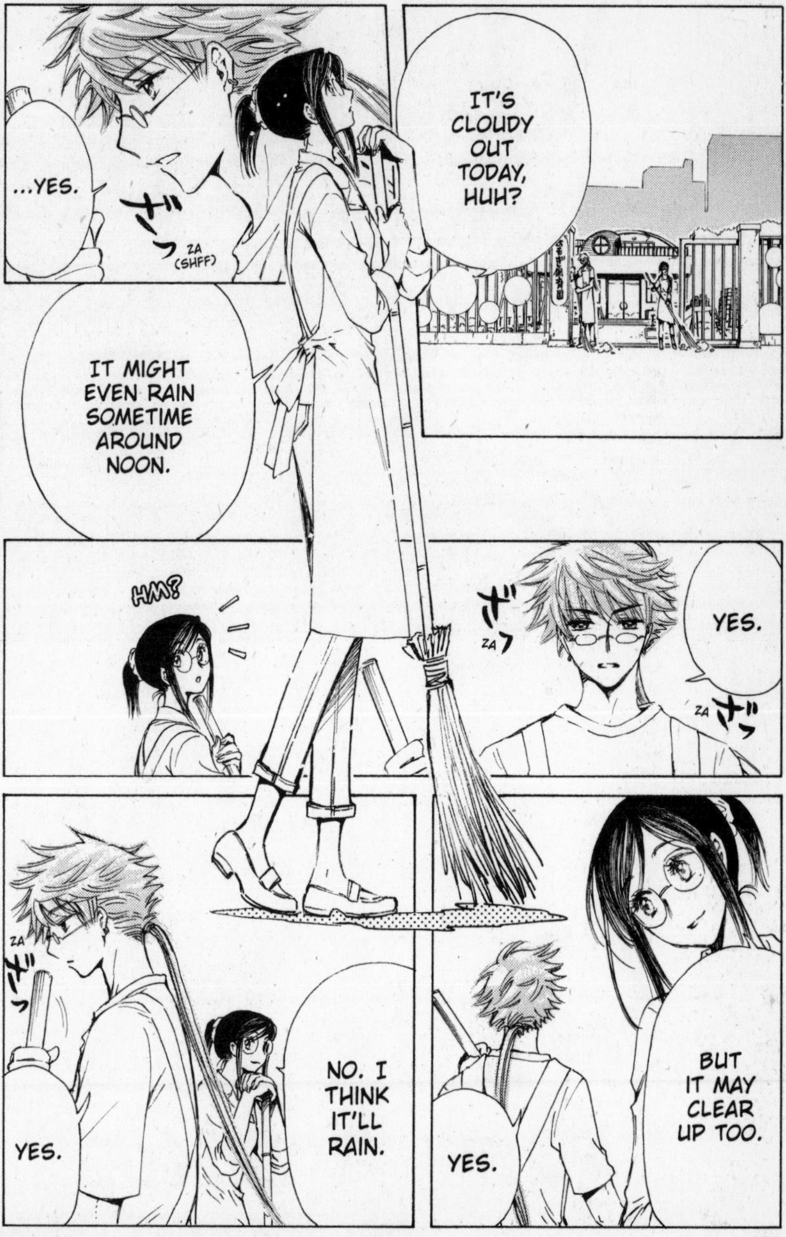
IT'S CLOUDY OUT TODAY, HUH?
...YES.
ZA (SHFF)
IT MIGHT EVEN RAIN SOMETIME AROUND NOON.
YES.
ZA
ZA
HM?
BUT IT MAY CLEAR UP TOO.
YES.
NO. I THINK IT'LL RAIN.
YES.
ZA

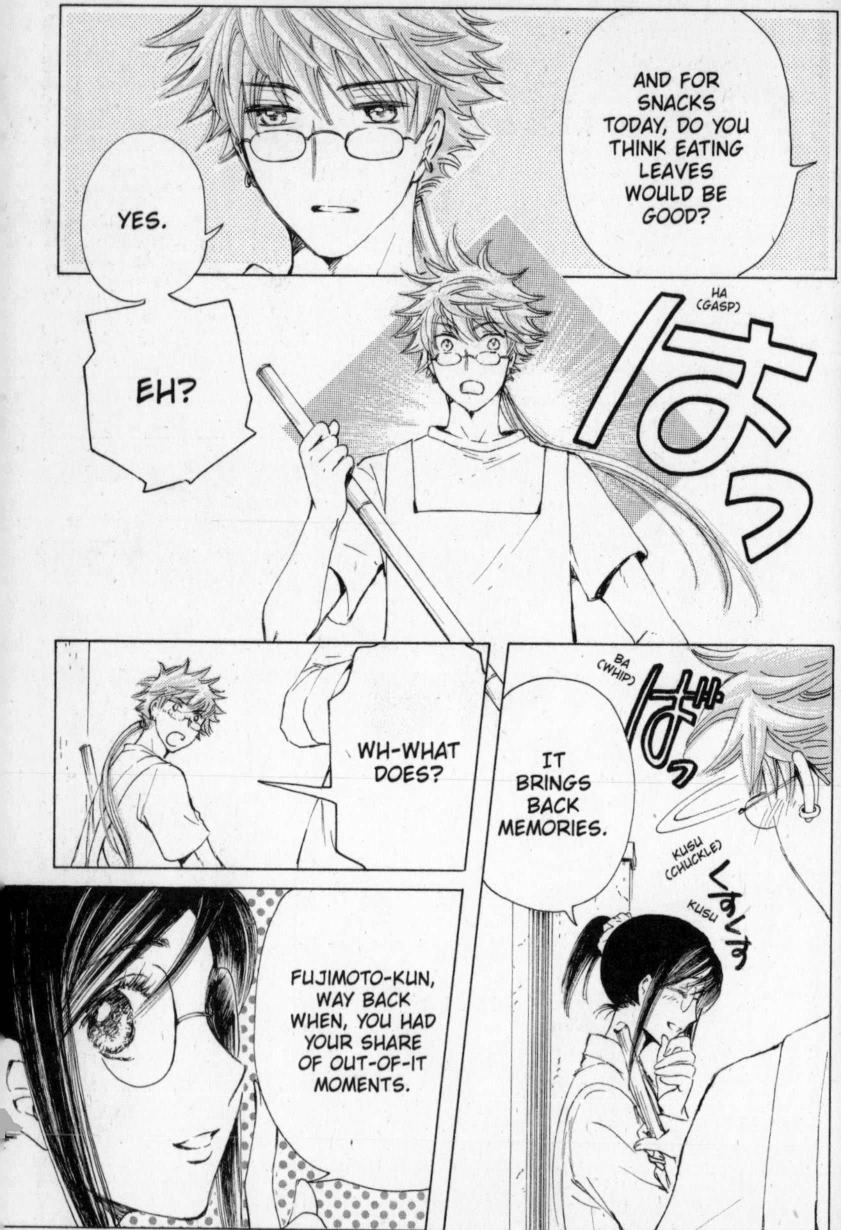
AND FOR SNACKS TODAY, DO YOU THINK EATING LEAVES WOULD BE GOOD?
YES.
HA (GASP)
はっ
EH?
BA (WHIP)
ばっ
IT BRINGS BACK MEMORIES.
KUSU (CHUCKLE)
KUSU
くすくす
WH-WHAT DOES?
FUJIMOTO-KUN, WAY BACK WHEN, YOU HAD YOUR SHARE OF OUT-OF-IT MOMENTS.

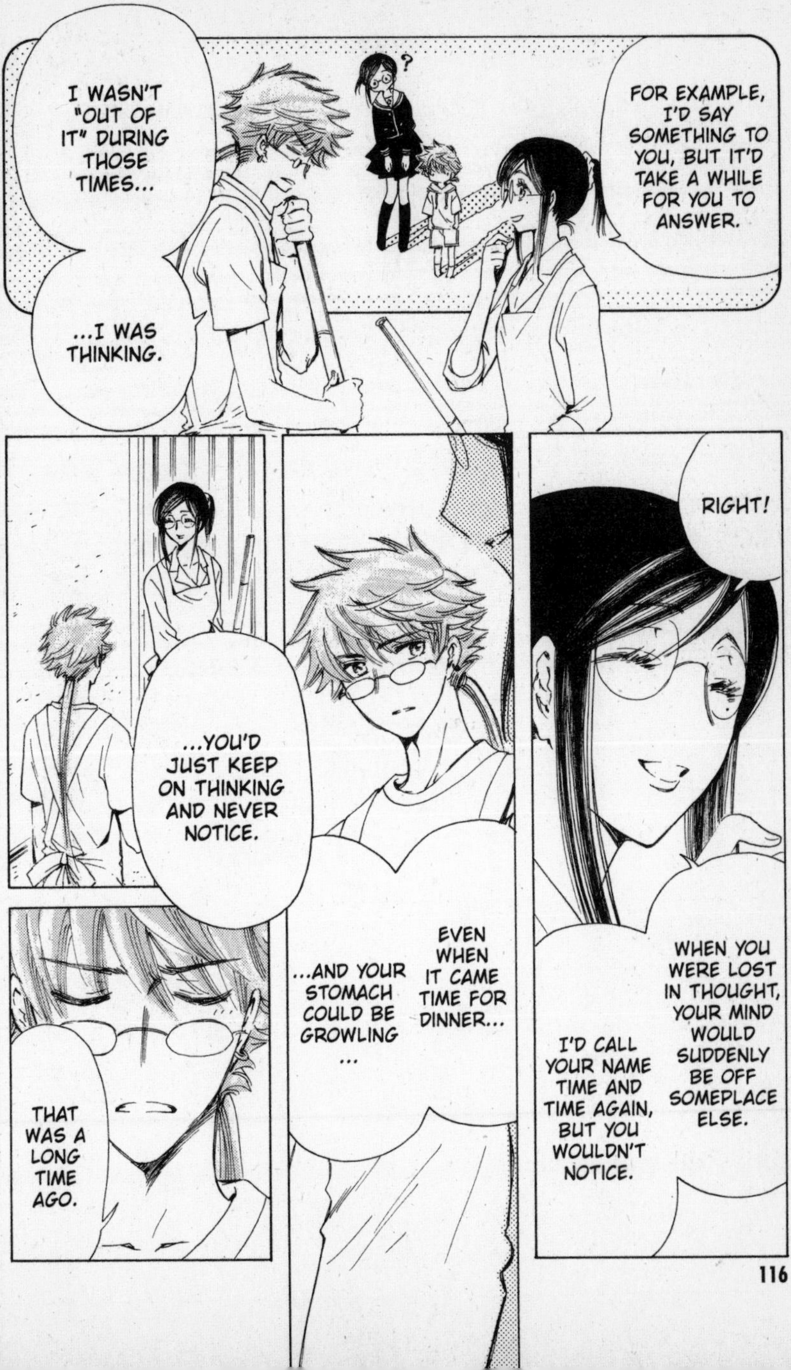
FOR EXAMPLE, I'D SAY SOMETHING TO YOU, BUT IT'D TAKE A WHILE FOR YOU TO ANSWER.
?
I WASN'T "OUT OF IT" DURING THOSE TIMES...
...I WAS THINKING.
RIGHT!
WHEN YOU WERE LOST IN THOUGHT, YOUR MIND WOULD SUDDENLY BE OFF SOMEPLACE ELSE.
I'D CALL YOUR NAME TIME AND TIME AGAIN, BUT YOU WOULDN'T NOTICE.
EVEN WHEN IT CAME TIME FOR DINNER...
...AND YOUR STOMACH COULD BE GROWLING...
...YOU'D JUST KEEP ON THINKING AND NEVER NOTICE.
THAT WAS A LONG TIME AGO.

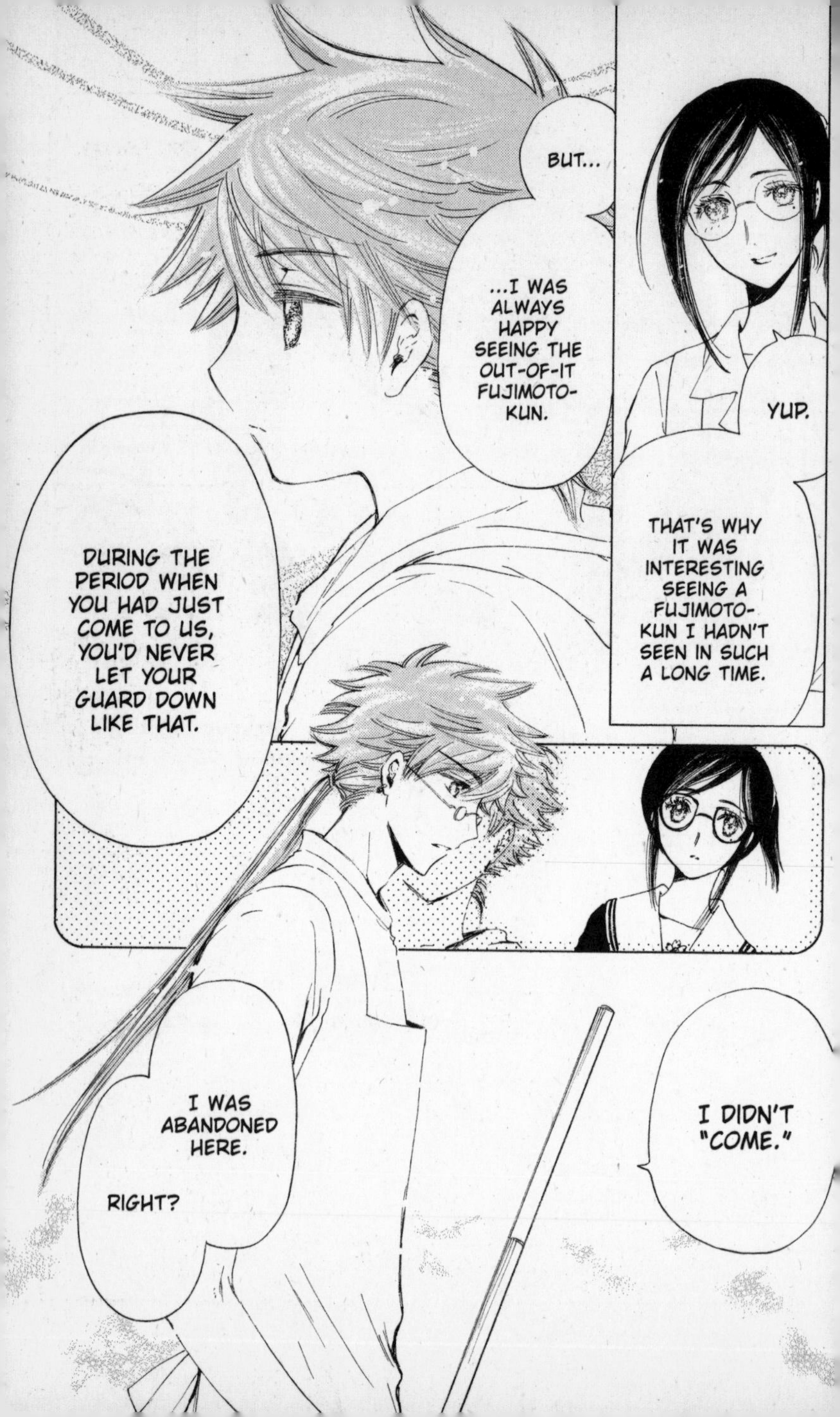
BUT...
...I WAS ALWAYS HAPPY SEEING THE OUT-OF-IT FUJIMOTO-KUN.
YUP.
THAT'S WHY IT WAS INTERESTING SEEING A FUJIMOTO-KUN I HADN'T SEEN IN SUCH A LONG TIME.
DURING THE PERIOD WHEN YOU HAD JUST COME TO US, YOU'D NEVER LET YOUR GUARD DOWN LIKE THAT.
I DIDN'T "COME."
I WAS ABANDONED HERE.
RIGHT?

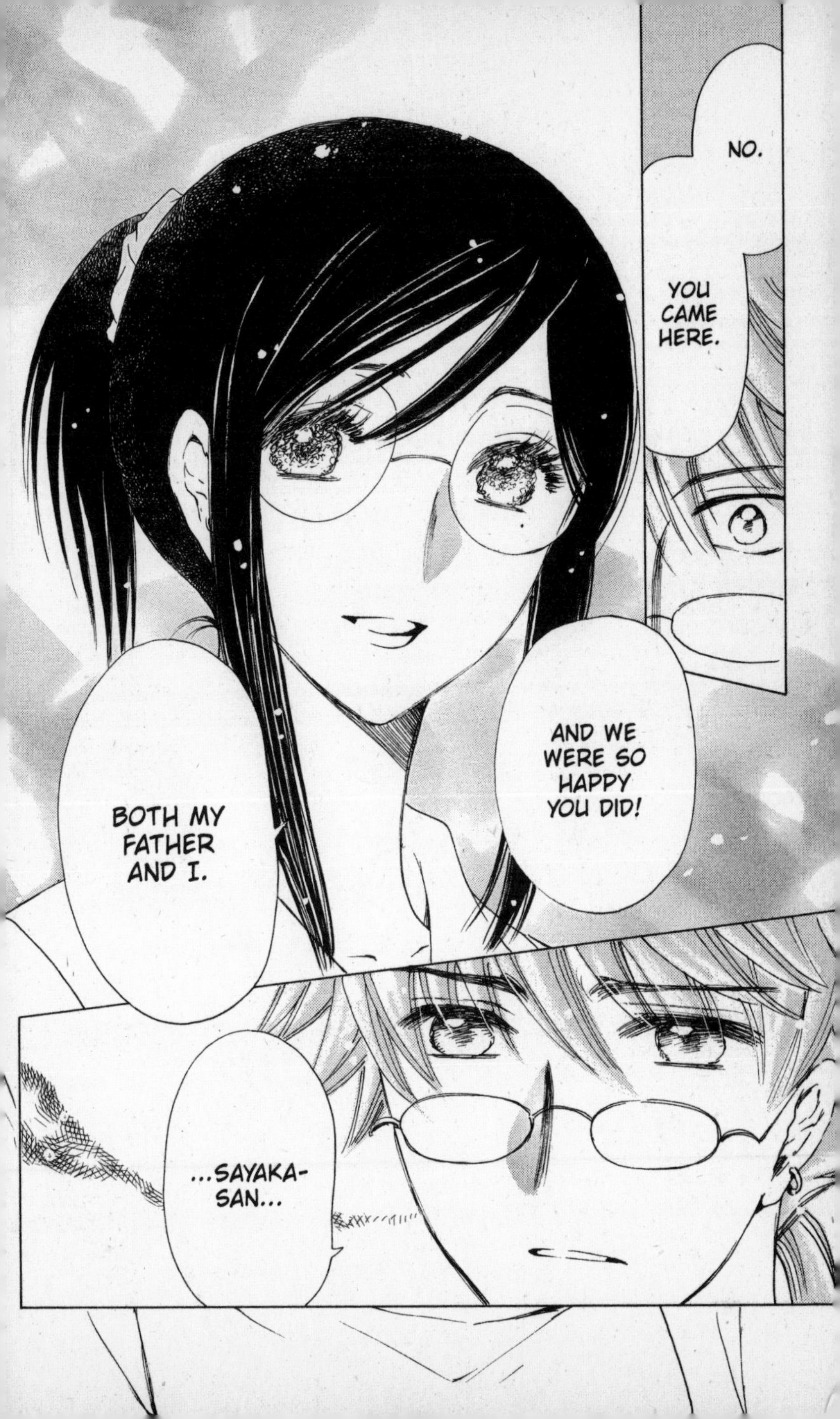
NO.
YOU CAME HERE.
AND WE WERE SO HAPPY YOU DID!
BOTH MY FATHER AND I.
...SAYAKA-SAN...

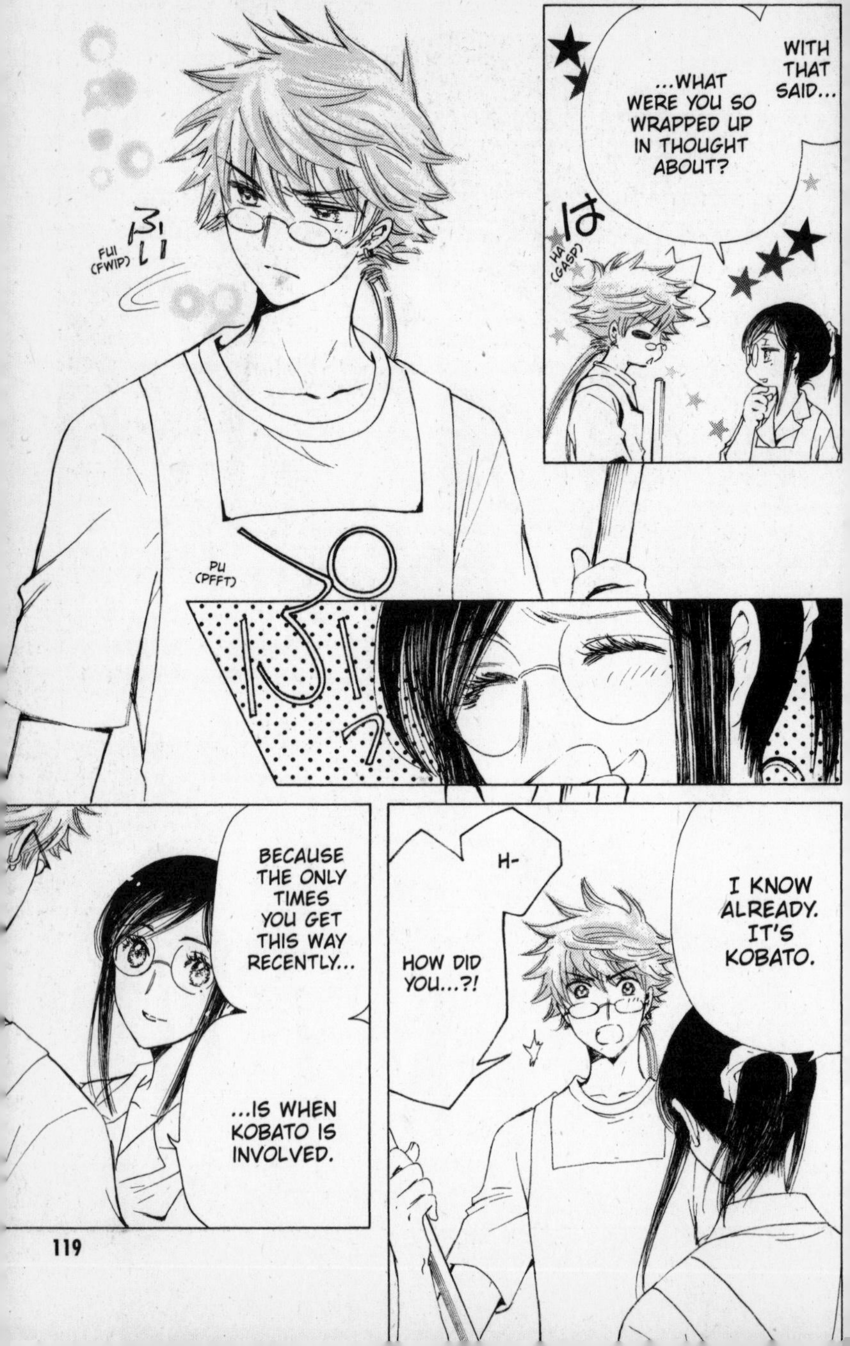
WITH THAT SAID...
...WHAT WERE YOU SO WRAPPED UP IN THOUGHT ABOUT?
は
HA (GASP)
ふい
FUI (FWIP)
PU (PFFT)
I KNOW ALREADY. IT'S KOBATO.
H-
HOW DID YOU...?!
BECAUSE THE ONLY TIMES YOU GET THIS WAY RECENTLY...
...IS WHEN KOBATO IS INVOLVED.

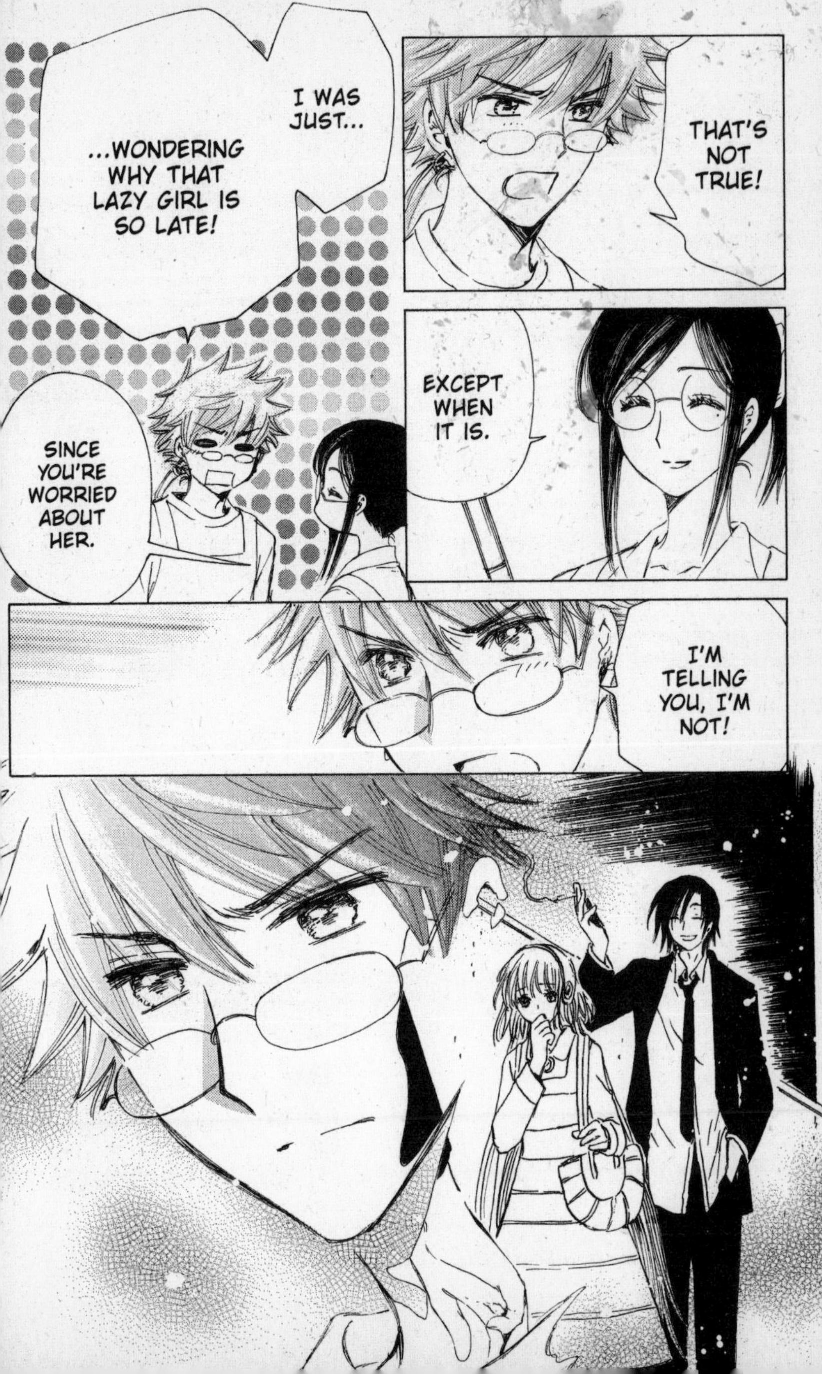
THAT'S NOT TRUE!
EXCEPT WHEN IT IS.
I WAS JUST...
...WONDERING WHY THAT LAZY GIRL IS SO LATE!
SINCE YOU'RE WORRIED ABOUT HER.
I'M TELLING YOU, I'M NOT!

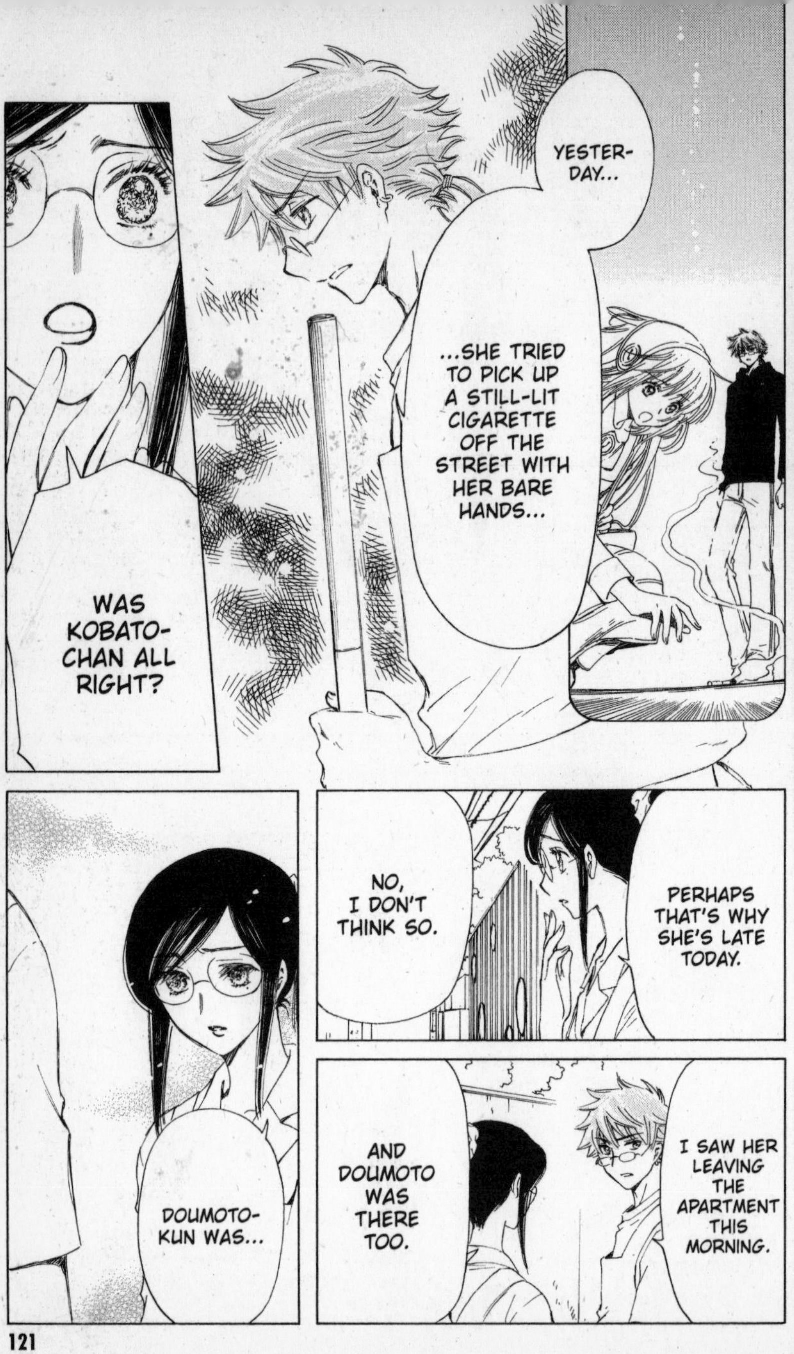
YESTER-DAY...
...SHE TRIED TO PICK UP A STILL-LIT CIGARETTE OFF THE STREET WITH HER BARE HANDS...
WAS KOBATO-CHAN ALL RIGHT?
PERHAPS THAT'S WHY SHE'S LATE TODAY.
NO, I DON'T THINK SO.
I SAW HER LEAVING THE APARTMENT THIS MORNING.
AND DOUMOTO WAS THERE TOO.
DOUMOTO-KUN WAS...

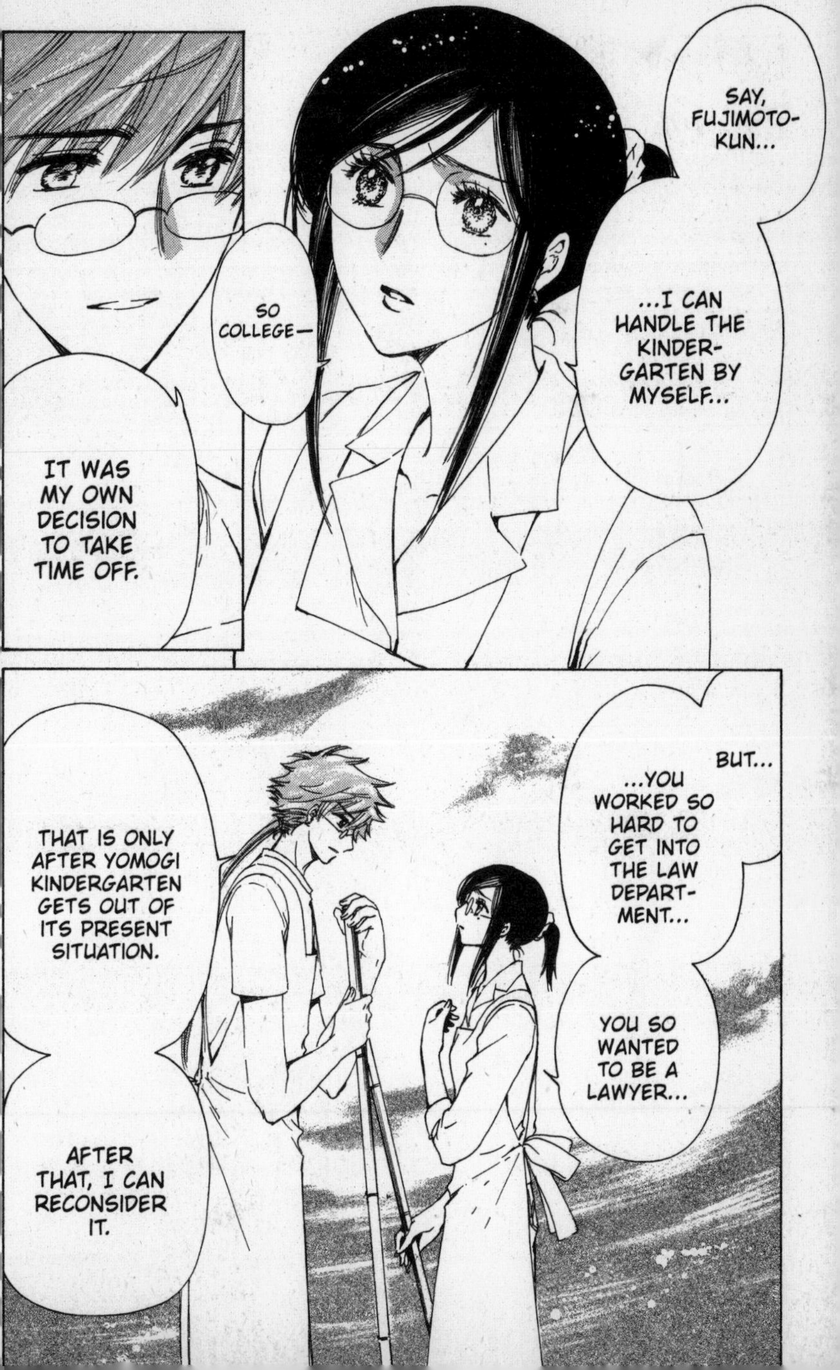
SAY, FUJIMOTO-KUN...
...I CAN HANDLE THE KINDER-GARTEN BY MYSELF...
SO COLLEGE—
IT WAS MY OWN DECISION TO TAKE TIME OFF.
BUT...
...YOU WORKED SO HARD TO GET INTO THE LAW DEPART-MENT...
YOU SO WANTED TO BE A LAWYER...
THAT IS ONLY AFTER YOMOGI KINDERGARTEN GETS OUT OF ITS PRESENT SITUATION.
AFTER THAT, I CAN RECONSIDER IT.

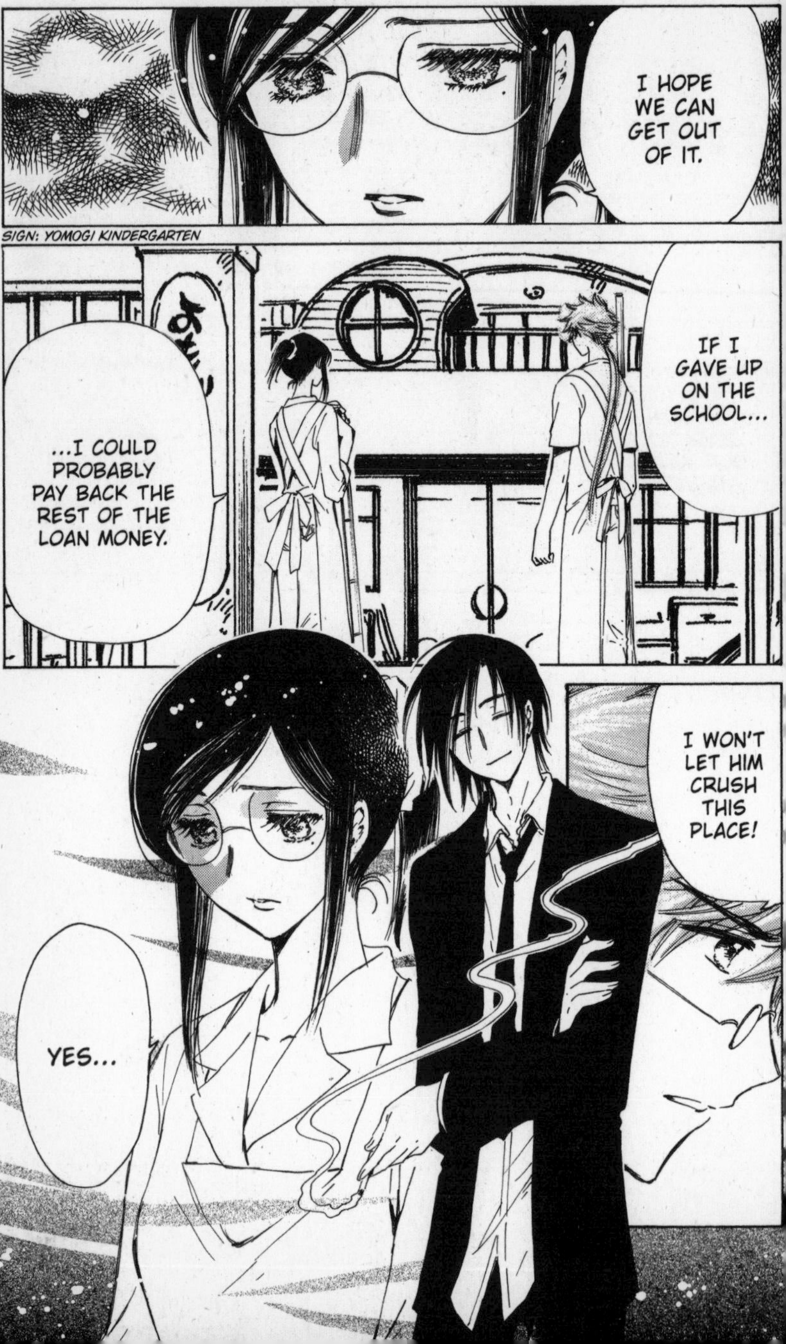
I HOPE WE CAN GET OUT OF IT.
SIGN: YOMOGI KINDERGARTEN
IF I GAVE UP ON THE SCHOOL...
...I COULD PROBABLY PAY BACK THE REST OF THE LOAN MONEY.
I WON'T LET HIM CRUSH THIS PLACE!
YES...

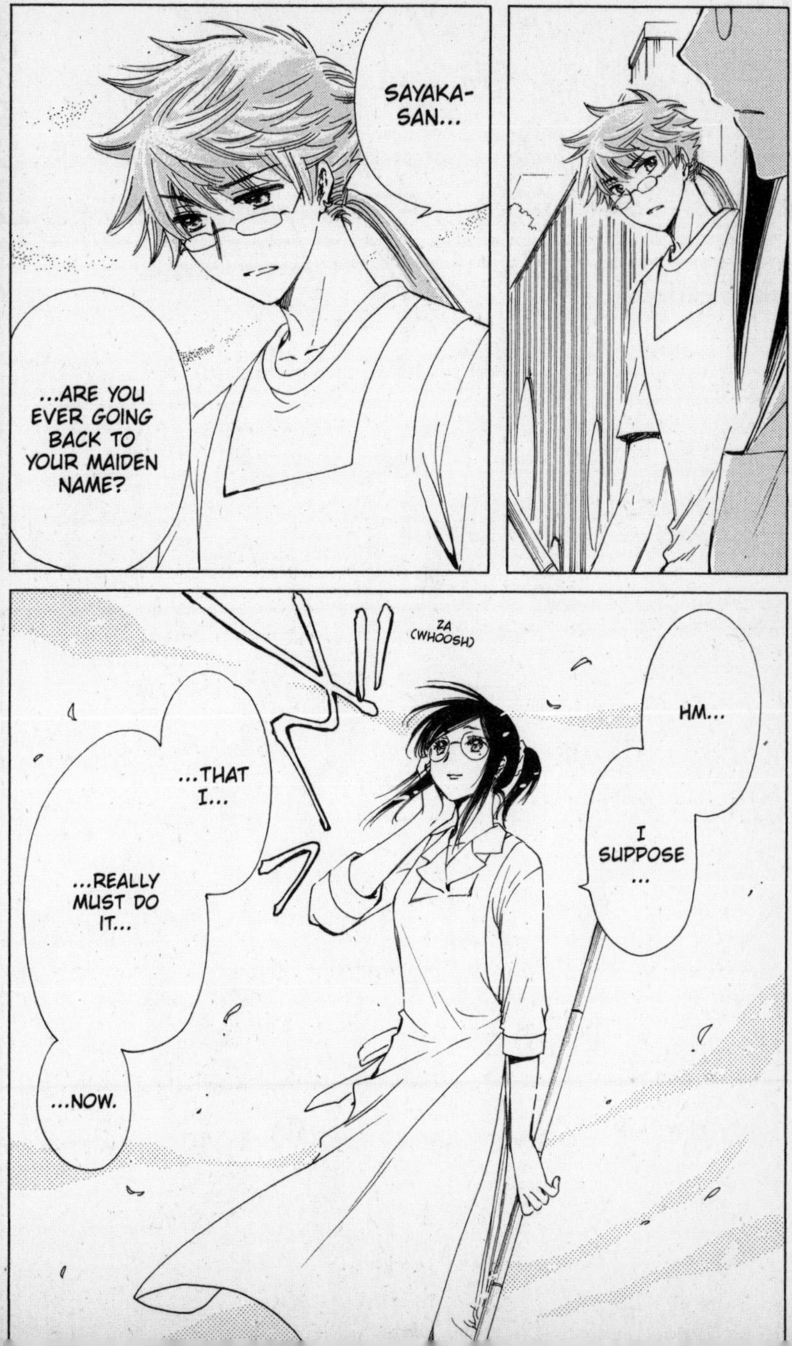
SAYAKA-SAN...
...ARE YOU EVER GOING BACK TO YOUR MAIDEN NAME?
ZA (WHOOSH)
HM...
I SUPPOSE...
...THAT I...
...REALLY MUST DO IT...
...NOW.

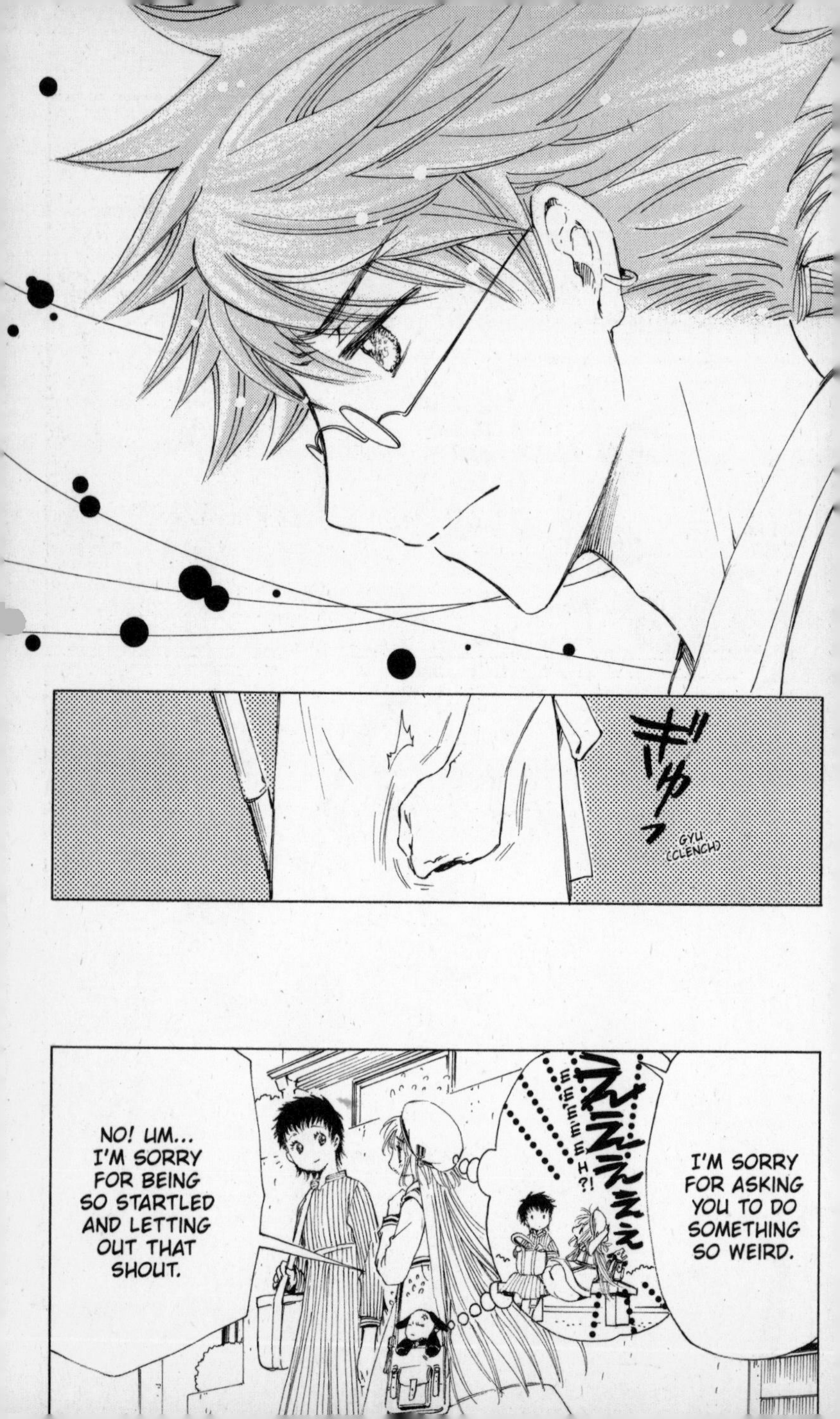
ギュッ
GYU (CLENCH)
I'M SORRY FOR ASKING YOU TO DO SOMETHING SO WEIRD.
EEEEEEH?!
NO! UM... I'M SORRY FOR BEING SO STARTLED AND LETTING OUT THAT SHOUT.

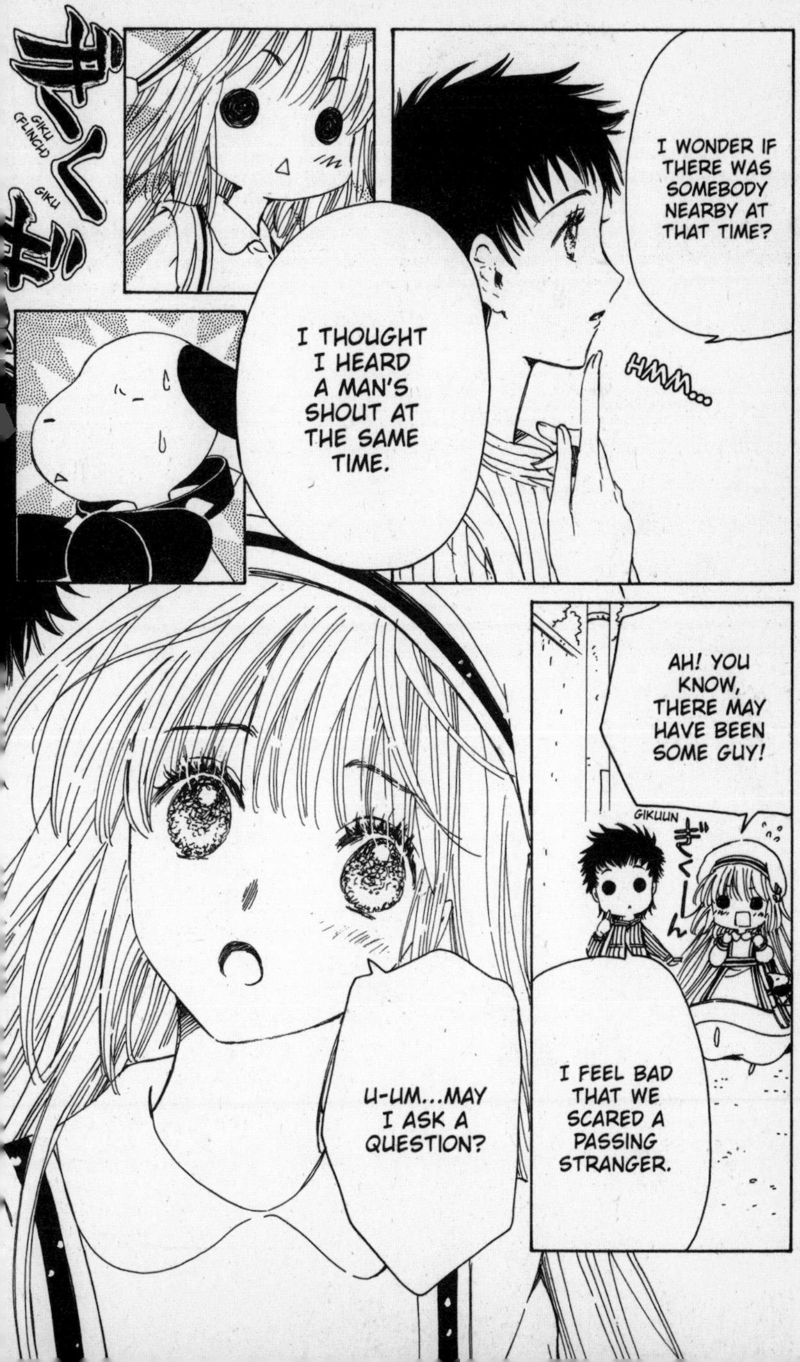
I WONDER IF THERE WAS SOMEBODY NEARBY AT THAT TIME?
HMM...
I THOUGHT I HEARD A MAN'S SHOUT AT THE SAME TIME.
GIKU (FLINCH)
GIKU
AH! YOU KNOW, THERE MAY HAVE BEEN SOME GUY!
GIKUUN
I FEEL BAD THAT WE SCARED A PASSING STRANGER.
U-UM...MAY I ASK A QUESTION?

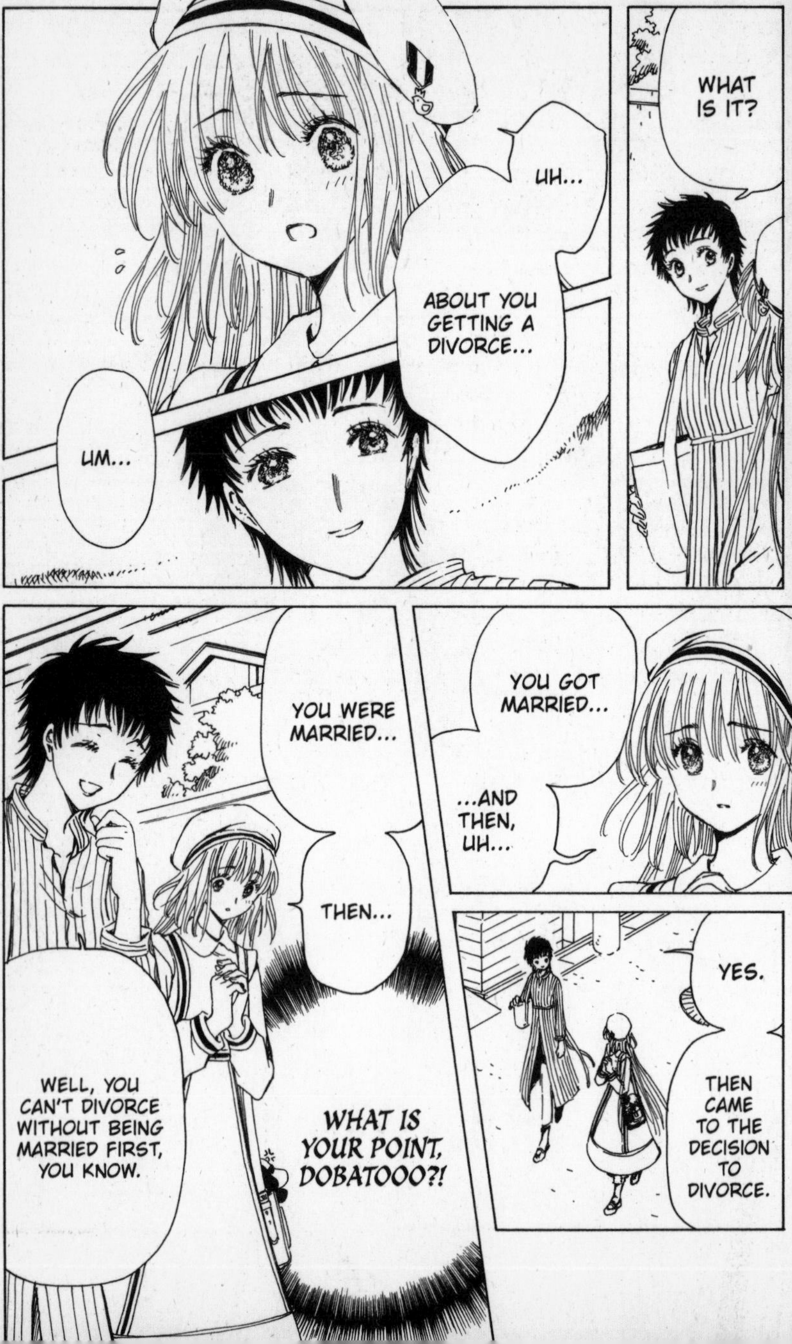
WHAT IS IT?
UH...
ABOUT YOU GETTING A DIVORCE...
UM...
YOU GOT MARRIED...
...AND THEN, UH...
YES.
THEN CAME TO THE DECISION TO DIVORCE.
YOU WERE MARRIED...
THEN...
WELL, YOU CAN'T DIVORCE WITHOUT BEING MARRIED FIRST, YOU KNOW.
WHAT IS YOUR POINT, DOBATOOO?!

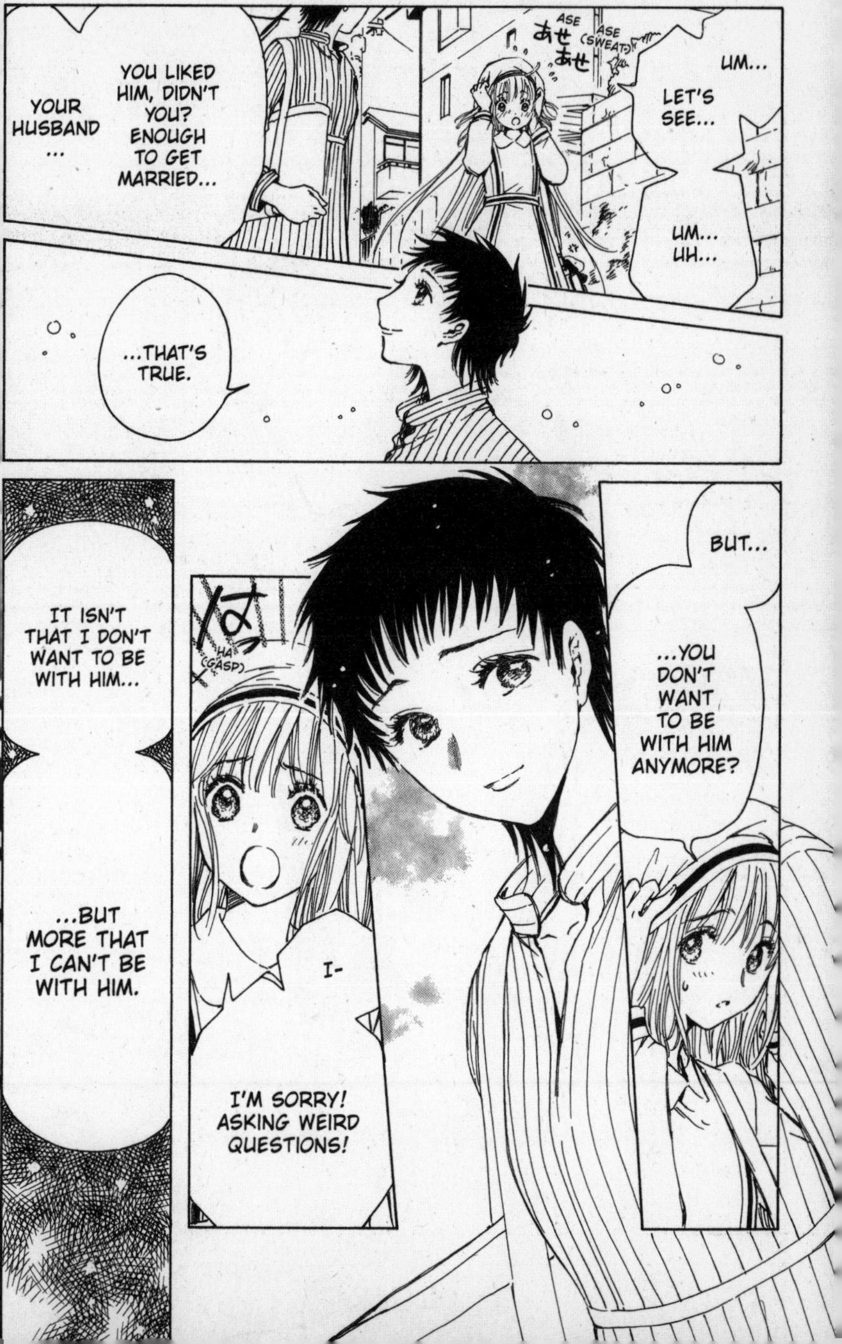

ASE
あせ
ASE (SWEAT)
あせ
UM...
LET'S SEE...
UM... UH...
YOU LIKED HIM, DIDN'T YOU? ENOUGH TO GET MARRIED...
YOUR HUSBAND...
...THAT'S TRUE.
BUT...
...YOU DON'T WANT TO BE WITH HIM ANYMORE?
は
HA (GASP)
I-
I'M SORRY! ASKING WEIRD QUESTIONS!
IT ISN'T THAT I DON'T WANT TO BE WITH HIM...
...BUT MORE THAT I CAN'T BE WITH HIM.

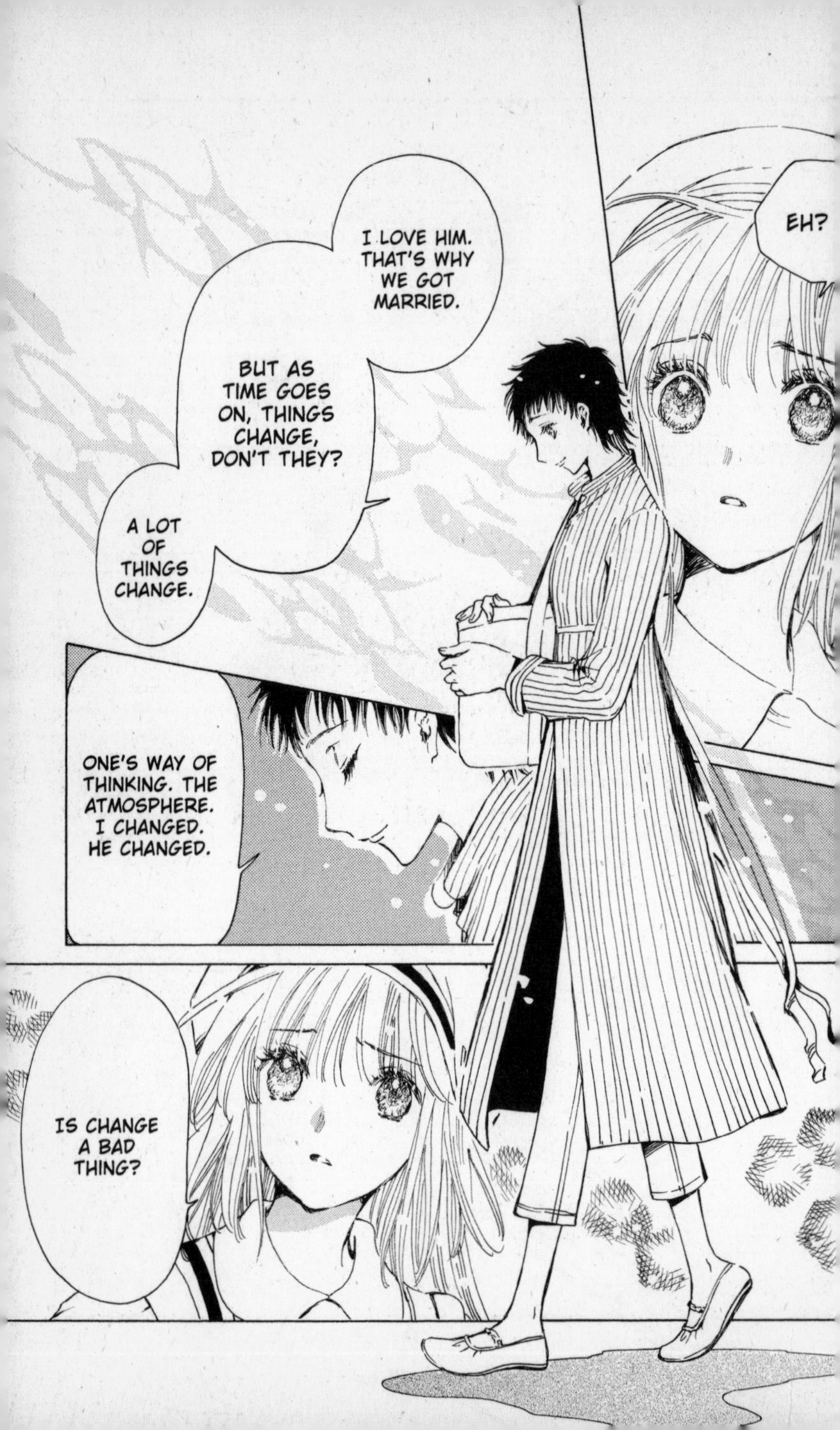
EH?
I LOVE HIM. THAT'S WHY WE GOT MARRIED.
BUT AS TIME GOES ON, THINGS CHANGE, DON'T THEY?
A LOT OF THINGS CHANGE.
ONE'S WAY OF THINKING. THE ATMOSPHERE. I CHANGED. HE CHANGED.
IS CHANGE A BAD THING?

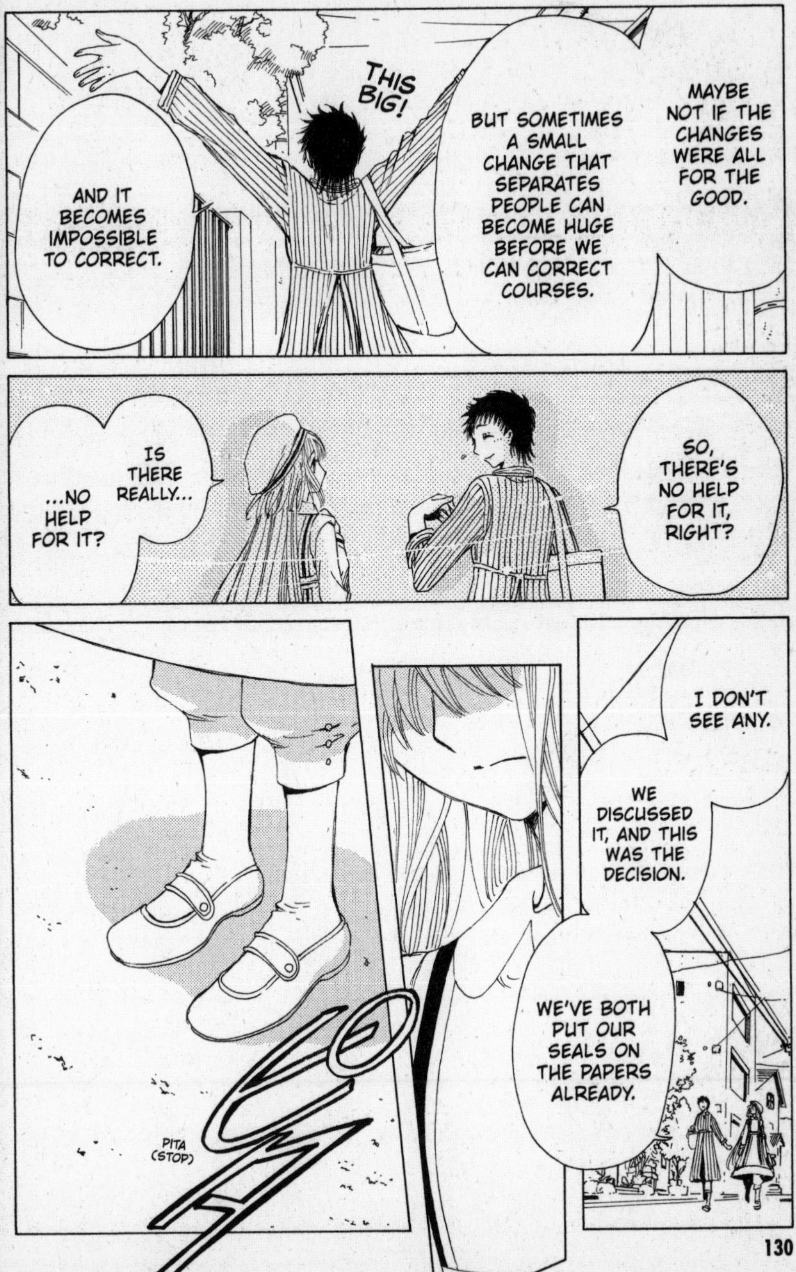
MAYBE NOT IF THE CHANGES WERE ALL FOR THE GOOD.
BUT SOMETIMES A SMALL CHANGE THAT SEPARATES PEOPLE CAN BECOME HUGE BEFORE WE CAN CORRECT COURSES.
THIS BIG!
AND IT BECOMES IMPOSSIBLE TO CORRECT.
SO, THERE'S NO HELP FOR IT, RIGHT?
IS THERE REALLY...
...NO HELP FOR IT?
I DON'T SEE ANY.
WE DISCUSSED IT, AND THIS WAS THE DECISION.
WE'VE BOTH PUT OUR SEALS ON THE PAPERS ALREADY.
PITA (STOP)

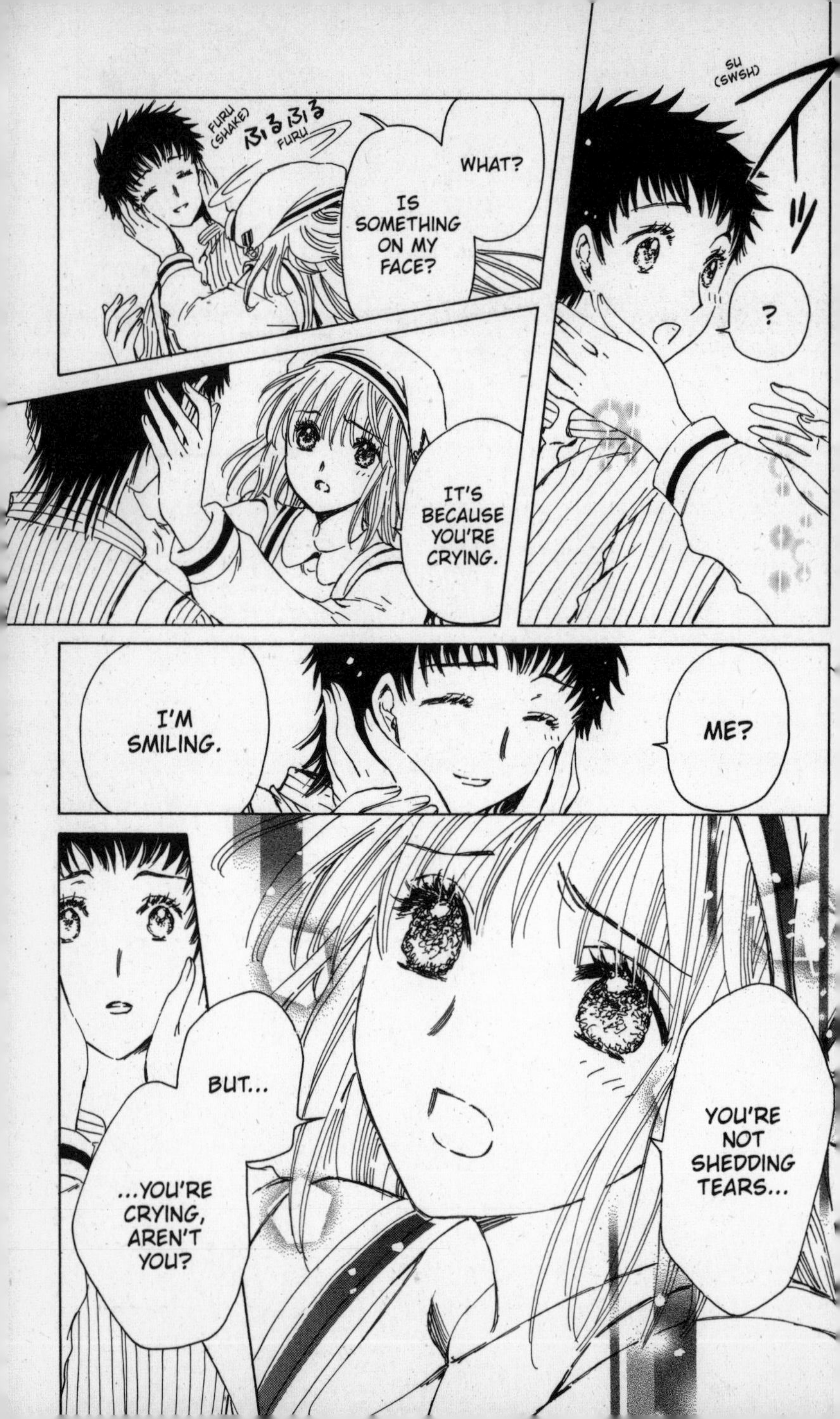
SU (SWSH)
?
FURU (SHAKE)
ふるふる
FURU
WHAT?
IS SOMETHING ON MY FACE?
IT'S BECAUSE YOU'RE CRYING.
ME?
I'M SMILING.
YOU'RE NOT SHEDDING TEARS...
BUT...
...YOU'RE CRYING, AREN'T YOU?

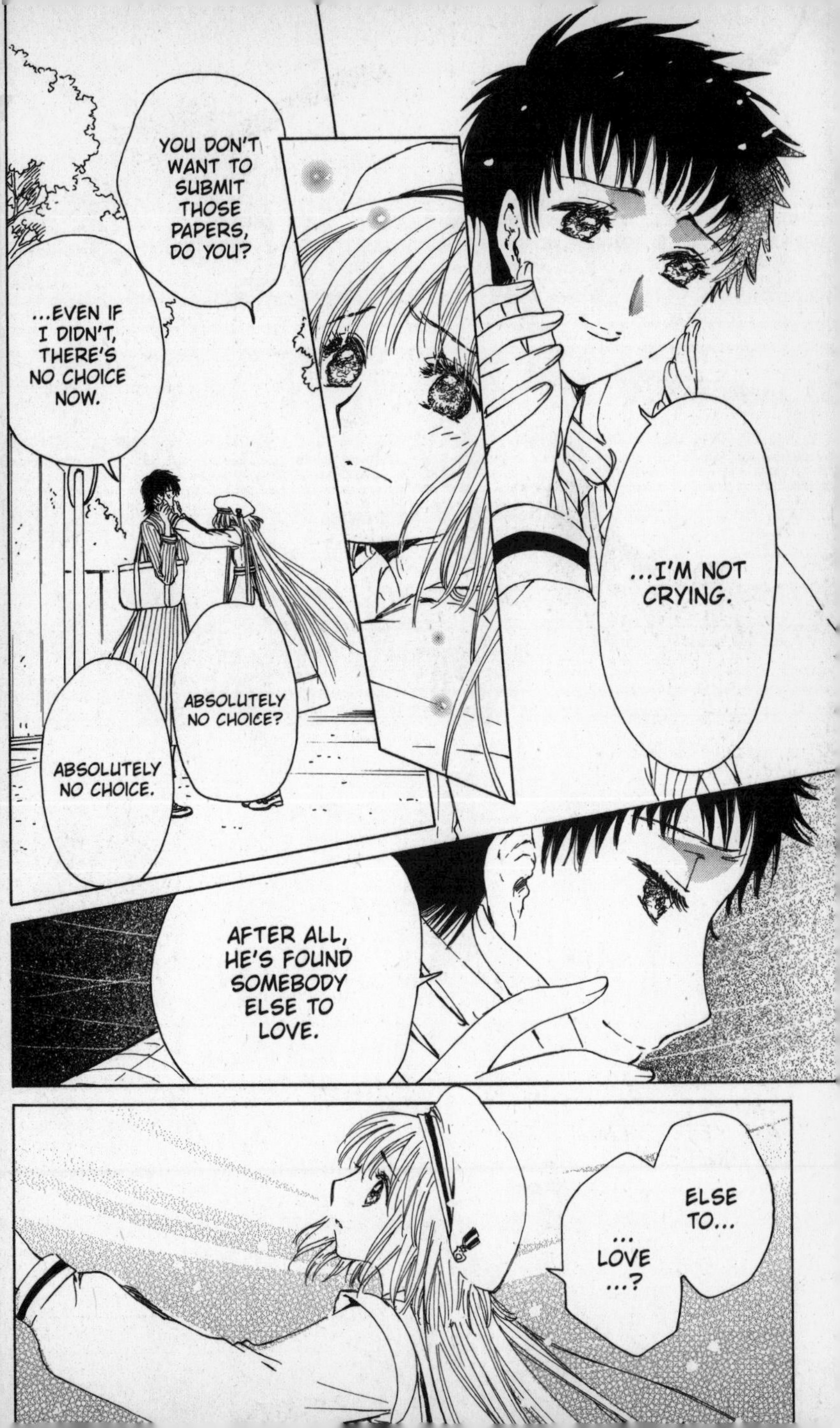
...I'M NOT CRYING.
YOU DON'T WANT TO SUBMIT THOSE PAPERS, DO YOU?
...EVEN IF I DIDN'T, THERE'S NO CHOICE NOW.
ABSOLUTELY NO CHOICE?
ABSOLUTELY NO CHOICE.
AFTER ALL, HE'S FOUND SOMEBODY ELSE TO LOVE.
ELSE TO...
...LOVE ...?

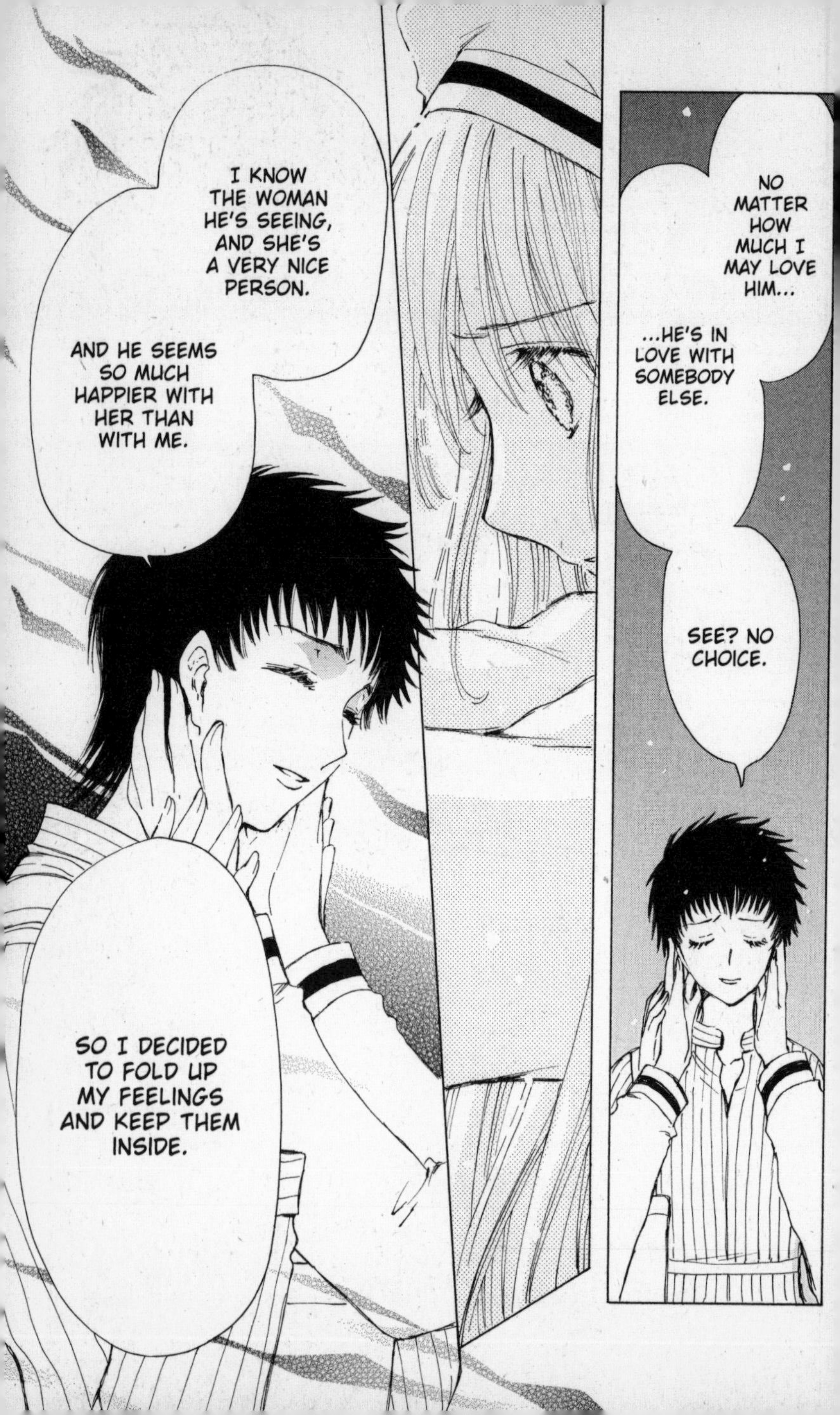
NO MATTER HOW MUCH I MAY LOVE HIM...
...HE'S IN LOVE WITH SOMEBODY ELSE.
SEE? NO CHOICE.
I KNOW THE WOMAN HE'S SEEING, AND SHE'S A VERY NICE PERSON.
AND HE SEEMS SO MUCH HAPPIER WITH HER THAN WITH ME.
SO I DECIDED TO FOLD UP MY FEELINGS AND KEEP THEM INSIDE.

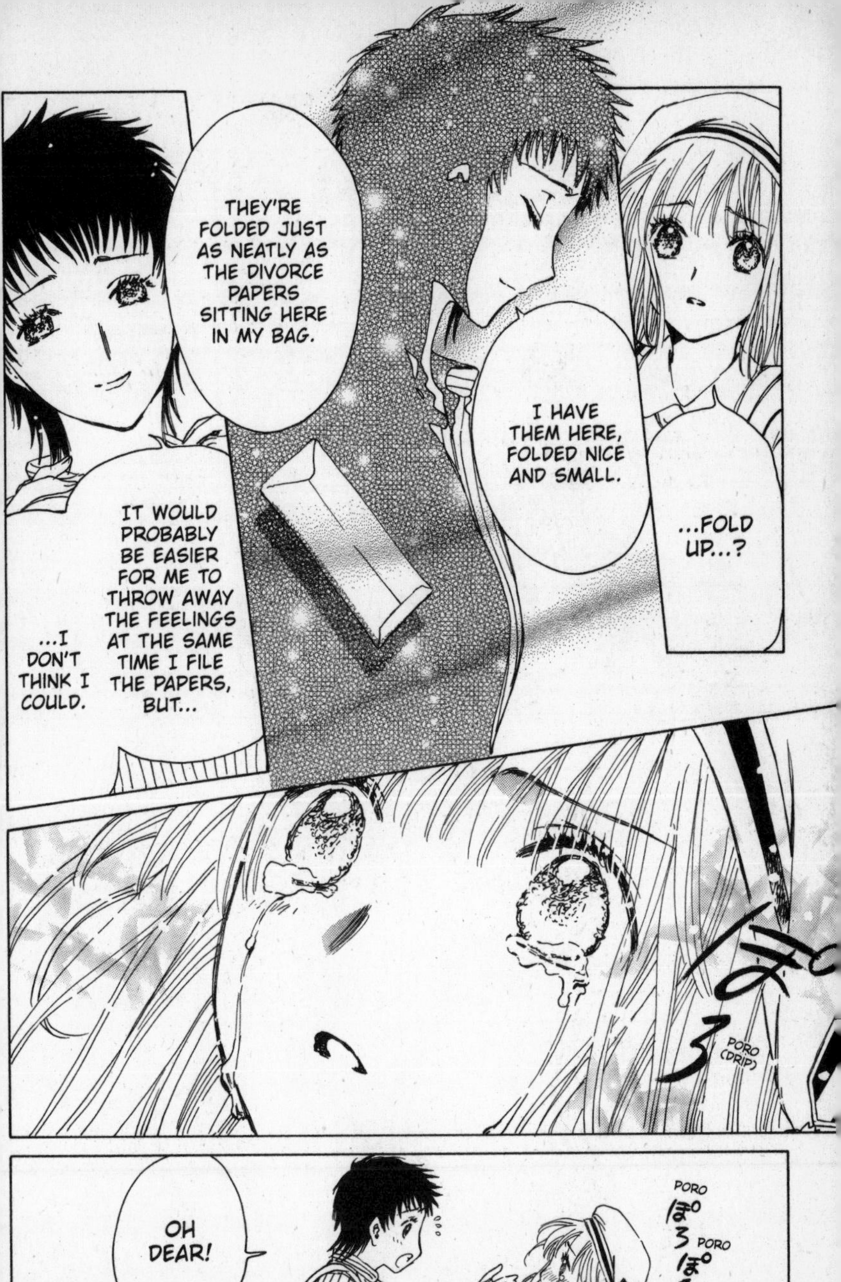
...FOLD UP...?
I HAVE THEM HERE, FOLDED NICE AND SMALL.
THEY'RE FOLDED JUST AS NEATLY AS THE DIVORCE PAPERS SITTING HERE IN MY BAG.
IT WOULD PROBABLY BE EASIER FOR ME TO THROW AWAY THE FEELINGS AT THE SAME TIME I FILE THE PAPERS, BUT...
...I DON'T THINK I COULD.
PORO (DRIP)
ぽろぽろ
PORO PORO
OH DEAR!

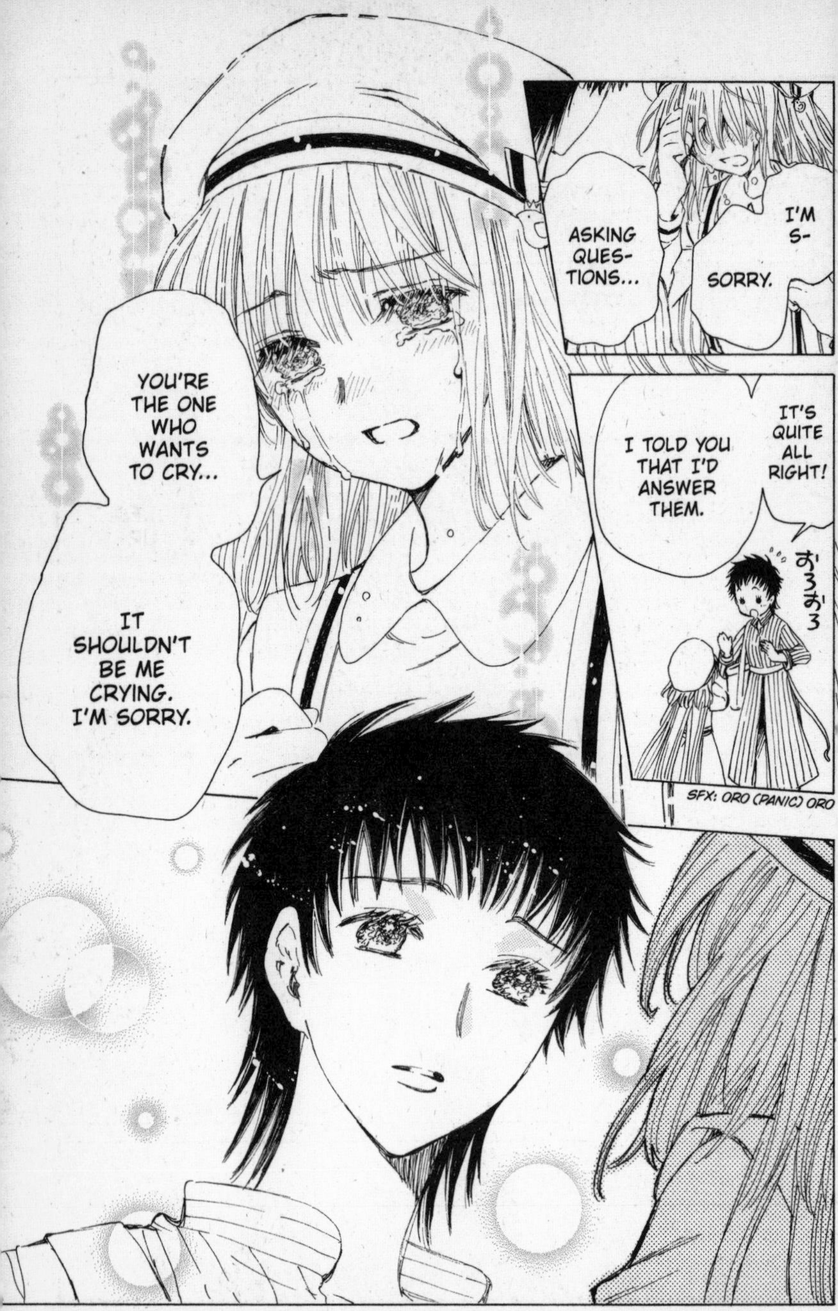
I'M S- SORRY.
ASKING QUES- TIONS...
IT'S QUITE ALL RIGHT!
I TOLD YOU THAT I'D ANSWER THEM.
おろおろ
SFX: ORO (PANIC) ORO
YOU'RE THE ONE WHO WANTS TO CRY...
IT SHOULDN'T BE ME CRYING. I'M SORRY.

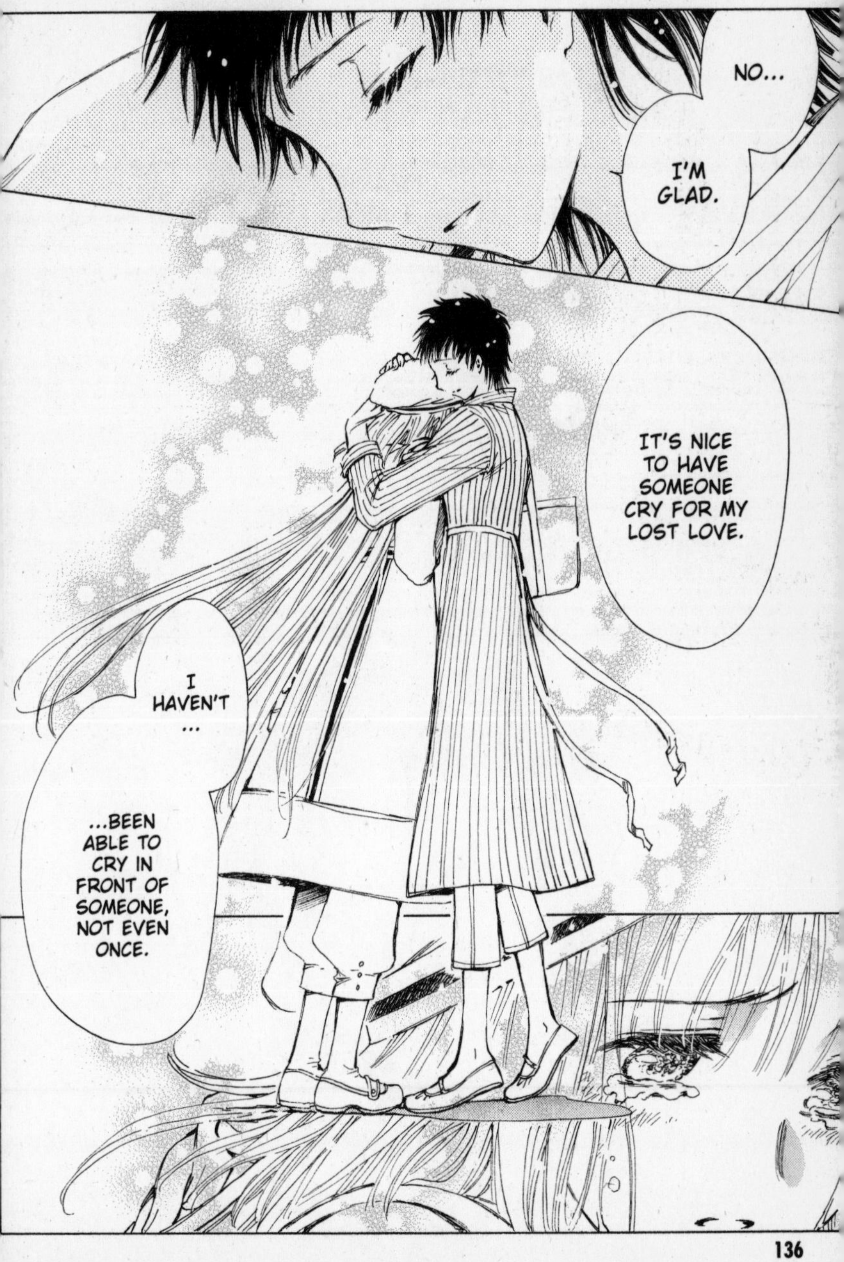
NO...
I'M GLAD.
IT'S NICE TO HAVE SOMEONE CRY FOR MY LOST LOVE.
I HAVEN'T ...
...BEEN ABLE TO CRY IN FRONT OF SOMEONE, NOT EVEN ONCE.

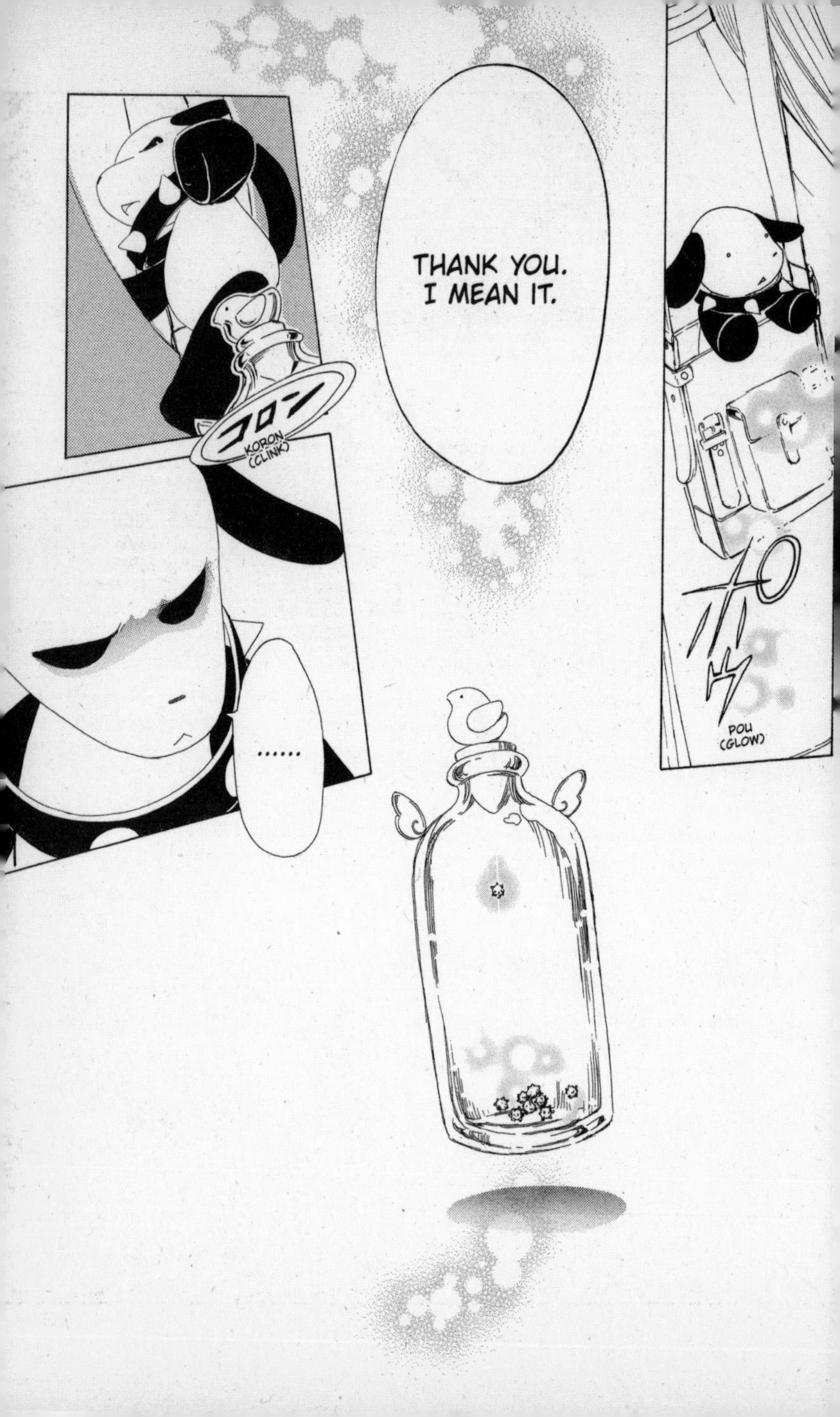
POU (GLOW)
THANK YOU. I MEAN IT.
コロン
KORON (CLINK)
......

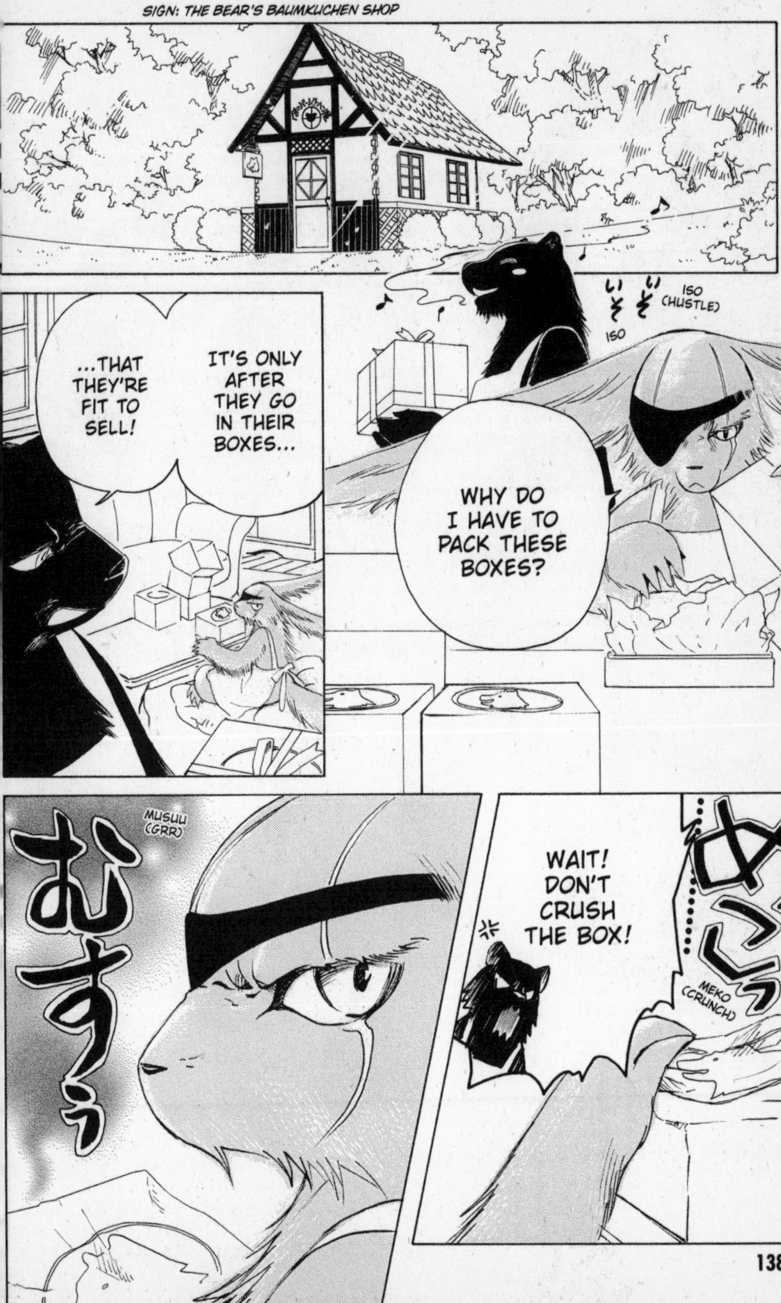
SIGN: THE BEAR'S BAUMKUCHEN SHOP
いそ いそ
ISO (HUSTLE)
ISO
WHY DO I HAVE TO PACK THESE BOXES?
IT'S ONLY AFTER THEY GO IN THEIR BOXES...
...THAT THEY'RE FIT TO SELL!
めこっ
MEKO (CRUNCH)
WAIT! DON'T CRUSH THE BOX!
むすぅ
MUSUU (GRR)

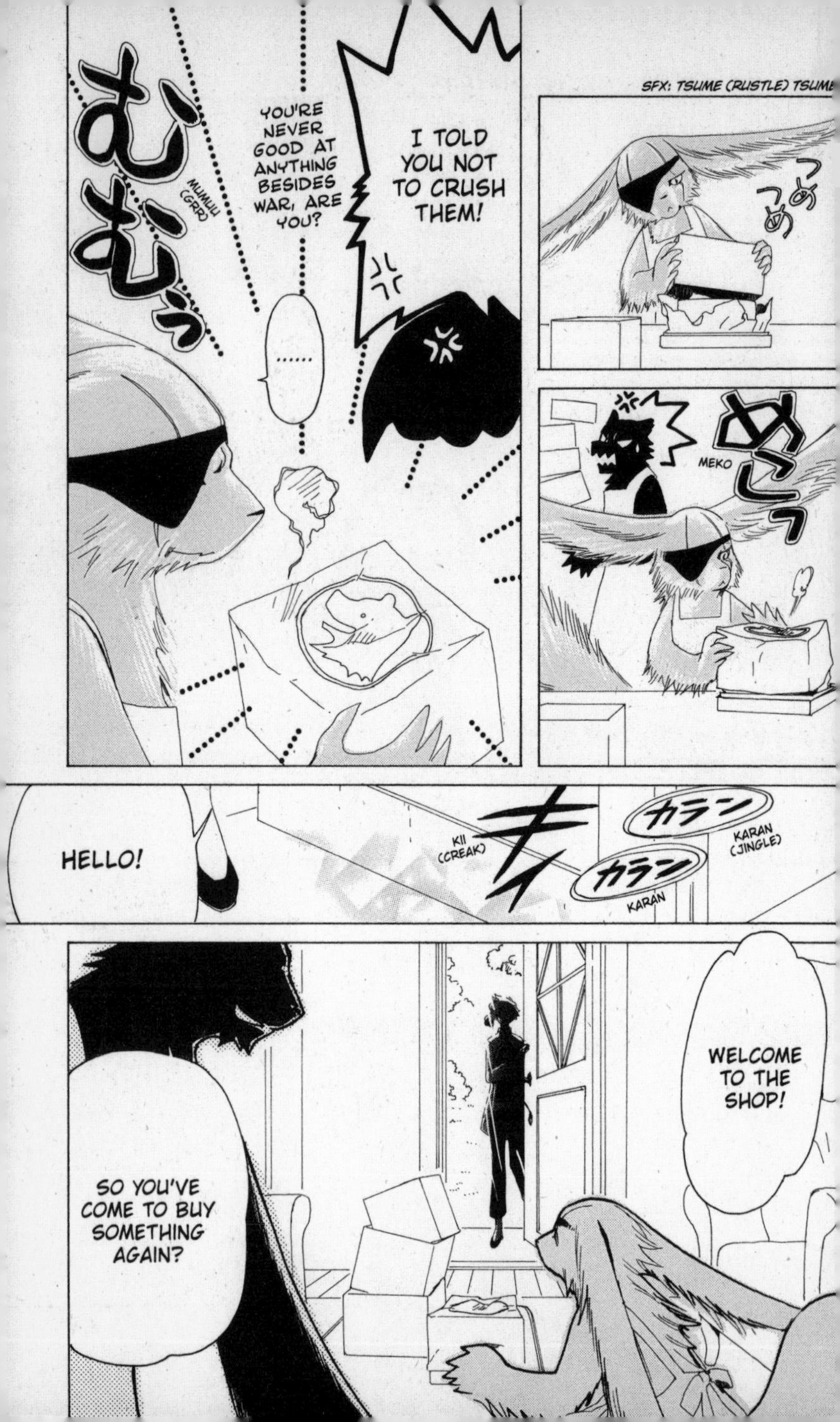
SFX: TSUME (RUSTLE) TSUME
つめつめ
めこっ
MEKO
I TOLD YOU NOT TO CRUSH THEM!
YOU'RE NEVER GOOD AT ANYTHING BESIDES WAR, ARE YOU?
……
むむっ
MUMUU (GRR)
カラン
KARAN (JINGLE)
カラン
KARAN
キィ
KII (CREAK)
HELLO!
WELCOME TO THE SHOP!
SO YOU'VE COME TO BUY SOMETHING AGAIN?

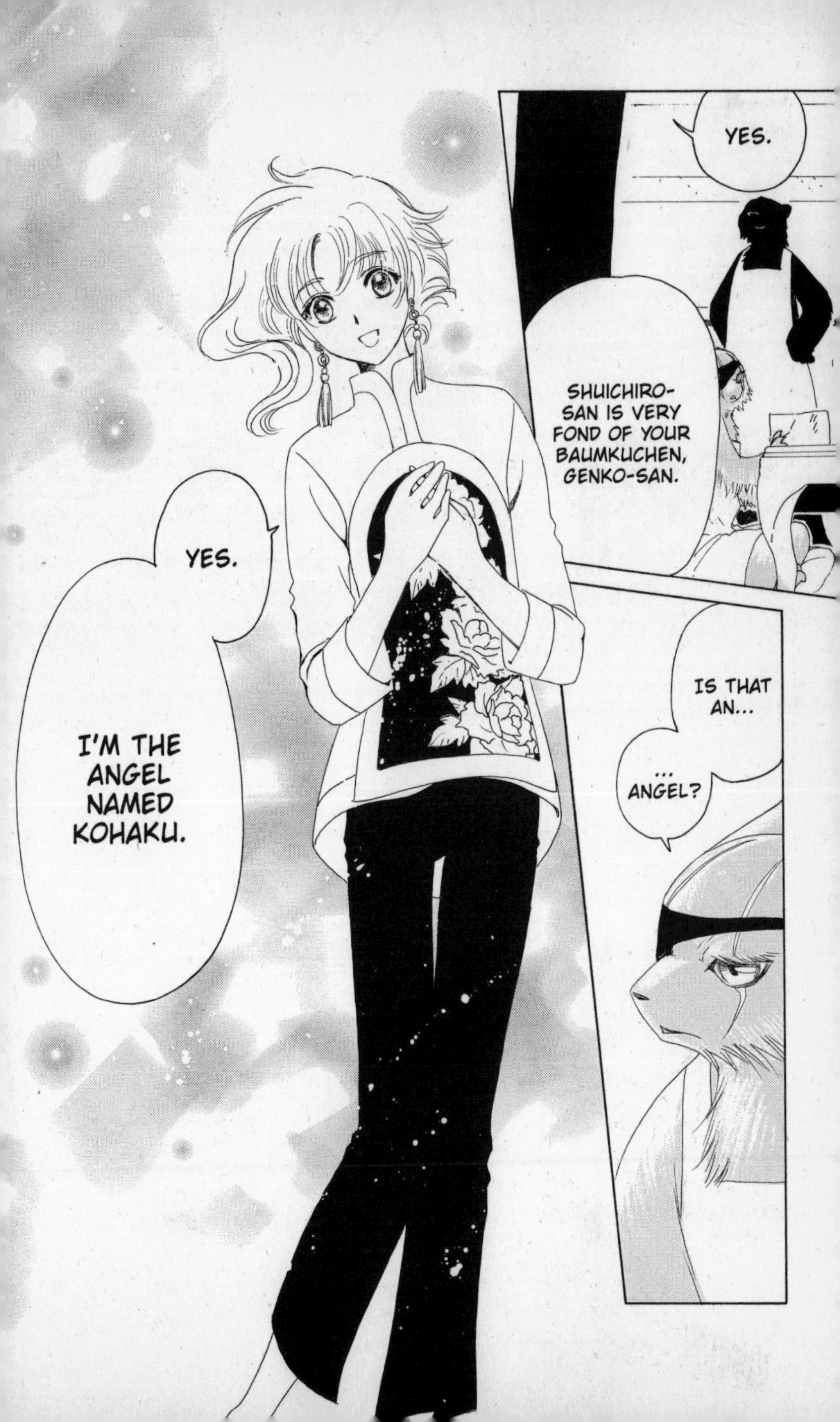
YES.
SHUICHIRO-SAN IS VERY FOND OF YOUR BAUMKUCHEN, GENKO-SAN.
IS THAT AN...
...ANGEL?
YES.
I'M THE ANGEL NAMED KOHAKU.

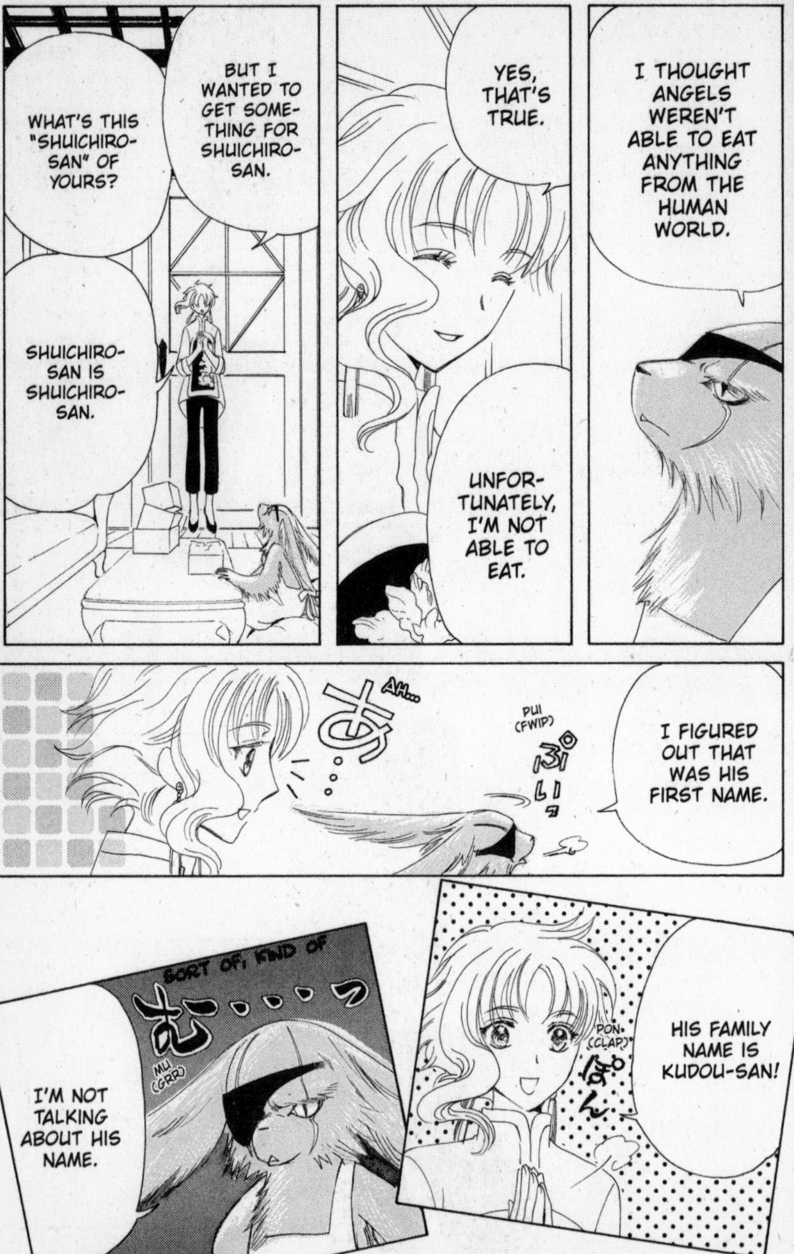
I THOUGHT ANGELS WEREN'T ABLE TO EAT ANYTHING FROM THE HUMAN WORLD.
YES, THAT'S TRUE.
UNFORTUNATELY, I'M NOT ABLE TO EAT.
BUT I WANTED TO GET SOMETHING FOR SHUICHIRO-SAN.
WHAT'S THIS "SHUICHIRO-SAN" OF YOURS?
SHUICHIRO-SAN IS SHUICHIRO-SAN.
I FIGURED OUT THAT WAS HIS FIRST NAME.
PUI (FWIP)
AH...
PON (CLAP)
HIS FAMILY NAME IS KUDOU-SAN!
SORT OF, KIND OF
MU (GRR)
I'M NOT TALKING ABOUT HIS NAME.

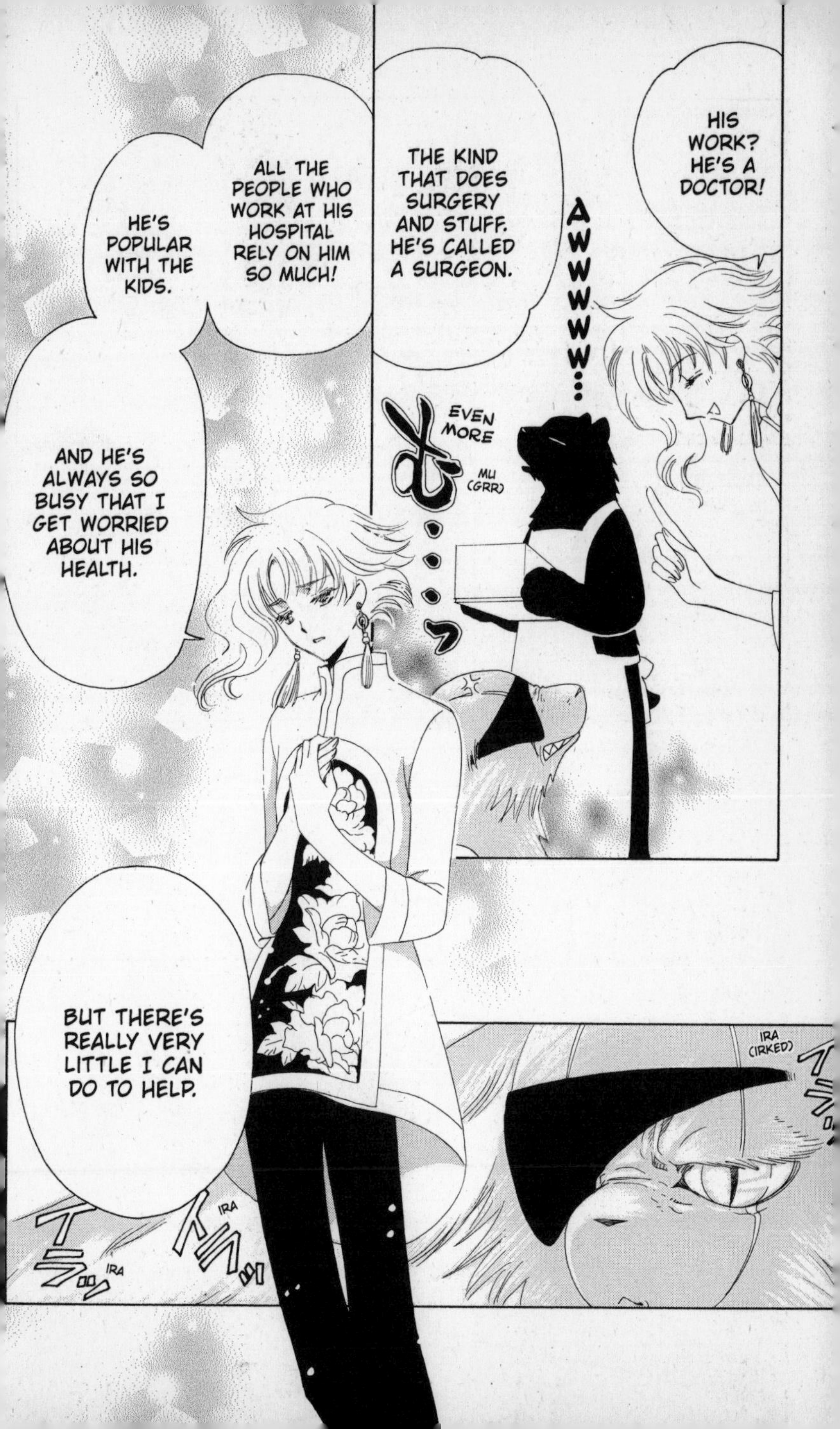
HIS WORK? HE'S A DOCTOR!
THE KIND THAT DOES SURGERY AND STUFF. HE'S CALLED A SURGEON.
AWWWWWW...
EVEN MORE
MU (GRR)
ALL THE PEOPLE WHO WORK AT HIS HOSPITAL RELY ON HIM SO MUCH!
HE'S POPULAR WITH THE KIDS.
AND HE'S ALWAYS SO BUSY THAT I GET WORRIED ABOUT HIS HEALTH.
IRA (IRKED)
BUT THERE'S REALLY VERY LITTLE I CAN DO TO HELP.
IRA
IRA

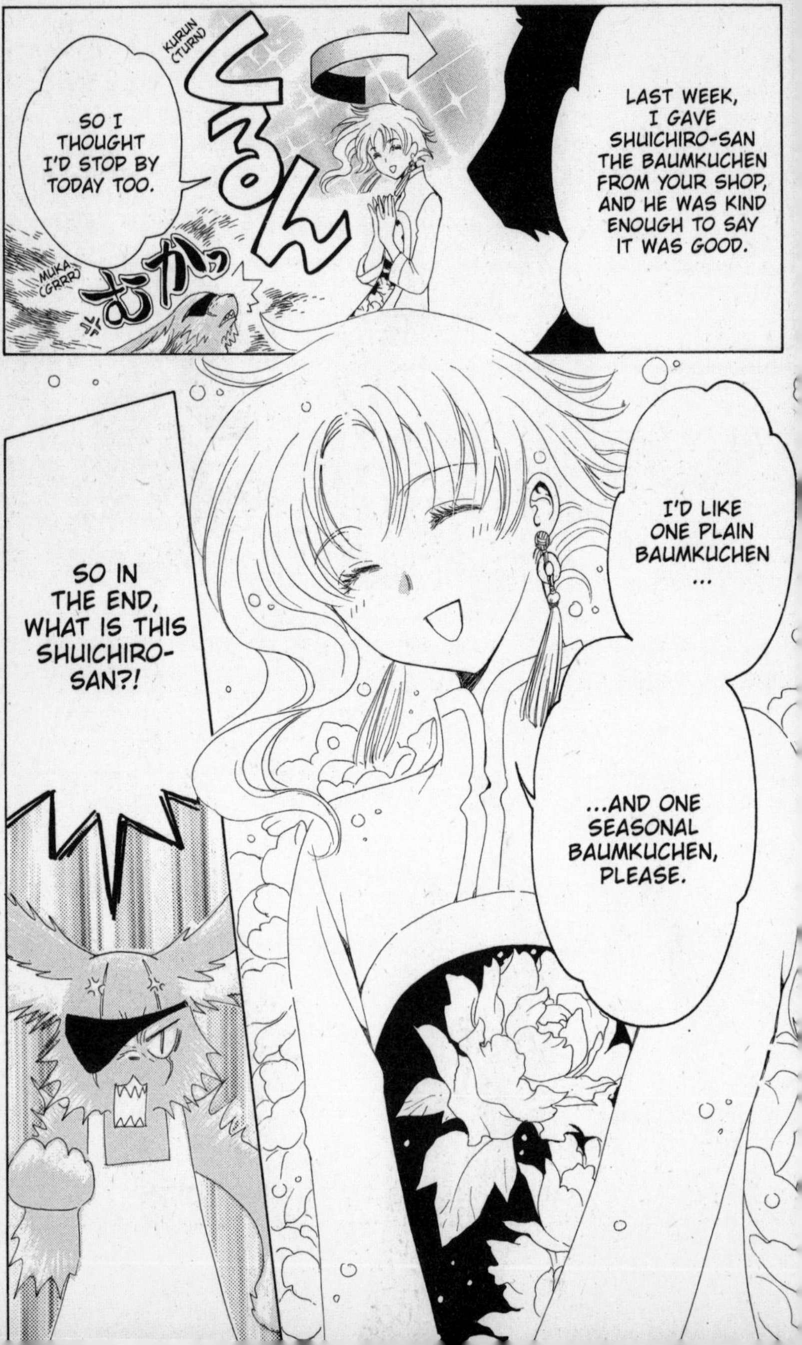
LAST WEEK, I GAVE SHUICHIRO-SAN THE BAUMKUCHEN FROM YOUR SHOP, AND HE WAS KIND ENOUGH TO SAY IT WAS GOOD.
KURUN (TURN)
くるん
SO I THOUGHT I'D STOP BY TODAY TOO.
MUKA (GRRR)
むかっ
I'D LIKE ONE PLAIN BAUMKUCHEN ...
...AND ONE SEASONAL BAUMKUCHEN, PLEASE.
SO IN THE END, WHAT IS THIS SHUICHIRO-SAN?!

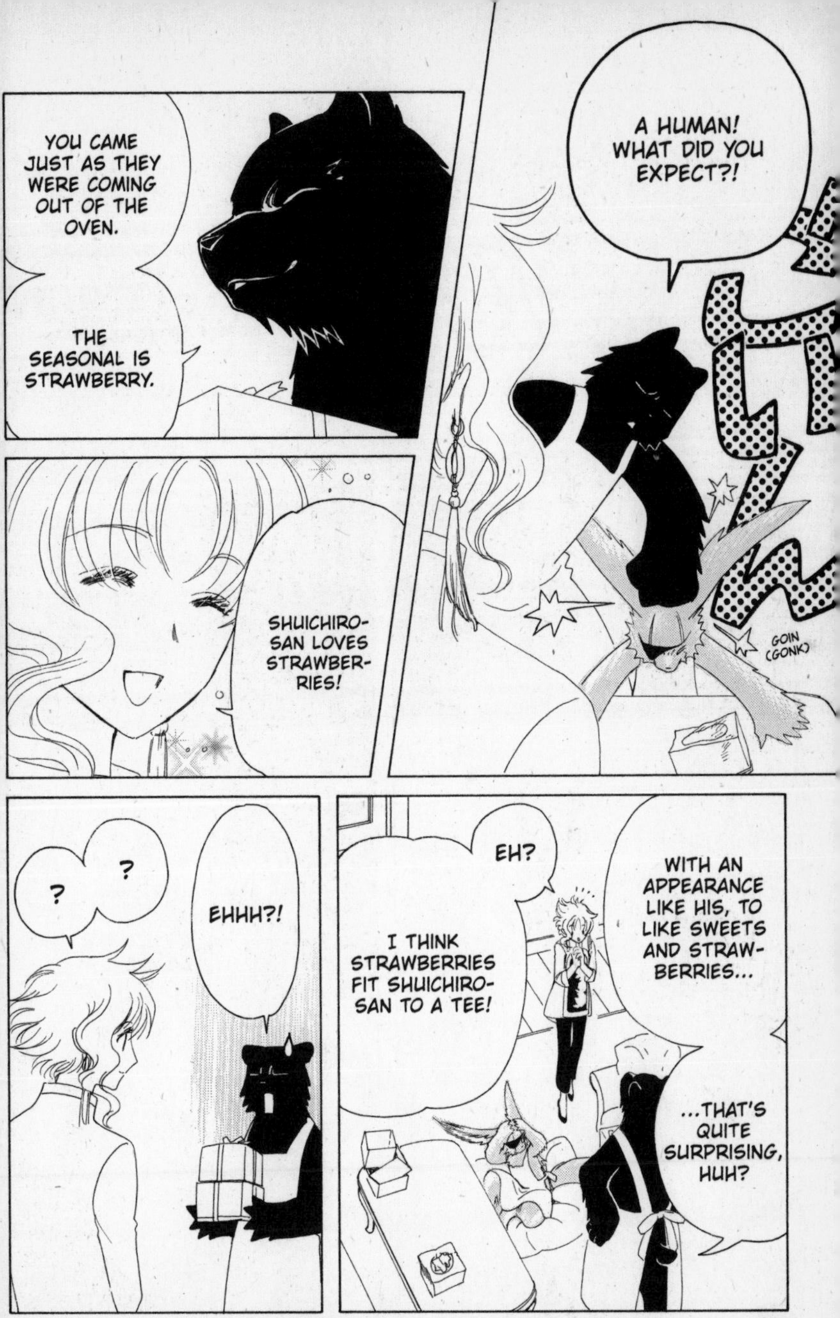
A HUMAN! WHAT DID YOU EXPECT?!
GOIN (GONK)
YOU CAME JUST AS THEY WERE COMING OUT OF THE OVEN.
THE SEASONAL IS STRAWBERRY.
SHUICHIRO-SAN LOVES STRAWBER-RIES!
WITH AN APPEARANCE LIKE HIS, TO LIKE SWEETS AND STRAW-BERRIES...
...THAT'S QUITE SURPRISING, HUH?
EH?
I THINK STRAWBERRIES FIT SHUICHIRO-SAN TO A TEE!
EHHH?!
? ?

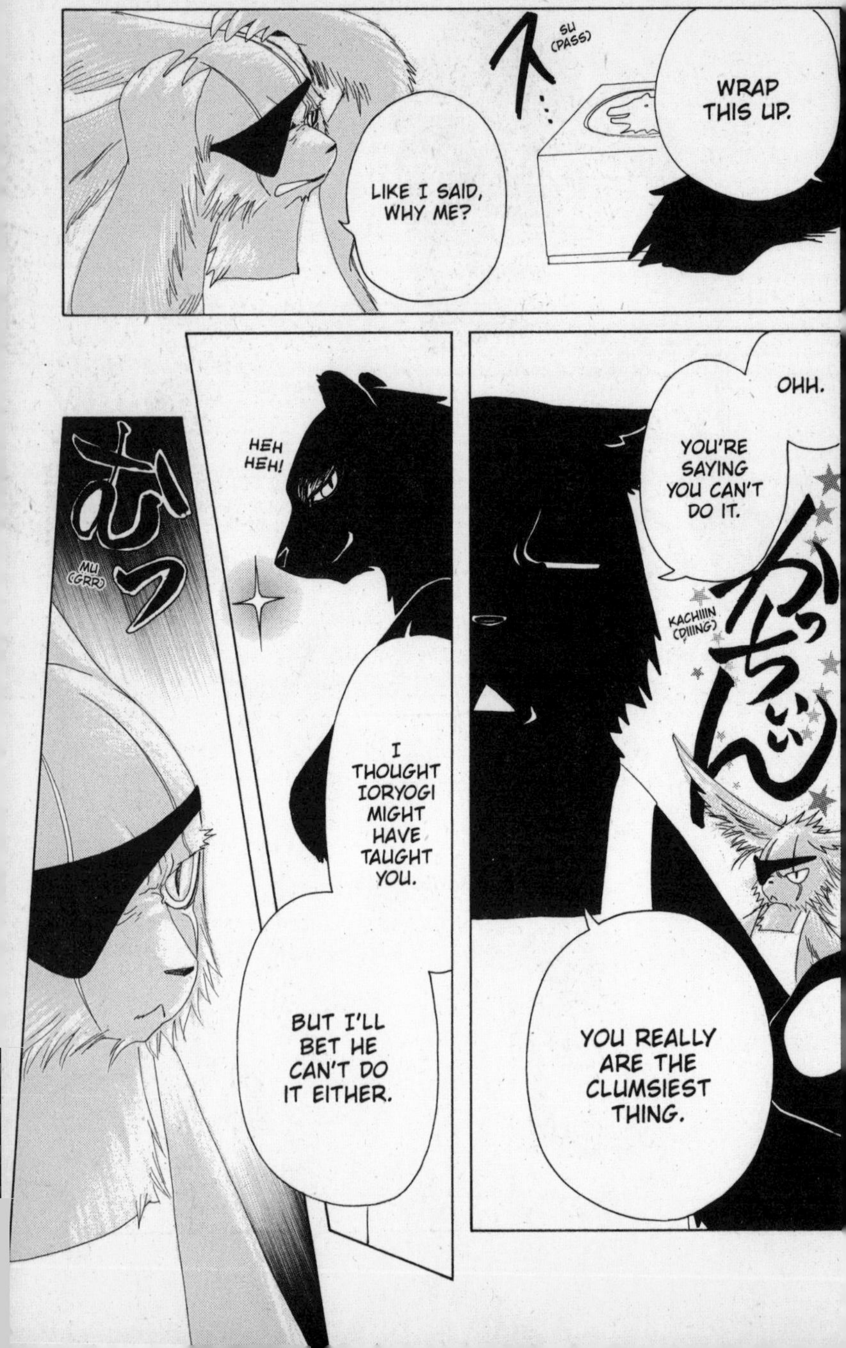
WRAP THIS UP.
SU (PASS)
LIKE I SAID, WHY ME?
OHH.
YOU'RE SAYING YOU CAN'T DO IT.
かっちぃん
KACHIIIN (DIIING)
YOU REALLY ARE THE CLUMSIEST THING.
HEH HEH!
I THOUGHT IORYOGI MIGHT HAVE TAUGHT YOU.
BUT I'LL BET HE CAN'T DO IT EITHER.
むっ
MU (GRR)

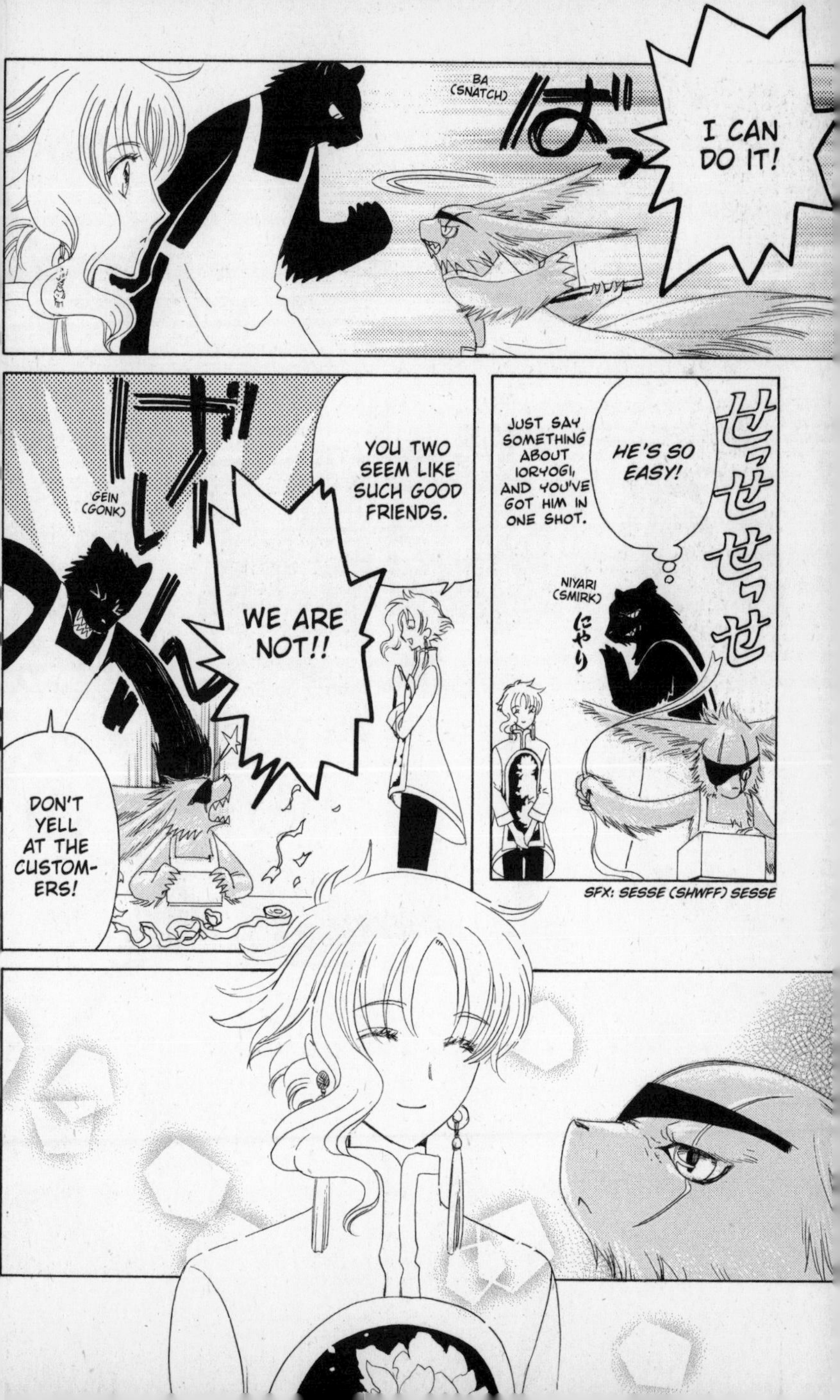
I CAN DO IT!
BA (SNATCH)
ばっ
せっせせっせ
HE'S SO EASY!
JUST SAY SOMETHING ABOUT IORYOGI, AND YOU'VE GOT HIM IN ONE SHOT.
NIYARI (SMIRK)
にやり
SFX: SESSE (SHWFF) SESSE
YOU TWO SEEM LIKE SUCH GOOD FRIENDS.
WE ARE NOT!!
GEIN (GONK)
DON'T YELL AT THE CUSTOMERS!

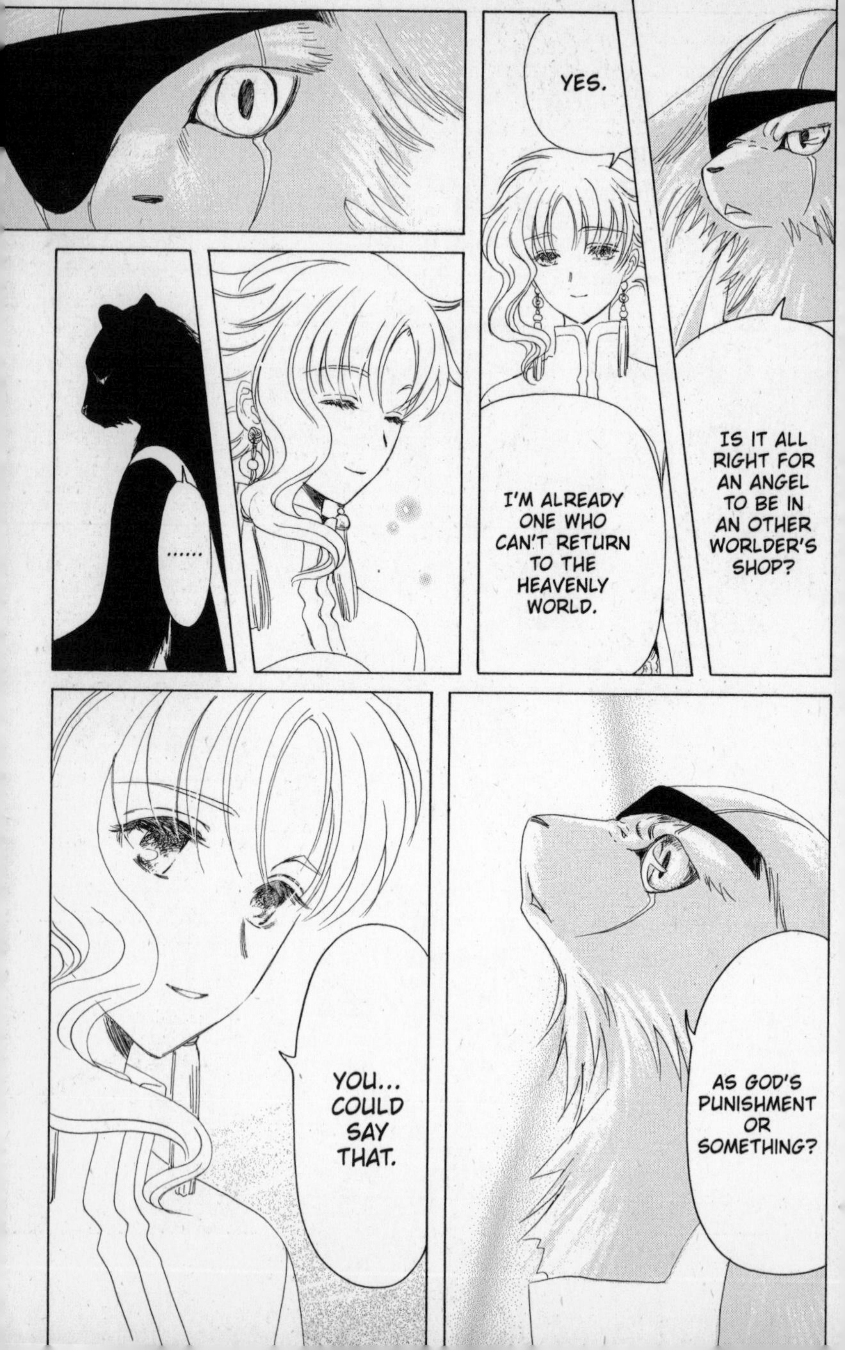
IS IT ALL RIGHT FOR AN ANGEL TO BE IN AN OTHER WORLDER'S SHOP?
YES.
I'M ALREADY ONE WHO CAN'T RETURN TO THE HEAVENLY WORLD.
......
AS GOD'S PUNISHMENT OR SOMETHING?
YOU... COULD SAY THAT.

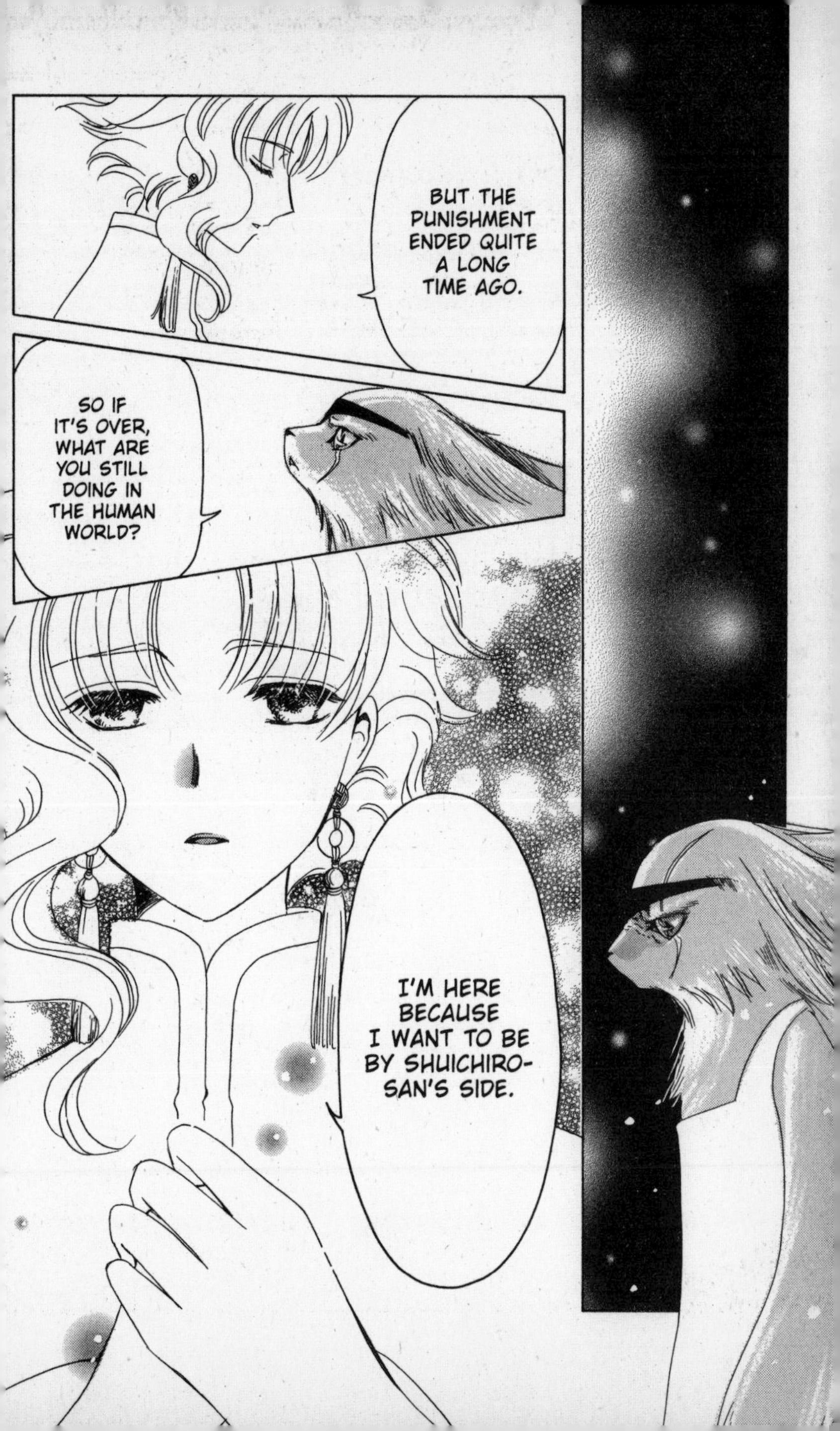
BUT THE PUNISHMENT ENDED QUITE A LONG TIME AGO.
SO IF IT'S OVER, WHAT ARE YOU STILL DOING IN THE HUMAN WORLD?
I'M HERE BECAUSE I WANT TO BE BY SHUICHIRO-SAN'S SIDE.

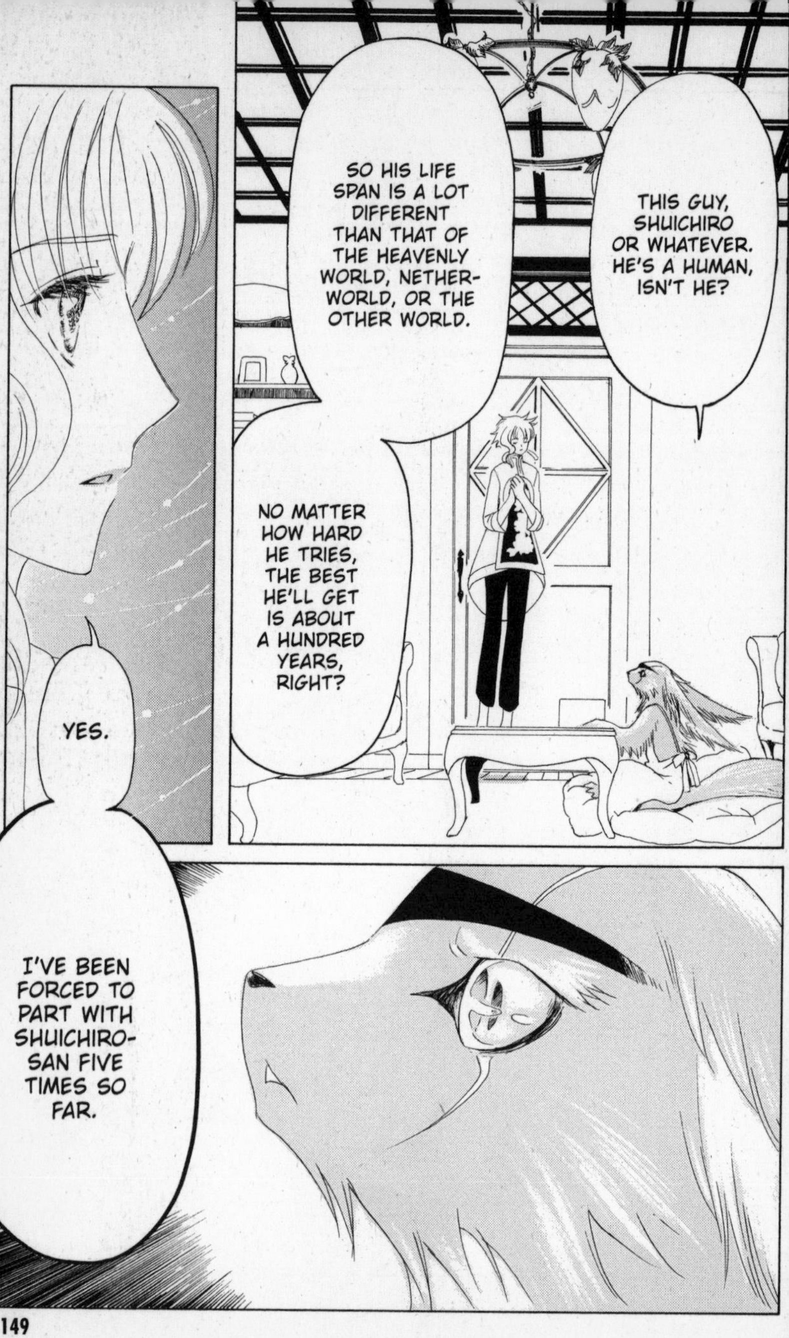
THIS GUY, SHUICHIRO OR WHATEVER. HE'S A HUMAN, ISN'T HE?
SO HIS LIFE SPAN IS A LOT DIFFERENT THAN THAT OF THE HEAVENLY WORLD, NETHER-WORLD, OR THE OTHER WORLD.
NO MATTER HOW HARD HE TRIES, THE BEST HE'LL GET IS ABOUT A HUNDRED YEARS, RIGHT?
YES.
I'VE BEEN FORCED TO PART WITH SHUICHIRO-SAN FIVE TIMES SO FAR.

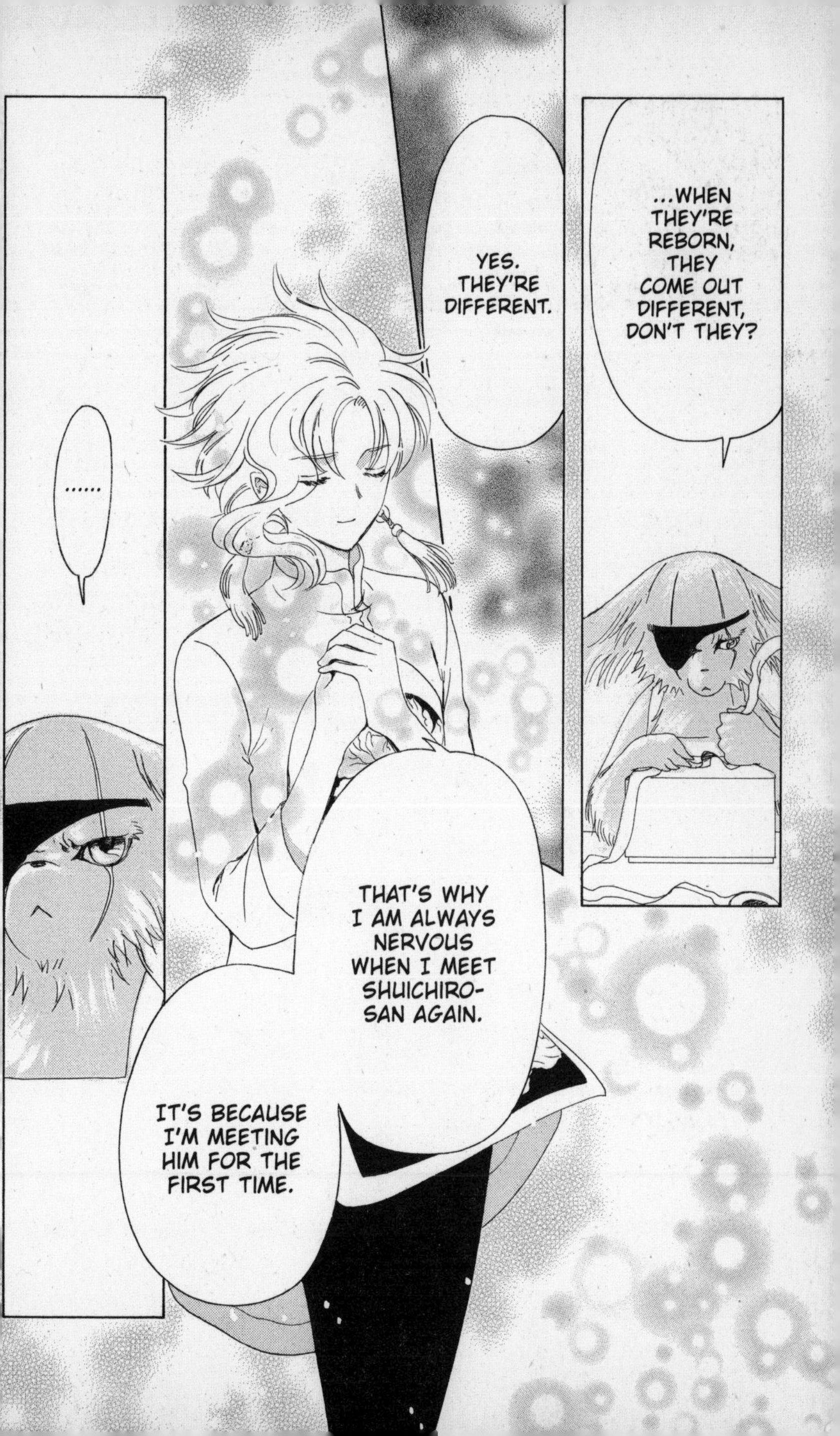
...WHEN THEY'RE REBORN, THEY COME OUT DIFFERENT, DON'T THEY?
YES. THEY'RE DIFFERENT.
......
THAT'S WHY I AM ALWAYS NERVOUS WHEN I MEET SHUICHIRO-SAN AGAIN.
IT'S BECAUSE I'M MEETING HIM FOR THE FIRST TIME.

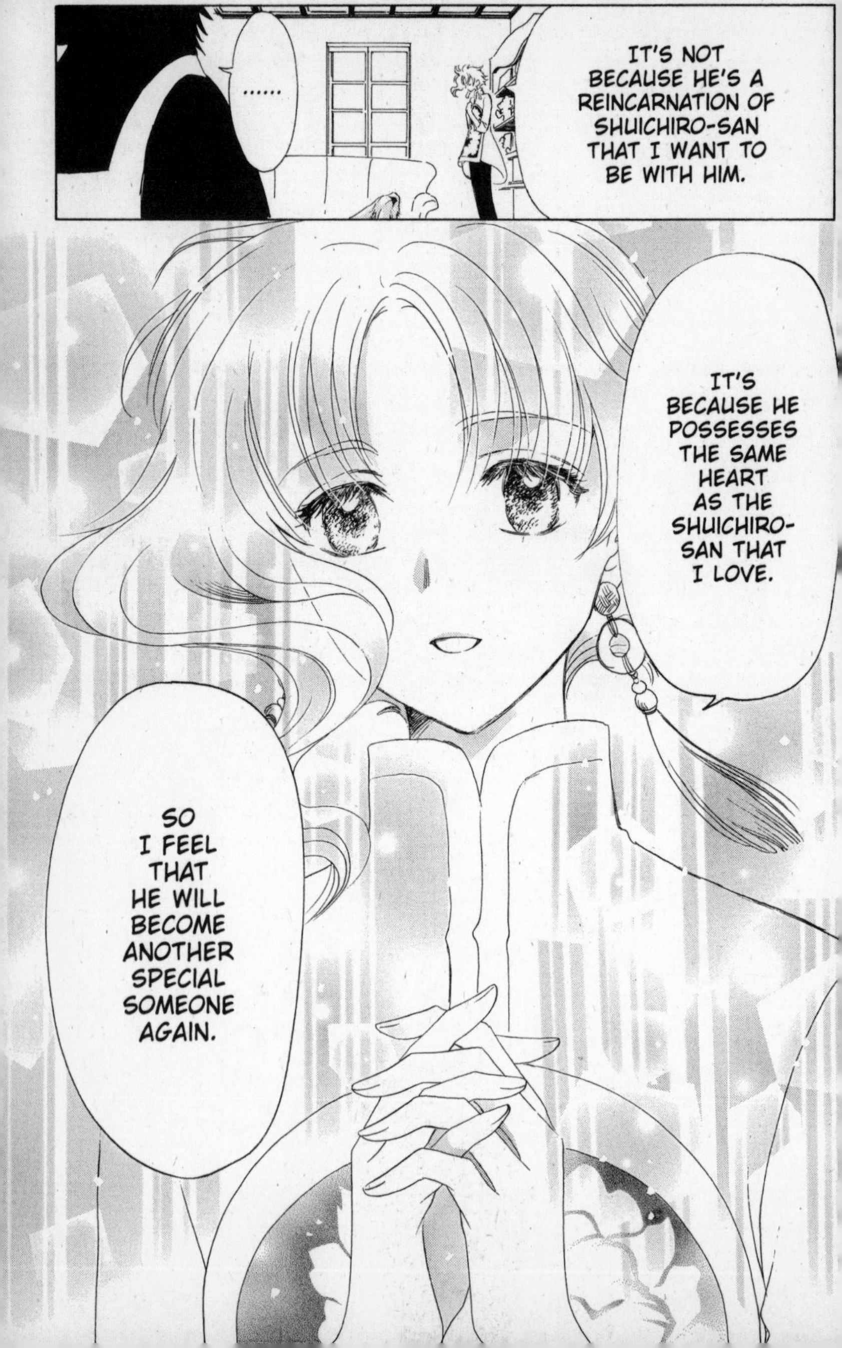
IT'S NOT BECAUSE HE'S A REINCARNATION OF SHUICHIRO-SAN THAT I WANT TO BE WITH HIM.
......
IT'S BECAUSE HE POSSESSES THE SAME HEART AS THE SHUICHIRO-SAN THAT I LOVE.
SO I FEEL THAT HE WILL BECOME ANOTHER SPECIAL SOMEONE AGAIN.

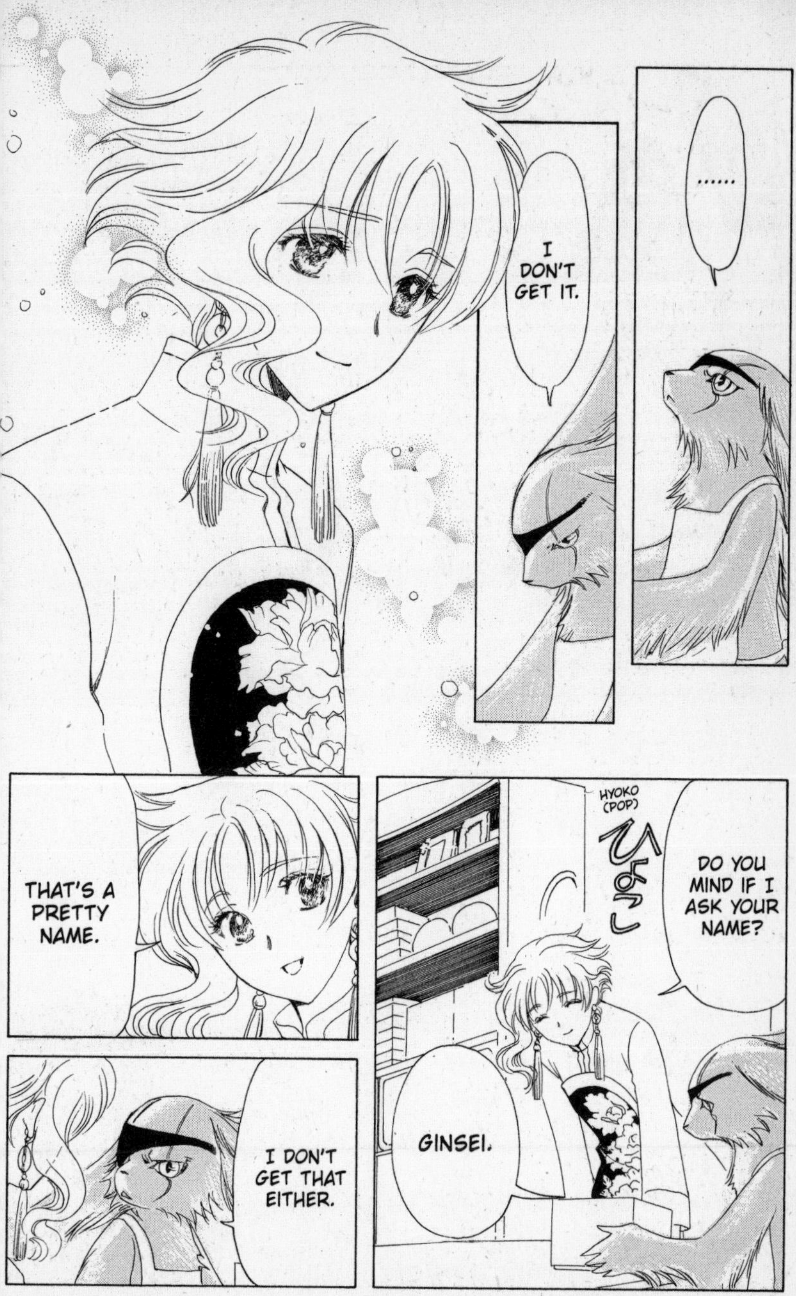
......
I DON'T GET IT.
DO YOU MIND IF I ASK YOUR NAME?
HYOKO (POP)
ひょっ
GINSEI.
THAT'S A PRETTY NAME.
I DON'T GET THAT EITHER.

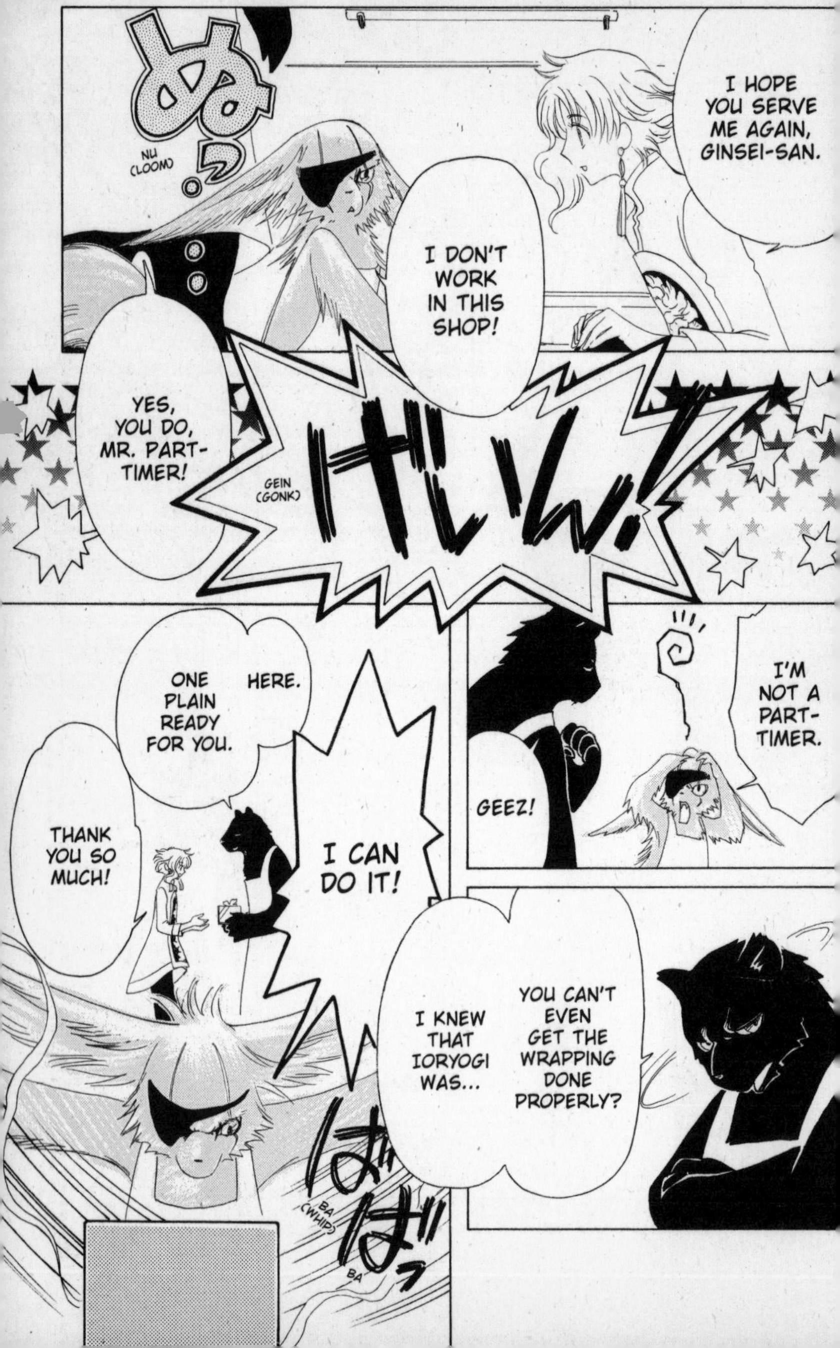
I HOPE YOU SERVE ME AGAIN, GINSEI-SAN.
I DON'T WORK IN THIS SHOP!
NU (LOOM)
GEIN (GONK)
YES, YOU DO, MR. PART-TIMER!
I'M NOT A PART-TIMER.
GEEZ!
YOU CAN'T EVEN GET THE WRAPPING DONE PROPERLY?
I KNEW THAT IORYOGI WAS...
HERE.
ONE PLAIN READY FOR YOU.
THANK YOU SO MUCH!
I CAN DO IT!
BA (WHIP)
BA

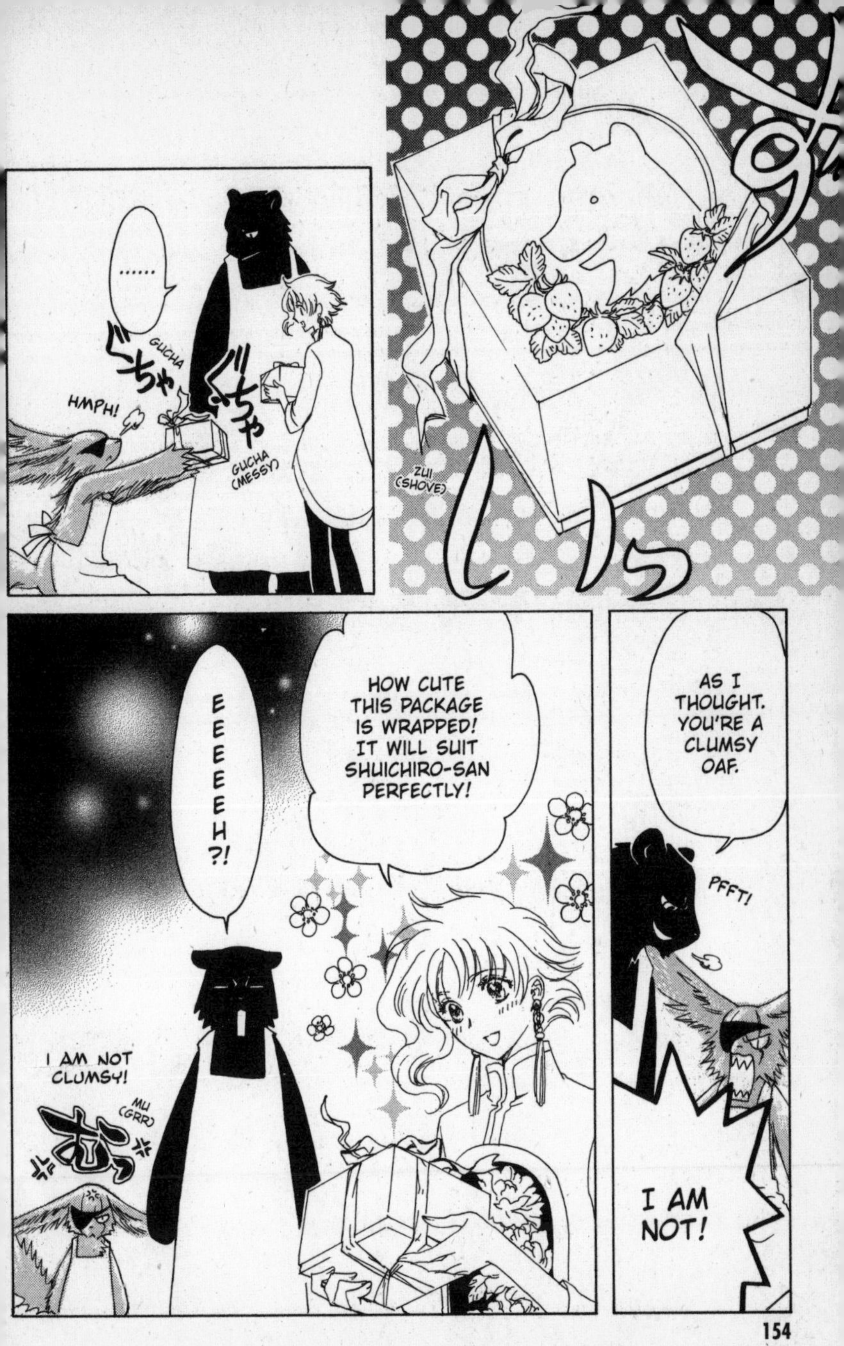
ZUI (SHOVE)
......
ぐちゃ
GUCHA
HMPH!
ぐちゃ
GUCHA (MESSY)
AS I THOUGHT. YOU'RE A CLUMSY OAF.
PFFT!
I AM NOT!
HOW CUTE THIS PACKAGE IS WRAPPED! IT WILL SUIT SHUICHIRO-SAN PERFECTLY!
EEEEEEH?!
I AM NOT CLUMSY!
MU (GRR)

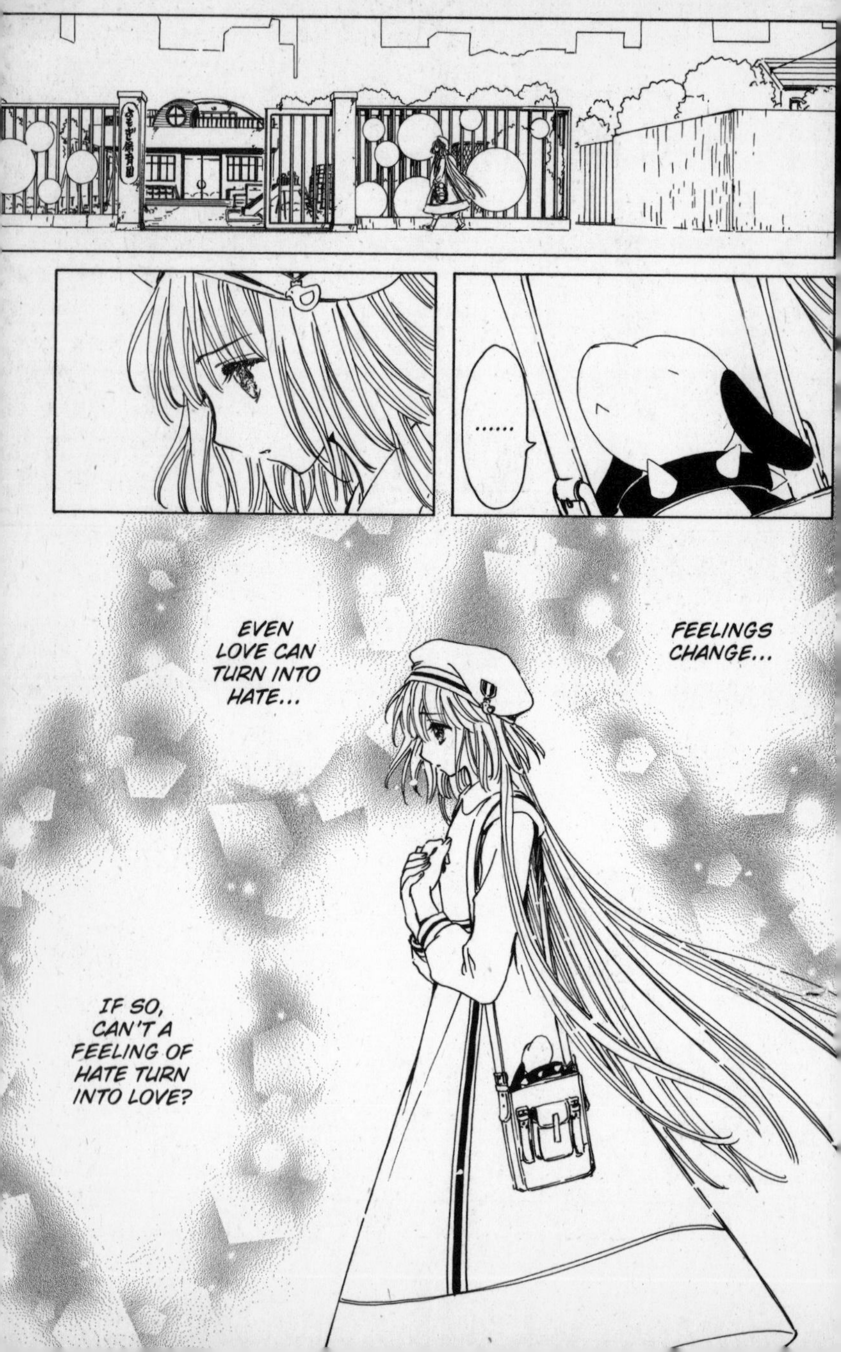
......
FEELINGS CHANGE...
EVEN LOVE CAN TURN INTO HATE...
IF SO, CAN'T A FEELING OF HATE TURN INTO LOVE?

SIGN: YOMOGI KINDERGARTEN

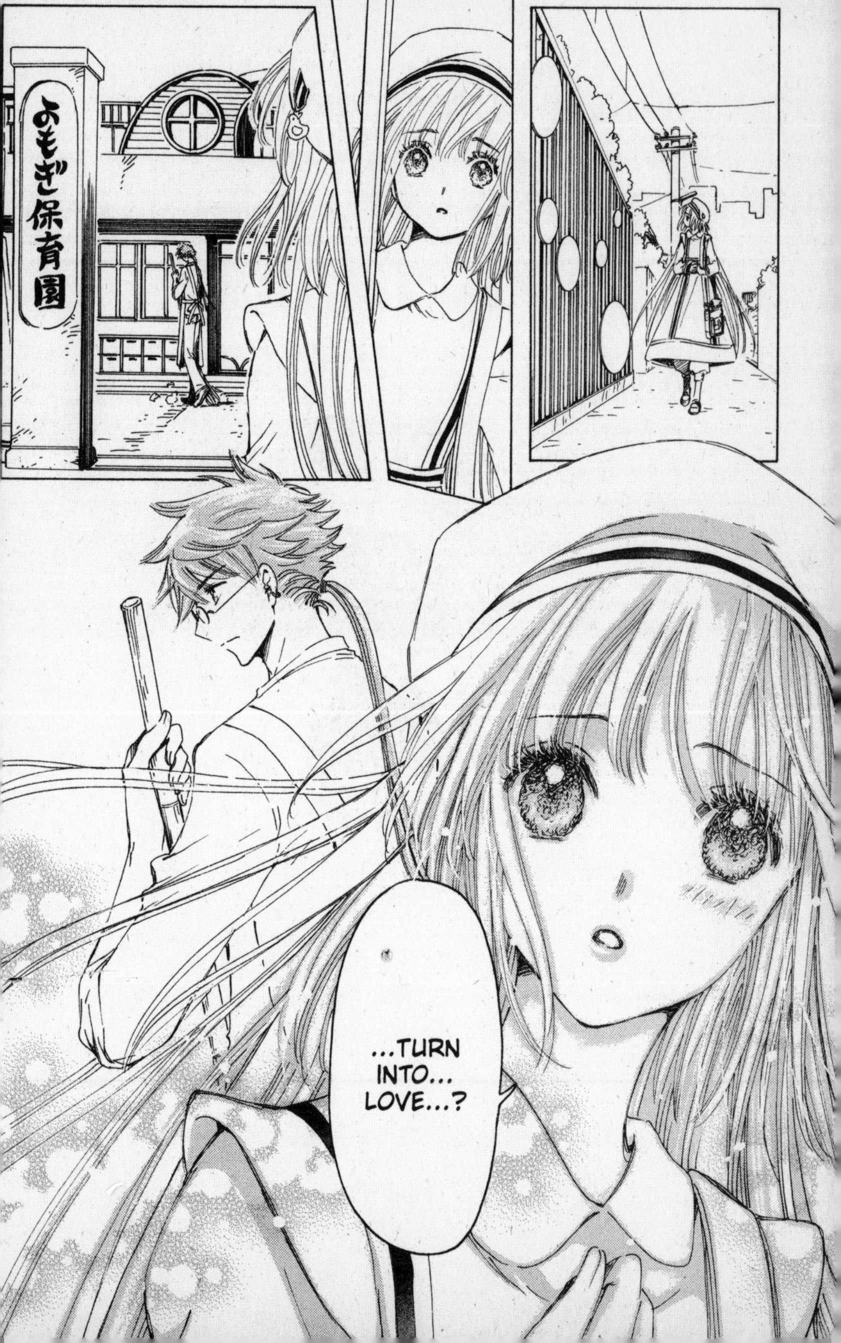
よもぎ保育園
...TURN INTO... LOVE...?

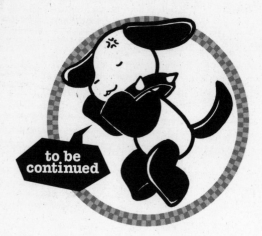

to be
continued

TRANSLATION NOTES

COMMON HONORIFICS

no honorific: Indicates familiarity or closeness; if used without permission or reason, addressing someone in this manner would constitute an insult.

***-san*:** The Japanese equivalent of Mr./Mrs./Miss. If a situation calls for politeness, this is the fail-safe honorific.

***-sama*:** Conveys great respect; may also indicate that the social status of the speaker is lower than that of the addressee.

***-kun*:** Used most often when referring to boys (though it can be applied to girls as well), this indicates affection or familiarity. Occasionally used by older men among their peers, but it may also be used by anyone referring to a person of lower standing.

***-chan*:** An affectionate honorific indicating familiarity used mostly in reference to girls; also used in reference to cute persons or animals of either gender.

Page 42 - ***Bad night vision***
There is a word for "bad night vision" in Japanese, *torime*. Literally the kanji mean "bird eyes."

Page 53 - ***Iorogi***
Ioryogi's old name, Iorogi, uses three kanji with a meaning of "five hundred gods."

Page 54 - ***Ginsei***
The kanji for *gin* in Ginsei's name means "silver," and the one of the meanings for *sei* is "life."

Page 70 - ***Yakusoku***
"Running gag" is a pretty-close-but-not-exact translation for an Osakan comedy word, *yakusoku*. See the notes in Volume 2 for details.

Page 73 - ***Way you called his name***
Kobato is referring to the fact that Doumoto didn't use honorifics when he called Fujimoto by name. A lack of honorifics usually means a friendly relationship.

Page 74 - ***Polite***
Kobato's self-introduction and deep bow is the way you are supposed to greet people in polite Japanese society. It's also a way that isn't seen too often these days and so is surprising when one does see it.

Page 134 - ***Divorce papers***
In Japan, when it is an equitable divorce (both partners agree to divorce) the process is very simple. Just obtain a Rikon Todoke paper, fill out the required areas, have the required number of legal seals (hand-carved stamps that only an individual carries)—usually one seal from each of the parties in the divorce and those of two witnesses—and finally turn in the paper to the local city hall for processing. The woman in this story has already filled out the paper and gotten the required seals. She is now heading to the local city hall.

Page 144 - ***Sweets***
Tough, manly men are not supposed to like sweet things. That stereotype is prevalent in western nations as well, but it is especially prominent in Japan.

Kobato.

Can't wait for the next volume? You don't have to!

Keep up with the latest chapters of some of your favorite manga every month online in the pages of YEN PLUS!

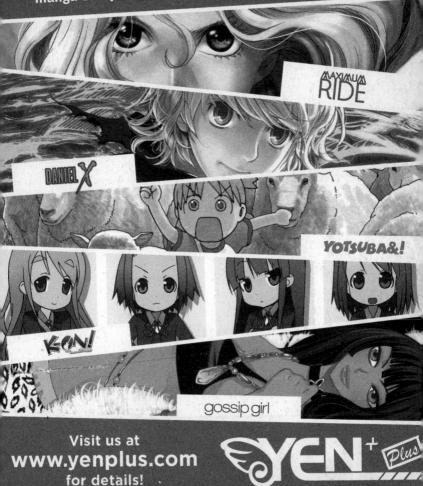

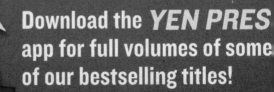

KOBATO. ④

CLAMP

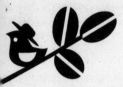

Translation: William Flanagan • Lettering: Alexis Eckerman

KOBATO. Volume 4 © 2009 CLAMP. First published in Japan in 2009 by KADOKAWA SHOTEN Co., Ltd., Tokyo. English translation rights arranged with KADOKAWA SHOTEN Co., Ltd., Tokyo through TUTTLE-MORI AGENCY, INC., Tokyo.

Translation © 2011 by Hachette Book Group, Inc.

Yen Press
Hachette Book Group
237 Park Avenue, New York, NY 10017

www.HachetteBookGroup.com
www.YenPress.com

Yen Press is an imprint of Hachette Book Group, Inc. The Yen Press name and logo are trademarks of Hachette Book Group, Inc.

First Yen Press Edition: July 2011

ISBN: 978-0-316-17818-1

10 9 8 7 6 5 4 3 2 1

BVG

Printed in the United States of America